Radical Elegies

Bloomsbury Studies in Critical Poetics

Series Editor: Daniel Katz, University of Warwick, UK

Political, social, erotic, and aesthetic—poetry has been a challenge to many of the dominant discourses of our age across the globe. Bloomsbury Studies in Critical Poetics publishes books on modern and contemporary poetry and poetics that explore the intersection of poetry with philosophy, linguistics, psychoanalysis, political and economic theory, protest and liberation movements, as well as other art forms, including prose. With a primary focus on texts written in English but including work from other languages, the series brings together leading and rising scholars from a diverse range of fields for whom poetry has become a vital element of their research.

Editorial Board:
Hélène Aji, University of Paris Ouest-Nanterre, France
Vincent Broqua, University of Paris 8 - Vincennes/Saint Denis, France
Olivier Brossard, University of Paris Est Marne La Vallée, France
Daniel Kane, University of Sussex, UK
Miriam Nichols, University of the Fraser Valley, Canada
Peter Middleton, University of Southampton, UK
Cristanne Miller, SUNY Buffalo, USA
Aldon Nielsen, Pennsylvania State University, USA
Stephen Ross, University of Warwick, UK; Editor, Wave Composition
Richard Sieburth, New York University, USA
Daniel Tiffany, University of Southern California, USA

Titles in the series include:
Affect, Psychoanalysis, and American Poetry, John Steen
City Poems and American Urban Crisis, Nate Mickelson
Lyric Pedagogy and Marxist-Feminism, Samuel Solomon
A Black Arts Poetry Machine, David Grundy
Queer Troublemakers, Prudence Bussey-Chamberlain

Forthcoming titles:
Radical Elegies, Eleanor Perry

Radical Elegies

White Violence, Patriarchy, and Necropoetics

Eleanor Perry

BLOOMSBURY ACADEMIC
LONDON • NEW YORK • OXFORD • NEW DELHI • SYDNEY

BLOOMSBURY ACADEMIC
Bloomsbury Publishing Plc
50 Bedford Square, London, WC1B 3DP, UK
1385 Broadway, New York, NY 10018, USA
29 Earlsfort Terrace, Dublin 2, Ireland

BLOOMSBURY, BLOOMSBURY ACADEMIC and the Diana logo are
trademarks of Bloomsbury Publishing Plc

First published in Great Britain 2022
This paperback edition published 2024

Copyright © Eleanor Perry, 2022

Eleanor Perry has asserted her right under the Copyright, Designs and
Patents Act, 1988, to be identified as Author of this work.

For legal purposes the Acknowledgements on p. ix constitute an
extension of this copyright page.

Cover design by Eleanor Rose
Cover image © Studio Parris Wakefield/ Ikon Images

All rights reserved. No part of this publication may be reproduced or transmitted
in any form or by any means, electronic or mechanical, including photocopying,
recording, or any information storage or retrieval system, without
prior permission in writing from the publishers.

Bloomsbury Publishing Plc does not have any control over, or responsibility for, any
third-party websites referred to or in this book. All internet addresses given in this
book were correct at the time of going to press. The author and publisher regret
any inconvenience caused if addresses have changed or sites have ceased
to exist, but can accept no responsibility for any such changes.

A catalogue record for this book is available from the British Library.

A catalog record for this book is available from the Library of Congress.

ISBN:	HB:	978-1-3502-3606-6
	PB:	978-1-3502-3610-3
	ePDF:	978-1-3502-3607-3
	eBook:	978-1-3502-3608-0

Series: Bloomsbury Studies in Critical Poetics

Typeset by Integra Software Services Pvt. Ltd.

To find out more about our authors and books visit www.bloomsbury.com
and sign up for our newsletters

For JPV.
And
for the ungrievable dead and
those grievers whose broken hearts
have not mattered.

Contents

Acknowledgements	ix

	Introduction: Against genealogy	1
	White violence: The 'English elegy' and its colonial foundations	4
	Patriarchy: The intersectional biases of a genealogical approach	7
	Genealogy as necropoetics	18
	Radical elegies	20
	A note on positionality	24
	Notes	26
1	Ornate absences and rhetorical acts: The scholarly reception of elegies by Black and African American women poets	29
	Black elegies, white elegies: Prescriptive gestures	30
	Safe grief and dangerous grief	35
	Militant grief and the Black Aesthetic	42
	Radical Black women's elegy: Wheatley, Brooks, Clifton	48
	Notes	59
2	Resisting necrophilous white patriarchy: Elegies about racial injustice	61
	The limits of elegiac genealogy	62
	Red ooze, severed gaze and the maintenance of white masculinity: Elegies for Emmett Till	65
	Reflections, disintegrations, incendiary materials: Civil Rights elegies	79
	Necrophilous white state violence: Post-Civil Rights elegies	92
	Notes	112
3	Abstracted grief, precarious grief: Rethinking elegy via transfeminism and queer necropolitics	115
	Re-makings, multiplicities, displacements: Beyond binary concepts of gender	116
	Necropolitics: Precarity, dehumanization and grievability	118

	Abstract bodies and the complicit reader: Joshua Jennifer Espinoza's 'Poem (Let us Live)'	120
	Irregularity and memorial: Ryka Aoki's 'The Woman of Water Dreams'	128
	Body as site of colonial struggle: Qwo-Li Driskill's 'Pedagogy'	140
	Towards some conclusions	148
	Notes	151
4	Anti-museum, anti-archive and personal elegy: Writing the human back into being	153
	Mourning through the cracks: Fragile intimacy in Solmaz Sharif's 'Personal Effects'	157
	Inherited grief: Kay Ulanday Barrett's 'While looking at photo albums'	165
	Deafness and 'cure': Meg Day's 'Elegy in Translation'	170
	Postscript	176
	Note	176

References	177
Index	193

Acknowledgements

Many thanks are due to Simon Smith, David Herd, Nancy Gaffield, Carol Watts and David Stirrup for all of their time, attention and generous feedback during various early and later stages of this book's development.

I would also like to thank Dan Katz and the editors and publishers at Bloomsbury – Ben Doyle, Lucy Brown, Laura Cope – for their support and guidance throughout the publication process. And I am hugely grateful to the anonymous reviewers who provided such detailed and thoughtful feedback on this book's various draft iterations, and whose encouragement and suggestions helped to shape the book into its current form.

This book is the result of nine years of research on elegy and its scholarship. It would not have been possible without the extensive and unwavering encouragement, feedback and support from my partner, colleague and collaborator, Juha Virtanen.

The third party copyrighted material displayed in the pages of this book is done so on the basis of 'fair dealing for the purposes of criticism and review' or 'fair use for the purposes of teaching, criticism, scholarship or research' only in accordance with international copyright laws, and is not intended to infringe upon the ownership rights of the original owners.

Introduction: Against genealogy

As a poetic articulation, elegy offers a means of marking a loss, a death – or perhaps multiple losses, multiple deaths – in a public or communal way; and of expressing the complex emotions of personal and collective grief in response to that loss. The question of whose elegies are given primacy in cultural and literary discourse is a political one, because elegies reflect whose deaths are publicly marked and, by extension, whose lives are considered to have superlative value. Equally, elegies have the capacity to resist structural and systemic social inequalities for this same reason and, throughout history, have often done exactly this. And yet, elegy scholarship often tells a significantly different story, by and large focusing primarily on elegiac poetry written by, and about, white men.

While Diana Fuss's *Dying Modern* (2013) examines elegiac work by women (Emily Dickinson, Adelaide Crapsey, Stevie Smith, Elizabeth Bishop and Sylvia Plath, among others); and Melissa F. Zeiger's *Beyond Consolation* (1997) has chapters on women's elegies, women's breast cancer elegies and AIDS elegies, the majority of elegy scholarship texts focus principally on writers who are (often cis and/or straight) white men. Some texts include chapters on women's work and/or work by Black writers: Iain Twiddy's *Pastoral Elegy in Contemporary British and Irish Poetry* (2012) has one chapter on 'Contemporary Female Poets and Pastoral Elegy'; David Kennedy's *Elegy* (2007) has one chapter dedicated to 'Female elegists and feminist readers'; R. Clifton Spargo's *The Ethics of Mourning* (2004) has a chapter on Plath; as does Jahan Ramazani's *Poetry of Mourning* (1994) which also has one chapter on the work of Anne Sexton, Adrienne Rich and Amy Clampitt; one on Langston Hughes and a section on Michael S. Harper.[1] On the other hand, John B. Vickery's *The Modern Elegiac Temper* (2006) examines in detail the work of thirty-five white male poets and that of two women – Edna St Vincent Millay and Edith Sitwell. Dennis Kay's *Melodious Tears* (1990); Eric Smith's *By Mourning Tongues* (1977); W. David Shaw's *Elegy & Paradox* (1994); and Peter M. Sacks's *The English Elegy* (1985) do not make detailed reference to work either by women or by writers of colour. *The Oxford Handbook of the Elegy* (2010) has four chapters out of thirty-eight that focus on women's elegies (Shohet; Mellor; Helle; Schnell); one on Indigenous American Elegy (Krupat); and one on AIDS elegies (Chambers). In other words, the scholarly examinations of elegies that exist to date largely paint an overarching picture of elegy as a series of (often cis and straight) white male poets mourning the deaths of other white men. The voices of women, especially women of colour and trans women, are often marginalized or excluded from the canon. Certainly, it is nothing new to point out that canons of poetry reflect the gendered and racial inequalities of wider society. Writers of colour, Black writers, Critical Race theorists, queer writers and feminist writers have for years examined and critiqued exclusions and marginalizations that exist within literary canons. What is of particular interest in the case of elegy are the wider implications of these exclusions and marginalizations, namely whose losses – and whose griefs – have mattered enough to be publicly marked, and whose have not.

The exclusions and marginalizations of certain voices from the canon presented by elegy scholarship require a particular mechanics to sustain; namely the reproduction of certain rhetorical manoeuvres. It is common practice, in books of elegy scholarship, to use stock phrase structures like 'from [insert poet] to [insert more recent poet]' to provide shorthand for an overarching view of the elegiac tradition. Three of the most cited texts in elegy scholarship contain a phrase like this within their subtitle: consider Dennis Kay's *The English Funeral Elegy from Spenser to Milton* (1990); Peter M. Sacks's *Studies in the Genre from Spenser to Yeats* (1987); and Ramazani's *The Modern Elegy from Hardy to Heaney* (1994). This tendency is also often taken up in the texts themselves. Ramazani, for instance, uses 'from Moschus to Spenser and Tennyson,' 'from Moschus to Swinburne' and 'from Moschus and Milton to Shelley, Tennyson, and Swinburne' (1994: 178; 221; 298). Sacks gives us 'from the time of Bion beyond that of Mallarmé,' and 'from Virgil to Stevens'; and describes Milton as 'joining company with Theocritus, Virgil, Sannazaro, and Spenser' (1987: 28; 187; 91). This shorthand framing of elegiac tradition reflects an understanding of elegy as a genealogy: a chronological map that spans from the ancient Greek pastoral *Idylls* of Theocritus (along with poems attributed to Moschus and Bion) to a handful of European – in many cases, English – writers (hence the 'English elegy'); and then, in some cases, to English and Anglo-American Modernist writers and contemporary poets, who also happen to be mostly white. It is, in other words, an understanding of elegy as a pedigree or literary system of rank that might be traced through a lineage of poetic ancestors.

In this way, the texts which are presented as embodying the 'genre' of elegy – in other words, the elegiac canon – reflect a line of constructed poetic inheritances, whereby white, male poets take up the mantle of their poetic predecessors by lamenting – in poetic form – the death of another white man (often another white, male poet). Celeste M. Schenck describes this literary act as a 'gesture of aspiring careerism,' which produces a 'poetry of ambition, focusing […] on issues of literary succession and poetic potency' (1986: 14–15). Simply put, a genealogy of elegy depicts, as Kennedy emphasizes, 'men mourning the untimely deaths of other men' (2007: 10). As Andrea Brady has suggested, these 'patrilineal constructions of literary inheritance' – often augmented by the incorporation of inheritance metaphors within the poems themselves – consist specifically of elite, Oxbridge-educated male poets (2006: 136–7). We might, for instance, consider the scholastic origins of canonical poets like Edmund Spenser (Pembroke College, Cambridge); John Milton (Christ's College, Cambridge); Percy Bysshe Shelley (University College, Oxford); Matthew Arnold (Balliol College, Oxford); and Algernon Charles Swinburne (Balliol College, Oxford).

It is upon the poetic work of this supposed lineage – or genealogy – of white, largely English, men that the majority of elegy scholarship focuses: the Renaissance poets Spenser (see Sacks 1987; and Kay 1990), Milton (see Sacks 1987; Shaw 1994; Smith 1977; and Kay 1990) and John Donne (see Shaw 1994; and Kay 1990); and the poets of the 'English tradition': Thomas Gray (see Sacks 1987; and Smith 1977), Shelley (see Sacks 1987; Shaw 1994; and Smith 1977), Alfred, Lord Tennyson (see Sacks 1987; Shaw 1994; and Smith 1977), Swinburne (see Sacks 1987; and Zeiger 1997), Arnold (see Shaw 1994; and Smith 1977) and Thomas Hardy (see Sacks 1987; Ramazani 1994; and Zeiger 1997). Some texts extend their scope to include more contemporary Anglo-American or Irish writers. Ramazani examines Wallace Stevens, Langston Hughes, Sylvia Plath, Anne Sexton, Adrienne Rich and Amy Clampitt; while Iain Twiddy examines, among others, Eavan Boland, Nuala Ní Dhomhnaill, Paula Meehan and Penelope Shuttle.[2] These examples notwithstanding, an understanding of elegy as a genealogy which maps chronologically from Greek pastoral poets to the 'English tradition' and its Modernist and contemporary legacies largely underpins existing elegy scholarship. Even texts which do not adopt a genealogical framework, such as Fuss's *Dying Modern* (2013), or which acknowledge issues of misogyny in the existing scholarship, like Zeiger's *Beyond Consolation* (1997), are not entirely free of the genealogical model. Fuss's text offers three alternative traditions or genealogies (deathbed poems, corpse poems and aubades) while Zeiger uses the 'English elegy' as a critical starting point in her introduction.

Framed as providing a study of elegy that is *from* an ancient Greek or Roman poet *to* a more contemporary poet, a genealogical model or framework implies an inclusion of all that is in-between. In other words, it implies an all-encompassing quality; an exhaustiveness: elegy *from* its origins *to* its contemporary iterations. However, what this phrasing points away from is the fact that it is not possible to be all-encompassing in scope within the space of a single book; certain choices have to be made in terms of which elegies to represent within any given text. In short, this genealogical framework points away from what is excluded. And this becomes more troubling when we consider that an elegy publicly and poetically mourns the loss of a person. Canonizing an elegy bestows significance upon that loss and confers esteem upon the way in which that person is poetically mourned. It gives focus and value to certain ways of articulating loss. And it defines whose lost lives are worthy of lamenting.

In this way, by prioritizing elegies by and about white men, elegy scholarship operates as what Judith Butler refers to as a 'normative framework,' that establishes 'what life will become worthy of being mourned' and 'whose life, if extinguished, would be publicly grievable' (2016: 53; 75). Or, to put it another way, it establishes and maintains the 'pervasive forms of inequality that establish some lives as disproportionately more livable and grievable than others' (Butler 2020; 17). It is a framework which implies a common experience of grief shared by all humanity while, in actuality, that common experience is – as we shall see – constructed on principles of whiteness, masculinity and heteronormative binaries of gender. While elegy scholarship may occasionally make space for voices that do not conform to these identity parameters, it does so only if those voices can be assimilated into this pre-established notion of a supposedly universal common grief experience. It does not, in other words, acknowledge elegies that articulate ways in which grief and loss may be experienced *because of* society's privileging of whiteness, masculinity and heteronormative binaries of gender.

White violence: The 'English elegy' and its colonial foundations

What is conspicuously overlooked in a genealogical understanding of elegy is that the highly revered 'English elegy' was founded in the age of the British Empire and consequently its historical legacy is deeply enmeshed with colonial politics and ideals. Many of its key canonical figures either played roles in, or propounded ideas that contributed to, upholding imperialist and colonial politics. For instance, Spenser – the writer of 'Astrophel,' an elegy for Sir Philip Sidney – served under Lord Deputy Arthur Grey at the Siege of Smerwick Massacre and acquired land in the Munster plantation scheme that involved the confiscation of Irish lands by the English crown. In *A View of the State of Ireland* he promoted colonial policies that included 'general starvation, widespread confiscation of native lands, ruthless transportation of the innocent populace, and the establishment of military rule over the entire country' (Brady 1986: 17). His view that 'the Irish were worse than normal barbarians,' was based, in large part, on his belief that they were descended from North African Carthaginians (Kiernan 2008: 176).

Another example is Milton – writer of 'Lycidas,' an elegy for Edward King – who was a state servant for Oliver Cromwell's Commonwealth, and whose pamphlets (*Observations*, for instance, is understood as a 'fanatically anti-Irish' text) were instrumental in Cromwell's occupation of Ireland, which included massacres at Drogheda and Wexford (Raymond 2004: 319). According to Steven Jablonski, Milton 'not only accepted the principles behind the concept of natural slavery,' but also identified these so-called natural slaves 'with the black Africans' of the Old World (1997: 174). Though he is often better known for his writing on liberty, Jablonski argues that 'the idea of slavery was part of [Milton's] idea of liberty' and, by using Aristotle's theory that 'geography and climate dispose different peoples to different forms of rule,' Milton attempted to 'provide a rational and naturalistic explanation' for the idea (1997: 187, 177, 181).

Another example is Tennyson – writer of 'In Memoriam', an elegy for Arthur Henry Hallam – who was on the Governor Eyre Defense and Aid Committee, which supported Eyre's decision to arrest and hang Paul Bogle and George William Gordon. These two men were organizers of a march in Morant Bay in Jamaica to protest the unjust treatment of ex-slaves; a protest in which four hundred locals were killed. We might also consider Arnold – writer of 'Thyrsis', an elegy for Arthur Hugh Clough – who is widely known for using 'Victorian race science' in his series of essays titled *Culture and Anarchy*, and 'preposterous racialism' in his book *On the Study of Celtic Literature* (Caulfield 2016: 115).

The 'English elegy', then, is deeply enmeshed with the British colonial project. A genealogical understanding of elegy therefore privileges a very specific colonialist worldview; its supposed Englishness, to follow Vera M. Kutzinski, is a product of colonialism (1992: 552–3). In other words, its Englishness is a construction; a manufactured assemblage of aesthetic qualities that operate as a means of differentiating it, generically, from New World writing. While a genealogical scholarly approach often presents the 'English elegy' as a pre-established literary category against which all later elegies might be measured, it is better understood as a retrospectively organized set of texts chosen to reflect and promote certain English ideals: namely whiteness, masculinity, a classical education, a rejection of femininity and the moderation or restraint of emotion; ideals which are often later taken up and reflected in Modernist and contemporary elegies by British and Anglo-American poets.

For these reasons, a genealogical understanding of elegy can be submitted to a similar critique that political theorist Achille Mbembe applies to the museum or archive, in that it has not, historically 'been an unconditional place of reception for the multiple faces of humanity taken in its unity' (2019: 171). Like Mbembe's archive, it does not 'produce visibility,' but rather, a 'fundamental and reality-generating hallucination' (2019: 173). That is, it presents a curated illusion of humanity which is, very often, mistaken for reality. As with Mbembe's critique of Western culture in general, the ideals of the 'English elegy' have been 'hypostatized and placed on a pedestal,' and they have become 'the zero point of orientation,' for elegy scholarship just as, in Mbembe's view, the West has become the 'zero point of orientation' for the humanities more broadly (2019: 122). Western culture, Mbembe argues, presumes itself to be the 'only one to have symbolically overcome death,' just as the 'English elegy' – along with its more contemporary literary heirs and successors – presumes itself to be the only poetic articulation which is symbolically able to address loss (2019: 122). And, as a 'zero point of orientation' in genealogical approaches to elegy, the 'English elegy' is revered at the expense of other voices and perspectives on grief and loss; perspectives that are marginalized and excluded from the discourse (Mbembe 2019: 122).

If we interrogate genealogical approaches to elegy, we can discern some of the ways in which these marginalizations and exclusions take place. The purpose of doing so is not to blanketly disparage or devalue existing elegy scholarship, but rather to highlight the way in which a genealogical approach limits how elegy might be understood. As we shall see, a genealogical approach often leads to the uncritical adoption of certain biases towards whiteness, masculinity and heteronormative conceptions of gender. These biases, which may be subtle or overt in nature, are pervasive throughout elegy scholarship and they have two principal effects. Firstly, they promote and sustain the idea that white men represent the standard and universal version of human subjectivity in relation to grief and loss. And secondly, they cumulatively enact what Butler calls a 'violence through omission' (2006: 34). They establish which lives 'will become worthy of being mourned,' or 'publicly grievable,' and which will not (2016: 75). When certain deaths are not publicly marked, Butler asserts, those deaths disappear 'in the ellipses by which public discourse proceeds' (2006: 35). These biases, in other words, prevent us from perceiving what is excluded from the discourse: whose losses are not voiced and whose deaths are not marked. They prevent us from seeing, as Sara Ahmed puts it, 'how some broken hearts matter; how some do not' (2014a: para 11). Just like the genealogical framing of elegy scholarship as representing *from* an origin *to* a contemporary point, these biases distract from what is conspicuously absent from the discourse.

Patriarchy: The intersectional biases of a genealogical approach

Kimberlé Crenshaw's description of intersectionality provides a useful framework for understanding the multiple ways in which biases within elegy scholarship operate as a means of marginalizing and excluding certain voices. As Crenshaw points out, we are conditioned to think about forms of marginalization and exclusion 'along a single categorical axis,' which overlooks those who may be 'multiply-burdened,' by different forms of marginalization and exclusion (1989: 140). Thus, while the following transhistorical overview of elegy's – and elegy scholarship's – various embedded biases follows a loosely categorized structure (i.e. gender, race and class), this categorization represents a compartmentalization of what is, as Crenshaw notes, 'a much more complex phenomenon' (1989: 140). For elegists whose work is potentially subject to multiple biases, the 'intersectional experience is greater than the sum' of the individual categories of bias, as I will demonstrate later in this section and in Chapter 1 (1989: 140).

We will begin by examining elegy scholarship's patriarchal biases. Critical writing on elegies by women is often sequestered into separate chapters, as if 'women's elegy' constituted a sub-category that is somehow distinct from a supposed 'elegy proper'. Kennedy's *Elegy* (2007), for instance, discusses women elegists within a separate chapter, as does Zeiger's *Beyond Consolation* (1997). Ramazani's *Poetry of Mourning* dedicates two chapters out of nine to women's elegies; one on Sylvia Plath and one grouping together the work of Anne Sexton, Adrienne Rich and Amy Clampitt under the title of 'family elegy' (1994: 294). Other texts – including Sacks's (1987) and Smith's (1977) – refer to women's elegy only briefly, or indeed, not at all. Women's elegiac work thus often remains proportionately underrepresented.

These gendered biases manifest not only through principles of focus (i.e. whose work warrants a chapter of critical writing), but also in the language used to describe elegiac work. Numerous texts, for instance, adopt the semantic habit of gendering as masculine the neutral terms 'elegist' or 'poet' (Sacks 1987: 9, 22; Shaw 1994: 44, 48, 50–1; Smith 1977: 5, 10, 12; Kennedy 2007: 21; Watkin 2004: 8). This serves to present the idea that, in the main, these roles are filled by men; and that when they are filled by women, it is an exception rather than the rule. As a rhetorical gesture, this perpetuates institutional notions of masculine superiority, implying that women are something other than the standard within elegiac writing.

Such use of gendered language is further exemplified in a tendency for the use of heavily gendered metaphors. For example, Kennedy suggests that in writing an elegy, the elegist 'claim[s] membership of a *band of brothers*' and 'bring[s] back something for *the benefit of all men*' (2007: 30; emphasis mine). Goldberg claims that '[t]he *pregnant* body of poetry *is the text written by men*,' and describes Jonson's elegy for Shakespeare as '*muscular masculine labor*,' and '*manly* poetic forging' (Goldberg 2010: 500; 502; emphasis mine). Gendered language like this explicitly serves to demarcate the elegiac tradition as a homosocial, masculinized mode from which women are semantically excluded (other than, as in Goldberg's pregnancy metaphor, as an absent figurative symbol of creative [re]productivity). Elegy, these metaphors tell us, is an inherently masculine creative domain.

When elegies by women are discussed, they are often described as somehow less controlled and less dignified than men's elegies. To cite an example, Shaw describes Emily Dickinson's use of domestic symbolism within her elegiac poetry by stating that '[w]ith *housewifely* instinct, [she] puts love away, like a dish, until eternity,' and goes on to describe her as 'an *officious housekeeper*' (1994: 119; emphasis mine). He describes Christina Rossetti's elegiac themes as 'spinsterish,' and refers to both Dickinson and Rossetti as 'the two spinsters,' whose work uses '*homely* details to *domesticate* death and fear of the unknown' (1994: 120; 122; emphasis mine). By doing so, Shaw relegates the thematic content of their work to the realm of the domestic. While domestic themes may be politically engaged, for instance highlighting social inequalities entrenched within domestic spaces such as the erasure of feminized labour, women's lack of agency and sovereignty in heteropatriarchal marriage structures, or reproductive injustices, Shaw is not pointing towards these possibilities in his description. Instead, he subtly belittles Dickinson's and Rossetti's poetry. Words like 'housewifely,' and 'housekeeper' equate their writing with domestic tasks, implicitly understood here as trivial in nature. 'Homely' implies domestic, but also a lack of sophistication and beauty. The word 'spinster' carries pejorative connotations of prudishness and repression. Thus, his use of coded language operates as a means of demeaning their work because it is deemed – by Shaw – to be lacking in worldly wisdom and substance; unrefined; prim; inhibited; and/or relegated to the sphere of the private. To borrow from Jane Gallop's description of the split between so-called 'women's issues (love, family, sexuality) and "serious" subjects,' it is a means of relegating the work of women writers to 'the suburbs of intellectual life' (1988: 8).

It is also common to see women's elegies described in such a way as to imply they are not worthy of critical attention, citing reasons of predictability, lack of authenticity or of having little critical value. For instance, Anne K. Mellor suggests that, when women writers have adopted the pastoral mode, 'their efforts have often seemed to *lack authentic emotion*, to be *merely workmanlike exercise*' (2010: 444; emphasis mine). This implies that their poems are lacking in importance and value; efficient but simple or plain; and executed without flourish, as a kind of habit or form of training. Moreover, she claims that in the elegies of Charlotte Smith, Letitia Landon and Felicia Hemans, grief is 'not so much an emotion as a *literary performance*,' implying that the emotions they articulate in their poems are inauthentic, constructed fictions (2010: 450; emphasis mine).

We might also consider the tendency to categorize women's elegies as complaints. Crewe describes the complaint as 'sometimes voiced by inconsolable women,' while 'in contrast, a male speaker typically voices the pastoral elegy'; and Curran portrays Charlotte Smith's poetry as 'sonnet of complaint,' which he describes as 'a man's genre' at the time (Crewe 2010: 519; Curran 2010: 243). Mellor describes the female complaint as 'a literary form that both articulates the suffering of women and represents those sufferings as inevitable and inescapable' (2010: 451). To sub-categorize women's elegies in this way is a means of tacitly downgrading their articulations of grief to the status of a minor grievance. As Juliana Schiesari has pointed out, the woman's complaint has historically been perceived as 'mere chatter and thus as less dignified,' than work in the patriarchal tradition, and as such it is 'not granted the same extraordinary virtue and wisdom' (1992: 55). Lauren Berlant similarly highlights that 'it is not the woman who first calls her self-articulation a complaint,' but rather that 'the patriarchal social context in which she makes her utterance hystericizes it for her, even before she speaks' (1988: 243). To categorize a woman's elegy as a complaint, then, is to represent it as inferior to, or less important than, 'elegy proper'.

Gender biases are also starkly visible in texts that suggest women and men grieve differently according to a gendered binary. For instance, Zeiger cites G.W. Pigman III's book *Grief and English Renaissance Elegy*, to suggest that 'denial of loss, grief, and fear' are, to a degree, 'constitutive of masculinity' (1997: 12–13). Mellor adheres to a similar framework by drawing on Doka and Martin's psychology text *Men Don't Cry... Women Do* (2000). In doing so, she argues that men tend to be 'instrumental grievers,' who experience 'grief as an intellectual rather than an emotional experience' and who 'channel' their grief 'into physical activities'; in contrast, women are described as 'intuitive grievers,' who 'frequently and spontaneously express their grief through outbursts and weeping,' and who articulate their grief as 'feelings in the form of tears, depression, anxiety, loss of appetite, inability to concentrate, anger or irritability' (Martin and Doka cited in Mellor 2010: 443).

In an analysis of *The Winter's Tale* by Shakespeare, Crewe outlines what he calls a 'cultural policing of grief,' that adheres to a similar binary: the idea that '[e]xcessive grieving is feminine, while the imposition of control and maintenance of propriety are masculine' (2010: 521). This kind of elegiac '[m]anliness,' he goes on, 'protects the dignity of death, even the plain fact of death, against figurative prolixity, denial, and sentimental trivialization' (2010: 521). He further argues that these more 'impersonal' and 'disciplined' forms of elegy are considered 'decorous,' within the practice of this cultural policing (2010: 522). What he terms 'dignified, manly minimalism' – that which seeks to 'maintain a sense of proportion' – is, he posits, considered in opposition to 'extravagance,' and 'sentimental temptation' (2010: 528). This description of cultural policing clearly maps out a deeply entrenched binary framework that underpins the ways in which elegies are frequently read. The description of men's elegies as 'minimalist,' and as maintaining a sense of 'proportion' associates them with simplicity, modesty, balance and symmetry. The suggestion that adopting these aesthetic traits protects death from 'prolixity, denial, and sentimental trivialization,' implies that an excess of language – i.e. wordiness or verbosity – might be understood as an excessive or disproportionate response to death (Crewe 2010: 521). It is implied that responses to loss which express emotion (for instance, those that express tenderness, sadness or nostalgia) perform a trivialization; a devaluing of the seriousness of death. What underlies this framework is the tacit belief that measured language and moderation (understood and presented as a masculine aesthetic) is, in its proportion, more balanced, fair and impartial – in essence, more truthful – than the use of prolixity and expression of sentiment or feeling in elegy (understood and presented as a feminine aesthetic) (Crewe 2010: 528).

Further, this latter aesthetic is understood as inaccurate, inauthentic and exaggerated because of its 'excesses' of words and emotions.

In summary, then, genealogical approaches present elegies written by white men as authoritative and objectively truthful. Elegies written by poets who are *not* white men are often, in contrast, devalued as inauthentic simply because they might reflect different responses to grief and loss. As Schiesari notes, '[t]he canon legitimates certain linguistic practices without ever examining *what* the conditions for linguistic legitimation are,' and as such it 'legitimates itself through an imaginary literary historicity precisely because it does not recognize certain articulations of disempowerment' (1992: 188–9; emphasis author's). In other words, an elegiac genealogy established and maintained *by* white men reflects and legitimizes the poetic articulations and experiences *of* white men. This genealogy is uncritically presented as an authentic aesthetic and thematic standard, despite – or as Schiesari argues, *because of* – the fact that it marginalizes and excludes certain voices.

So far, we have explored a number of scholarly biases that privilege the work of white men in relation to the work of writers who might be grouped under the category of women elegists. In other words, we might understand it as a brief outline of elegy scholarship's patriarchal biases. However, to follow Crenshaw again, 'ideological and descriptive definitions of patriarchy are usually premised on the white female experience' (1989: 156). To present such an outline without also considering the multiple additional biases against women elegists of colour would address only 'white female experiences' of bias in elegy scholarship (Crenshaw 1989: 144).

The marginalization of women elegists of colour may arise as a consequence of both gender bias and/or racial bias or a fusion of the two whose elements cannot be fully disentangled (Crenshaw: 149). As in the case studies in Chapter 2, the examples listed here focus on the work of Black and African American women elegists. This should not overlook the fact that elegies by writers of other ethnicities and racial identities – such as those by Asian, African, West Asian and North African, Caribbean, Latinx, Chicanx and Indigenous writers (with the acknowledgement that, as categories, such terms are overly broad and generalizing) – are also significantly marginalized and excluded from genealogical approaches, often to the extent that they are not mentioned at all. This renders investigation of any rhetorical devices employed as a means of maintaining that marginalization and exclusion extremely difficult, since there are few or no examples to interrogate. What this lack of examples demonstrates is a significant and invisibilized structural bias within elegy discourse, which systematically and conspicuously omits voices by writers of colour in general; and women writers of colour in particular. This bias raises necessary questions about whose voices are represented within elegy discourse: whose losses are not voiced; and whose deaths are not marked within scholarly representations of elegy.

To acknowledge racial biases within elegy scholarship is not to say that women writers of colour are not critically addressed at all. Fuss, for instance, refers to Frances Ellen Watkins Harper in a discussion of deathbed poems; while Vickery mentions Lucille Clifton's elegy for Malcolm X in a discussion of elegies for major cultural figures (Fuss 2013: 17; Vickery 2006: 74). Zeiger dedicates significant space to Audre Lorde's breast cancer elegies and mentions the work of Alice Walker (1997: 135–65; 136). Ramazani includes several references: Gwendolyn Brooks's 'Of De Witt Williams on his way to Lincoln Cemetery'; Phillis Wheatley and Mary Weston Fordham; and Henrietta Cordelia Ray are all acknowledged (1994: 17; 295; 297). *The Oxford Handbook of The Elegy* – described on its dustjacket blurb as 'the single most comprehensive study of its subject,' and as including thirty-eight chapters covering a 'remarkable historical breadth' – makes very few substantial references to work by women of colour, particularly when you consider the scope of this claim (Weisman 2010).[3] And Shaw (1994); Spargo (2005); Kennedy (2007); Sacks (1987); Smith (1977); and Kay (1990) contain no significant references to work by women of colour. It is also worth noting that many of the aforementioned references are brief in scope and there are no chapters dedicated solely to the elegiac poetry of an individual woman poet of colour in any of the books listed above.

The marginalization and exclusion of poetic work by Black women is not, by any means, limited to elegy scholarship; and must be understood as intrinsically enmeshed with colonial ideas. It is well known that Thomas Jefferson critically dismissed the poetic work of Phillis Wheatley, claiming that she was not a poet at all, a position that was maintained by a number of critics from the late nineteenth century onwards.[4] Sold into slavery at an early age to a family in Boston, over half of Wheatley's thirty-nine published poems (and a quarter of her unpublished ones) are elegies. However, in *Notes on the State of Virginia*, Jefferson claimed that she was not a poet and condemns her work as 'below the dignity of criticism,' basing his argument on his belief that among Black people there 'is misery enough, God knows, but no poetry' (1785: 150).

While Chapter 1 of this book takes a detailed look at the rhetorical mechanics employed by elegy scholars and literary critics to marginalize and exclude Black women's elegies from genealogical constructions, it is nonetheless worth noting here that some contemporary scholarly writing about Black women elegists' work does not deviate far from the critical dismissal Jefferson levelled at Wheatley's poetry. For example, *The Oxford Companion to Women's Writing in the US* has an entry on Henrietta Cordelia Ray – who wrote several elegies including one for Abraham Lincoln and one for Robert G. Shaw – that describes her work as 'sentimental lyrics on hackneyed themes,' and as 'spinning her fanciful lyrics in intricate designs' (Kapai 1995: 745). These descriptions portray Ray's work as overly emotional, unimaginative, whimsical and full of cliché. Despite having written poems that memorialized leaders of the struggle for racial equality, she is criticized for 'ignoring the current issues affecting her race' (Kapai 1995: 745). Finally, the entry ends with a troubling assertion: that '[i]t is not surprising […] that she is remembered primarily for being an accomplished poet at a time when few black women could boast of such a distinction' (Kapai 1995: 745). In this way, the entry frames her work entirely in terms of the fact that she is a Black woman writing 'at a time' when few Black women were critically acknowledged (Kapai 1995: 745). This subtly erases any skill or talent in her work and suggests instead that her renown is a consequence only of her race and gender. In a similar way, Mary Weston Fordham's work is described in *Notable Black American Women* as 'largely uninspired' (Carney Smith 2006: 234). The book states '[w]hat emotional force exists in her lyrics is undercut by sentimentality and a derivative mode' (Carney Smith 2006: 234). This description overlooks significant praise her work received from Civil Rights activist Booker T. Washington and the literary critic William S. Braithwaite.

The marginalization and exclusion of elegies by Black women – and women of colour more broadly – may be understood, in terms borrowed from Kutzinski, as a tendency for genealogical conceptions of elegy to 'implicitly hold[…] fast to […] internal boundaries that demarcate race, class, and gender differences' (1992: 554). It is a tendency that reflects what Toni Morrison highlights in her argument that the American literary canon is not '"naturally" or "inevitably" "white,"' but 'studiously so' (1988: 139). John K. Young identifies a similar scholarly propensity for perceiving texts by Black writers as not 'meriting bibliographical attention,' resulting in a lack of knowledge that 'affects both how editors construct the literary past, […] and how editorial theorists envision their own practice' (2010: 22). In other words, the upshot of constructing a genealogy of elegy in which women elegists of colour are largely absent preserves and sustains the idea that their work is not worthy of critical attention. In short, it creates a sequence of reciprocal cause and effect, in which their work is not critically examined because it has not historically been critically examined.

Genealogical constructions of elegy sustain, to borrow Young's phrasing, 'an implicit connection between whiteness and aesthetic value,' that enables 'the continued neglect of minority literature as worth preserving' (2010: 18).

In addition to gender and racial biases, it is impossible to understand genealogical approaches to elegy without acknowledging the class biases upon which they are founded. Elegiac genealogies that designate Greek pastoral poetry as elegy's point of origin implicitly embed within their structure ideologies that privilege the white, wealthy, educated, urban male poet; ideologies that interlace and overlap with gendered and racial biases. Ancient Greek pastoral poetry depicted an idealized version of nature that, as Jeffrey Hammond emphasizes, incorporates a 'nostalgia for better times' (2010: 209). It is, in other words, a poetic fiction or, as Renato Poggioli terms it, a 'product [...] which each neoclassical age has reshaped in its own fashion' (1975: 3). Referring to English pastoral elegy, Watterson describes this representation of nature as the 'nostalgic product of sophisticated urban writers whose vision of the countryside and its inhabitants is informed by their own self-conscious alienation from both' (2010: 135). Historically, pastoral poetry was, in other words, almost exclusively written by aristocratic urban male poets who glorified the simple rural lifestyle of the male βουκόλος – the shepherd or goatherd – and employed this rhetorical figure as a personification of the idyllic alternative to their own upper-class lifestyle (Gutzwiller 1991: 177).

As Poggioli highlights, pastoral poets envisioned this rural figure as one who enjoyed the 'blessings of idleness even more than the rich man' (1975: 4–6). The βουκόλος operated as a symbol representing a romanticized notion of poverty as a condition that 'saves man from the blight of fear,' the 'slavery of desire' and the 'burdens of wealth' (Poggioli 1975: 11). The pastoral mode, then, operated as an idealization of the worker; one that depicted the life of the herdsman as more fortunate and more privileged than that of the aristocrat. It thus functioned as a means of erasing and obscuring the true nature of poverty within a highly unequal system of social classes. Kathryn J. Gutzwiller asserts that the figure of the herdsman in pastoral poetry was 'always the "other," a figure of another class (slave or hireling),' who represented the 'social and intellectual inferior' of the pastoral poet (1991: 23; 161). She argues that Theocritus's 'Idyll 5,' for instance, embodies the conversion of a 'rustic speech form,' into one of literary art, in which the figure of the 'illiterate,' and 'ignorant,' herdsman is appropriated by the scholar-poet for the amusement of the 'sophisticated reader' (1991: 136). Figures of poverty are depicted in such a way as to 'allow the intended reader to experience aesthetic pleasure by laughing at them from a position of superiority' (Gutzwiller 1991: 7). In other words, classical pastoral poetry not only appropriated and idealized the figure of the herdsman, but also explicitly mocked his lack of education and social sophistication.

Poggioli argues that this romanticization of the rural male worker also functioned as a means of reinforcing inequalities of gender. The figure of the herdsman is inseparable from a concept of desire that not only privileged the happiness of men but depicted that happiness as 'the fulfillment of the passion of love,' and associated it 'with the consummation of man's erotic wishes' (1975: 12–13). Thus, the idyllic realm of the pastoral poem promoted an 'ideal of absolute erotic anarchism,' in which there existed no obstacles to masculine sexual desire (Poggioli 1975: 43). This, in turn, normalized depictions of sexual violence towards both women and men as a means of achieving male happiness through *eros*. Female figures within this romanticized context operated as allegories for the short-lived seasons of the year and as such 'must always be endowed [...] with beauty as well as youth' (Poggioli 1975: 48–50). Older women, particularly those who fell in love with younger men, were conversely portrayed as 'grotesque' and 'ridiculous,' and were depicted in roles such as that of the 'scorned woman,' 'witch' or 'siren' (Poggioli 1975: 272; 49; 52). Within this pastoral desire dynamic, women must always reject male advances, since in 'yielding to man's desire, woman loses the very charms by which she attracts him' (Poggioli 1975: 171). Women, in other words, are only understood as desirable in pastoral poetry when they are rejecting a man's advances. Thus, the male desire dynamic of the pastoral poem contains no space for the possibility of female consent. In this way, the pastoral idyll operates as a model of society designed for the pleasure and happiness of men only. It is, as Poggioli terms it, a 'private masculine world where woman is not a person but a sexual archetype' (1975: 16).

The rhetorical figure of the herdsman and the Arcadian rural idyll are tropes rarely employed within the context of contemporary elegies. Nonetheless, genealogical approaches to elegy continue to celebrate and revere the use of pastoral frameworks without acknowledging or addressing the social inequalities they uphold. Curran, for instance, describes Shelley's 'reclamation' of the Greek pastoral as 'astonishing' while Gray asserts that Arnold's reconfiguring of pastoral conventions has a 'mysterious power' (Curran 2010: 249; Gray 2010: 283). Watterson describes a collection of pastoral elegies celebrating Sidney as establishing his 'mythical status as the flower of Elizabethan chivalry'; and Bonnie Costello describes Robert Frost's use of the 'consoling power of pastoral,' as defined by 'its simplicity, its integration of human and natural worlds, [and] its emphasis on song' (Costello 2010: 325; Watterson 2010: 145). The choices of words here, such as 'astonishing,' 'mysterious,' 'mythical' and 'consoling power,' imply the belief that conventions of the pastoral – as employed by English elegists and their literary heirs – have an intrinsic and inexplicably occult, mystifying or enigmatic potency that does not require further critical investigation. They demonstrate an idealized view of the pastoral mode and its qualities that overlooks any of the economic relations upon which it is based.

Elegy's economic relations have always had implications that affected who had the opportunity to write them, as well as who they were written for and about. In Renaissance England, both writers and publishers were dependent on aristocratic and royal patronage for financial support, prestige, endorsement and legitimization (Marotti 1991: 1–26). Such patronage would have been difficult to obtain as a woman, without affiliations with – or themselves being – members of the aristocracy. Notable exceptions include Emilia Lanier – writer of 'The Description of Cooke-ham' – who was born into minor gentry and, as the mistress of patron of the arts and theatre Henry Carey, was provided with a patronage of £40 a year in the late sixteenth century. Similarly, Mary Sidney Herbert, Countess of Pembroke – who wrote both 'To the Angell Spirit of the most excellent Sir Philip Sidney' and the 'doleful lay of Clorinda' (often attributed to Spenser) – was herself a renowned patron of writers in the early seventeenth century.[5] Many other women elegists wrote without any financial support whatsoever. Bathsua Makin, for instance – who wrote an elegy for Lady Elizabeth Langham – though highly educated and a vehement advocate of equal rights in education for women, was born into the middle class and suffered throughout her life with financial hardship. Similarly, Aphra Behn – the writer of 'On the Death of the Late Earl of Rochester,' and an elegy on the poet Edmund Waller – is thought to have spent time in a debtor's prison.[6] Other examples include Mary Collier – the so-called 'Washerwoman of Petersfield' – a working-class poet who wrote elegies for the poet Stephen Duck and the MP Norton Powlett; Mary Jones, the daughter of a cooper, who wrote 'Verses to the Memory of Miss Clayton,' and an epitaph for Lord Aubrey Beauclerk, the latter of which was published without her consent; and Anne Yearsley, an uneducated working-class poet who wrote, among others, 'Elegy, Written on the Banks of the Avon,' 'Elegy, on Mr. Chatterton,' 'An Elegy on Marie Antoinette, of Austria,' 'Elegy Sacred to the Memory of Lord William Russel' and 'Bristol Elegy'. It is no accident that genealogical constructions of elegy do not include significant references to these poets. Without endorsement or legitimization from aristocratic patronage, they are not afforded a place within the lineage of elegy's poetic ancestry. Like illegitimate children, they are disinherited from the elegy's family line.

The seventeenth-century change in elegy's economic relations provides us with an understanding of the means whereby certain elegies were characterized as legitimate, while others were dismissed and excluded as inauthentic. During this time, aristocratic patronage underwent a shift towards what Brady terms the 'commercialization of grief' (2006: 29). Funerals offered elegists an 'opportunity' to exhibit their work to potential 'employers or patrons,' thus providing conditions for what Brady terms a 'mercenary production of text' that led many to complain about the tendency of poets to 'Weepe for Gaine' (2006: 27; 29; W. Towers cited in Brady 2006: 29). She argues that these 'mercenary poets' were '[e]legiac slaves to occasion,' who wrote 'to serve their bodily needs, rather than to elevate themselves and their readers' (2006: 29; 30). This shift – from patrician patronage to a competitive literary marketplace – gave rise to a tendency for elegists to openly 'denounce other elegists' insincerity and venality,' and criticize their rivals as morally corrupt 'scheming mourners' (Brady 2006: 30). Accusations of greed and a lack of morals served as a means of devaluing the work of non-aristocratic – and non-aristocratically-funded – poets by dismissing as inauthentic any work that was written in order pay for basic human needs such as food and lodging.

These economic relations make permissible an understanding of elegy predicated upon principles of capital. In a system of aristocratic patronage, the poet is under the economic compulsion to sell their labour power to the aristocracy, for whom artistic patronage takes on a cultural value. The value of the elegy is in its capacity to fulfil the social need of providing solace and comfort to the bereaved, as well as to a wider community. In a commercial system, however, elegists are required to compete for patronage in a supposedly free market, where the act of writing an elegy is driven by monetary needs rather than by social ones. Since poets are required to produce more elegies to cover their basic human needs, this leads to an increase in elegy production, which in turn leads to a decrease in the cultural value of the elegy as a whole.

And just as in any capitalist model, a 'free market' inevitably leads to monopoly capitalism. And monopolized capital is stagnating capital, due to a lack of diversity of choice. Thus, the 'English elegy' – the lynchpin of genealogical constructions – represents a kind of cultural stagnation, offering only one perspective; one way of articulating grief through poetry.[7]

In summary, we can discern within genealogical approaches to elegy various intersecting and overlapping biases that privilege the poetic work of educated white men while excluding and marginalizing voices understood, in relation to this poetic work, as 'other'. How, then, can elegy scholarship begin to interrogate, destabilize and address these biases? To answer this, we might return to Crenshaw, who asserts that challenges to institutional hierarchies should not seek to protect individual sources of privilege; and that any approach that proceeds from a point of 'minor adjustments' will necessarily be limited (1989: 145). In short, we must go further than addressing each individual bias and instead challenge the genealogical foundations from which they arise.

A genealogical approach is a means of framing that, to borrow again from Butler, 'implicitly guides the interpretation,' in this case: whose work is worthy of critical attention, whose lives are worthy of being mourned and whose losses matter (2016: 8). As Butler points out, a frame 'never quite contain[s] the scene it was meant to limn,' and there is always something 'already outside' of it, which has 'made the very sense of the inside possible, recognizable' (2016: 9). Genealogical constructions, therefore, do not contain the entire picture of elegy and it is only by framing it in this genealogical way that the primacy of work by white men may be sustained. For Butler, when a frame is broken, 'a taken-for-granted reality is called into question, exposing the orchestrating designs of the authority who sought to control' it (2016: 12). These are, we might say, the principal aims of this book. Firstly, to break the constructed frame of genealogy which defines elegy scholarship; a frame that implicitly guides interpretations of elegy. And secondly, to question the 'taken-for-granted reality' which it upholds, in order to expose the 'orchestrating designs' that have heretofore controlled it (Butler 2016: 12).

Genealogy as necropoetics

Achille Mbembe's term 'necropolitics' – first outlined in an essay in 2003 and expanded in his 2019 book of the same name – describes the mechanisms of social and political power whose purpose is to determine 'who is able to live and who must die' (2019: 66). Arguing that Michel Foucault's notion of biopower does not offer a satisfactory explanation for the various 'contemporary forms of subjugating life to the power of death,' Mbembe offers the terms *necropolitics* and *necropower* to describe the structures that enable these forms of subjugation to play out (2019: 92).

Mbembe argues that the history of Western democracy has 'two bodies': the 'solar body,' which presents itself as ordered, 'peaceful, policed, and violence-free'; and the 'nocturnal body,' which is a history of violence, colonial conquest and war, and whose 'major emblems,' are 'the colonial empire and the pro-slavery state' as well as the 'camp and the prison' (2019: 22; 16; 22; 27). Through the production of 'exceptions, emergencies, and fictionalized enemies,' contemporary systems of political and social power make permissible not only the '*material destruction of human bodies and populations,*' but also 'unique forms of social existence in which vast populations are subjected to living conditions that confer upon them the status of the *living dead*' (Mbembe 2019: 70; 68; 92; all emphases author's). Bodies deemed 'undesirable,' 'illegal, dispensable, or superfluous,' are subjected to this latter condition; one of 'instability' and constant watchfulness, in which individuals must constantly 'prove to others' their status as human (Mbembe 2019: 99; 96; 132; 132). This condition is also characterized by multiple rules and borders whose purpose is to create 'impassable places' and 'spaces of loss and mourning' (Mbembe 2019: 99). We might relate this condition of '*living death*' to Judith Butler's definition of precarity, as a 'politically induced condition in which certain populations suffer from failing social and economic networks of support,' and who are 'exposed to injury, violence, and death' as well as 'risk of disease, poverty, starvation, [and] displacement' (2016: 25–6).

Enmeshed and entangled with Western democracy's 'nocturnal body' – its history of colonial conquest and war – genealogical constructions of elegy reflect these same mechanics of power (Mbembe 2019: 22). Like Butler's example of the obituary, elegy functions as a means 'by which grievability is publicly distributed,' and therefore 'by which a life becomes, or fails to become, a publicly grievable life,' or, indeed, 'by which a life becomes noteworthy' (2006: 34). This notion of grievability is the means through which the question of 'who is [...] a recognizable and valuable human' is produced (Butler 2020': 58). As Butler argues, it is only through linguistic and cultural 'fields' that such grievability can be established, through the public registering of a loss (2020: 105). Like obituaries, elegies are a 'norm governing who will be a grievable human' and – like Butler's description of media reporting on lives lost in the World Trade Center – they 'stage the scene and provide the narrative means by which "the human" in its grievability is established' (2006: 37–8).

Thus, by principally presenting the deaths and losses of educated white men as publicly grievable and noteworthy and – by extension – presenting them as the most superlatively grievable persons, genealogical constructions of elegy subtly operate as a necropolitical instrument. They reflect a *necropoetics*: a system of principles, precepts and techniques – both poetic (within canonical elegies themselves) and rhetorical (in genealogical constructions of the tradition) – which serve to establish and maintain whose lives are publicly grievable and whose losses are noteworthy.[8] As we have seen, these poetical and rhetorical techniques are ones that frequently and repeatedly celebrate and revere whiteness, patriarchal forms of masculinity, heteronormative binaries, the rejection of femininity and the restraint of emotion. Thus, when a literary or cultural text presents ideas that support and maintain necropolitical social structures in this way, we may understand such texts as necropoetic.

Both Mbembe's and Butler's writing, on necropolitics and precarity respectively, are concerned specifically with war, colonialism, terror and militarization. This book examines elegies which challenge a necropoetic understanding of whose deaths may be grieved; elegies which articulate the various ways in which political and social powers render certain lives precarious, unstable and disposable. But, while it examines issues of white colonial violence and structures of white power, militarized forms of policing, prison-industrial and military-industrial complexes, its scope does not encompass all the various forms of elegy that might be understood as working against these necropoetics. There is further scope, for instance, to explore elegies of the plantation, the refugee camp, the prison, the detention centre, the border, the barricade and the benefits sanction.

This book offers a move towards destabilizing existing genealogical structures in order to reimagine how we might approach and understand elegies differently. Its purpose is to investigate the rhetorical means by which certain elegies have been marginalized and excluded from elegy discourse; to explore elegies that interrogate and critique structures of power (specifically white violence and patriarchy); and to examine possibilities for rethinking elegy beyond genealogical constructions. Nevertheless, there is without doubt, scope for more work to be done to address elegy's necropolitical and necropoetical structures beyond this book's parameters.

Radical elegies

Functioning as a critique of the genealogical frameworks of elegy scholarship, it should go without saying that this book is not a genealogy of elegy. It does not offer a poetic lineage of any kind, nor does it originate or depart from a particular historical point in order to arrive at another. It does not provide fixed definitions or categorizations. Its understanding of elegy is broad and inclusive but, by necessity, it cannot reflect elegy in all its multiple, various and nuanced iterations.

Genealogical approaches tend to define elegy as a form or a genre of poetry. While, in classical contexts, the term 'elegy' referred to a specific form – couplets consisting of a hexameter followed by a pentameter – it has a more flexible definition in modern contexts: as a poetry encapsulating loss and/or grief of various kinds. It includes, for instance, the death of a loved one; loss through separation, estrangement or exile; the loss or destruction of something in nature; the loss of an identity or culture; loss on a national or international scale; loss of the self, either literally (in that a poet might imagine themselves dying or address their imminent death) or figuratively (as a symbolic or metaphorical death); or the anticipation of a loss that has not yet taken place. Because of this semantic flexibility, elegy is better understood as a mode or mood rather than a form or genre. Van Der Auwera and Aguilar describe mood as a 'frame of mind,' or 'disposition,' and mode as a 'measure,' or 'manner' (2016: 2). They also associate mood with 'inclination of the mind,' and 'attitude' (2016: 15; 7). Owen Earnshaw describes mood as the 'background,' which 'determines how we can perceive the world,' while V. K. Chari describes the mood of a poem as that to which, 'an orchestration of a variety of major and minor emotional tones' are 'subordinated' (Chari 1976: 289–90; Earnshaw 2017: 1700). This book understands elegy as a mode or a mood; as any poetry that expresses a disposition or frame of mind conditioned by loss; or as the background of loss across which various other complex emotions play out. All of the elegies examined in this book may be understood as elegies according to this definition.

As we have seen, genealogical approaches to elegy are often constructed on principles of whiteness, patriarchy and heteronormativity. Though these approaches have, on occasion, included references to work by writers who are *not* cis straight white men, such work is often defined by its opposition to these categories; that is to say, it is defined by its 'not-whiteness'; its 'not-maleness'; or its non-heteronormativity. This creates a paradox in elegy scholarship's inclusion of work understood, within its own genealogical constructions, as 'other': when included – elegies by writers of colour, women's elegies, queer and trans* elegies – it is on the basis of a perceived difference which, when incorporated into the genealogy, is flattened out. This is what Morrison refers to as a 'gathering of a culture's difference into the skirts of the Queen'; a colonialist tendency to assimilate literary work within Eurocentric structures whose ideals are represented as universal (1988: 134). Genealogical constructions of elegy, in other words, make space for difference only if that difference can be assimilated into a notion of a common experience of grief and loss. They do not acknowledge elegies that voice ways in which grief and loss are experienced *because* of the principles upon which genealogical frameworks are constructed – namely whiteness, patriarchy, heteronormativity – for the simple reason that such elegies challenge the very notion of a common grief experience. Radical elegies, then, challenge the foundations upon which genealogical constructions of elegy are built.

The elegies examined in this book can be understood as radical in three ways. The first, and perhaps most obvious, relates to the various ways in which they depart from the aesthetic and thematic standards of canonical elegies; in other words, the 'English elegy' and its Anglo-American legacies. They are elegies written in response to social injustices, forms of oppression and erasure, and as such they represent what Mbembe – alluding to Frantz Fanon – describes as '[t]he celebration of the imagination produced by struggle' (2019: 141). They represent the 'breaking apart,' of 'old cultural sedimentations' (Mbembe 2019: 141). They embody language that 'perforates, and digs like a gimlet, that knows how to become a projectile' (Mbembe 2019: 189). Or, to borrow from Butler, they challenge the 'taken-for-granted reality' presented by genealogical approaches (2016: 12).

Secondly, they are radical because they advocate for fundamental social and political change, responding to injustices and discriminatory policies and practices. Many are written in resistance to necropolitical mechanisms that render certain lives precarious, unstable and disposable; and that render some lives publicly grievable but not others. In doing so, they assert the grievability of lives that are rendered precarious and/or have been erased and marginalized by necropolitical systems. As Butler argues, the act of recasting such precarious lives as grievable 'expose[s] their living status to those powers that threaten' them (2020; 24). The elegies explored in this book write against police and military brutality, carceral systems, the regulation of bodies, the erasure and marginalization of identities and forms of being. They write against borders and boundaries, against ableism, against dehumanization. They write about erasures and marginalizations, from a position of erasure and marginalization. They critique patriarchal structures, disturb gendered binaries and directly challenge white supremacy.

Finally, they are radical in the sense that they are vital; they write against necropolitical forms of death and towards life. They each embody a 'gesture of care as a practice of resymbolization,' finding new meanings and new ways of articulating grief in order to reject colonial systems and their 'manufacturing' of a 'panoply of suffering' (Mbembe 2019: 5). Writing out of struggle, they investigate possibilities 'of reciprocity and mutuality' (Mbembe 2019: 5).

The book begins with an in-depth examination of the mechanics used to sustain certain erasures and marginalizations within genealogical constructions of elegy; in other words, the rhetorical manoeuvres required to maintain an overarching picture of elegy as principally a poetry written by white men. Chapter 1 takes as its starting point a quote by Toni Morrison that asks '[w]hat intellectual feats had to be performed' in order to achieve the conspicuous absences of marginalized voices within certain literary traditions and how 'certain absences are so stressed, so ornate, so planned, they call attention to themselves' (1988: 136). In its focus on the critical reception of Black and African American women's elegies within elegy scholarship, the chapter calls attention to these intellectual feats through textual and paratextual analysis. Building on Young's identification of a tendency to package Gwendolyn Brooks's work as 'safe,' the chapter explores an implicit 'safe' vs. 'dangerous' binary often applied to Black women's work, in which 'safe,' is understood as unthreatening and unalienating to white readers; and 'dangerous' is understood as work which explicitly resists white authority. The chapter then examines the subversion of this binary in the framework of a Black Aesthetic, arising out of the Black Arts Movement. The final part of the chapter performs analyses of poems by Phillis Wheatley, Gwendolyn Brooks and Lucille Clifton, in order to foreground some of the subtle and overt ways in which they resist elegiac norms. The chapter ends by sketching out a brief – and necessarily partial – transhistorical list of further elegiac texts by Black, African American and multiracial women poets.

Chapter 2 explores issues that arise when attempting to address issues of marginalization and exclusion by subsuming marginalized elegies into genealogical frameworks. Further, it examines how differences might be adequately acknowledged beyond measuring according to the standards of the 'English elegy'. As a part of this exploration, the chapter analyses elegies that respond to racial injustice, violence and oppression, beginning with close readings of three elegies written in response to the murder of Emmett Till. These analyses reveal and explore glitches in the symbolic myths and rigid hierarchies of power upon which constructions of white masculinity depend; and outline a rhetorical economy that underpins white supremacist thought: that of violence against Black bodies in exchange for the 'protection' of an imagined white feminine purity. The chapter then shifts context to elegies written in the Civil Rights Era, specifically two elegiac responses to the murder of Martin Luther King, Jr. Finally, the chapter examines three poems from different post-Civil Rights contexts and, while connected by threads such as the critique of militarized forms of policing and white structures of power, the poems are examined in their specific contexts in order to pay attention to their individual, particular historical moments and means of articulation.

Investigating potential spaces that trans*feminist theory and queer politics open up for rethinking elegy beyond genealogical constructions, Chapter 3 maps out some of the issues that arise from reading elegy according to a gendered binary. Using as key frameworks both Mbembe's political theory of necropolitics and Haritaworn, Kuntsman and Posocco's *Queer Necropolitics* (2014), it examines three elegies by trans* writers whose poems critique the role of language and abstraction in the dynamic of transmisogynistic violence; interrogate trans* commemorative practices; resist the violence of social systems of regulation; highlight the threat of violence to which gender-non-conforming bodies are constantly subjected; underscore the nexus of precarities within which trans* bodies are situated; and construct potential spaces of resistance to patriarchal, heteronormative and colonial powers.

The final chapter unpacks Mbembe's concept of the anti-museum, tentatively examining possible new approaches to elegy that might resist genealogical constructions. Exploring Mbembe's term *radical hospitality* through Derrida's critique of the guest/host dynamic, the chapter explores how this might be applied in approaches to elegy in order to disrupt systems of ownership and literary lineage. The chapter ends with analyses of three personal elegies that variously explore resistant forms of myth-making, fragile intimacies through sites of commonality, diasporic familial loss, and the pathologizing violences experienced by D/deaf persons both socio-culturally and interpersonally.

A note on positionality

One element of white privilege (or 'white living,' as Claudia Rankine calls it in her 2020 book *Just Us*) is the privilege to choose when and where to engage with issues of race (2020: 27). It is the privilege to choose not to write or talk about it; not to include it in a book or syllabus or journal article or classroom discussion. Or, it is the privilege to talk and write about race and then go home and think about something else. To work against 'white living,' then – if one is white – is to constantly and necessarily examine how whiteness structures one's encounters, interactions and interpretations. It is to constantly remind oneself of these structures even if, and as, they are invisibilized; and as they shift in response to other cultural shifts. We might say, then, that to engage critically only with work by white writers is to be a scholar only of white literature. And we may equally make similar points about what might be termed 'straight living,' 'cis living' and 'able-bodied living.' Another facet of privilege is the capacity to engage discursively with violent discourses without the sustained emotional labour involved in navigating subjective lived experiences of those same discourses. In the interests of what Lindsay Eales and Danielle Peers – citing Eli Clare – term 'collective space care,' readers should therefore be advised that the content of this book engages extensively with these kinds of violent discourses within its analysis (2020: 164).

Genealogies – as a framework – can often obfuscate layers of privilege. Genealogical models by nature imply comprehensiveness; the 'from... to...' framing reflects range, scale and scope as if 'the whole gamut' of its subject is included under its rubric. Its structure gestures away from the fact that who and what is included within a text is a choice made by the author. The token inclusion, within genealogical scholarly approaches, of one or two marginalized writers, points attention away from all the other writers that have not been included. Worse, situated within a genealogical context that is otherwise largely white and male (as well as straight, cis and able-bodied), these inclusions imply that those who are included are a rarity or an exception to the so-called standard.

Structures of power are deeply ingrained, and they take time and work to deconstruct. But that deconstruction is necessary. It has always been necessary, as the radical elegies in this book make plain. And it is as necessary now as it has ever been. White privilege – or 'white living' (ditto 'straight living,' 'cis living' and 'able-bodied living') – requires that scholars, writers, teachers and publishers rigorously examine the ways in which ideologies of white supremacy, patriarchy, heteronormativity, ableism and necropolitics have been upheld – knowingly or unknowingly – within texts, curricula, syllabi, classrooms and so on, while also recognizing that nothing will be achieved without widespread structural change (Rankine 2020: 27).

As of early 2021, the UK Conservative Party has launched a 'full on war on woke,' a so-called 'Culture War' against campaigners, activists and academics who they believe 'focus too much on the protected characteristics [...] including race, sex and gender reassignment' (Casalicchio 2021: para 1). According to Equalities Minister Liz Truss, such a focus leads to the neglect of issues facing white working-class children, an argument that both erases the disadvantages faced by working-class children of other ethnic backgrounds and divisively sets in opposition different vulnerable social groups (Casalicchio 2021: para 5; Treloar 2021: para 6; para 13). Moreover, as attempts are made to decolonize curricula, critics on the right have lamented 'left-wing academics helping minority students to force their identity politics on the rest' of the population (Peters 2017: headline). British heritage organizations have been threatened with defunding by the British culture secretary Oliver Dowden if their projects focus 'too heavily on Britain's imperial history,' which the Common Sense Group (a team of over fifty Tory MPs) described as an '"ideologically motivated endeavour" to rewrite history' (Murray 2021: para 4; para 8). In this way, as many cultural attitudes about protected characteristics and marginalized identities shift in progressive directions, and institutions begin to reflect those changes, so social, cultural and political discourses on the right organize to suppress and resist those changes.

In the same way that curricula and heritage projects are reassessing cultural and social understandings of history and knowledge, it is both timely and necessary to reassess literary approaches to elegy; to examine whose voices have been heretofore excluded from canonical formations and why, and to devise ways to resituate and foreground those voices. It is time, in other words, to destabilize the boundaries that have, in genealogical constructions of elegy, circumscribed whose lives are publicly grievable and whose broken hearts matter.

Notes

1   Throughout this book, I capitalize the word 'Black' as it refers to racial or cultural identity, unless it is within a citation. Lorne Foster argues that the capitalization of the word 'Black' within language is a 'revolutionary linguistic act,' because it 'represents a perverse usage of the colonizer's language,' and operates as a 'type of negation or affirmation placed before ruling discourses that frame […] social reality' (2003: para 3). And Kathy English, Public Editor of the Toronto publication *The Star* points out in a 2017 article, that 'there are long-standing stylebook "rules" and conventions […] that have provided reasons for not capitalizing […] "Black"' in newspapers and publications, but that this requires updating in instances where the word describes an 'identity, community and culture' (2017: para 2; para 3).
2   Further examples include Zeiger's chapter on breast cancer elegies (1997); Anita Helle's chapter on 'Women's Elegies, 1834-Present' and Maeera Y. Shreiber's chapter on 'Kaddish: Jewish American Elegy Post-1945' in Weisman (2010); Krupat (2012); Zafar (2013); M. Hammond (2010); and Hartman's article on the poetry of Al-Khansa (2011).
3   Helle refers to Gwendolyn Brooks's elegy 'The Mother'; and names both Lucille Clifton and Audre Lorde in a list of poets who have written on the theme of breast cancer; Max Cavitch briefly mentions Phillis Wheatley as the 'first prolific African American elegist'; while Mellor names Wheatley as an example of a woman elegist who 'insist[s] on the conduct proper of a man,' that is 'often at odds with the

masculine virtues eulogised in male-authored elegies' (Cavitch 2010: 228; Helle 2010: 470; 473; Mellor 2010: 455).

4 See Henry Louis Gates, Jr (2003: 49–50).

5 It is worth acknowledging, in this particular example, that even when the latter poem *is* attributed to Herbert, elegy scholars often do so while labelling her a 'Spenserian poet,' thus implying her work is derivative of his, and in doing so eliding her individuality and poetic contribution (Kay 1990: n53).

6 Behn's work was – like that of many other seventeenth-century woman poets – critically discussed at the time in heavily misogynistic terms. For instance, Janet M. Todd describes how Eric Robertson wrote in 1883 that 'it is a "pity" that "mention should be made of so unsexed a writer as Mrs. Aphra Behn"; it is a "fearful task" to read through her "corrupt plays"' (Todd 1998: 47–8).

7 For more on monopoly capitalism and economic stagnation, see Keith Cowling (1995: 430–46).

8 While there is potential for the two terms to overlap, the term *necropoetics* should be semantically distinguished from Joyelle McSweeney's term *necropastoral*, which she describes as a 'political-aesthetic zone in which the fact of mankind's depredations cannot be separated from an experience of "nature" which is poisoned, mutated, aberrant, spectacular, full of ill effects and affects' (2014: para 6). Similarly, *necropoetics* should be distinguished from Cristina Rivera Garza's term, *necrowriting* outlined in her book *The Restless Dead: Necrowriting and Disappropriation* (Nashville: Vanderbilt University Press, 2020). The latter term describes 'corpse texts' and 'writing practices that both bear witness to and resist the violence and death resulting from the neoliberal state,' and which specifically employ a poetics of disappropriation, defined by communality, collective working practices and the explicit recognition of writing as labour (2020: 12; 5; 55).

1

Ornate absences and rhetorical acts: The scholarly reception of elegies by Black and African American women poets

In relation to the conspicuous absences of Black women's writing from literary scholarship, Toni Morrison asks '[w]hat intellectual feats had to be performed,' in order to achieve them (1988: 136). '[C]ertain absences,' she argues, 'are so stressed, so ornate, so planned, they call attention to themselves; arrest us with intentionality and purpose' (1988: 136). To achieve such absences, she suggests, certain rhetorical actions and critical positions are necessary. This same question may be levelled at genealogies of elegy in relation to the absence of critical attention paid to work by women of colour. As we have seen in the Introduction, such little attention as is paid is, in almost all instances, attention to elegies by Black and African American women writers. While Krupat covers elegiac work by Indigenous American women (including Linda Hogan and Jane Johnson Schoolcraft) (2012); and Hammond explores elegy in the context of Arabic women's poetry (2010), elegies by Asian, African, West Asian and North African, Caribbean, Latinx and Chicanx poets are so significantly marginalized and excluded from genealogical approaches that their work is often not mentioned at all. This renders investigation into any rhetorical devices employed as a means of maintaining that exclusion extremely difficult, since there are few or no examples to examine. It is for this reason that this chapter takes as its focus elegiac work by Black and African American women writers. This is not, however, to suggest that the marginalization and exclusion of work by women elegists of colour within genealogical approaches is limited to dichotomous Black and white racial constructions. The aim of this chapter is to highlight the rhetorical means – the 'intellectual feats,' to quote Morrison – that have been performed in order to maintain the conspicuous absence of work by Black women in genealogical approaches to elegy (1988: 136). In doing so, however, it should not be overlooked that there are means by which these and other absences are maintained that remain invisible, in particular the decision not to include any reference to work by women of colour whatsoever, as in the examples of Shaw (1994); Spargo (2005); Kennedy (2007); Sacks (1987); Smith (1977); and Kay (1990). In addition to the 'intellectual feats' explored within this chapter, we must be equally attentive to blanket omissions like these and the structural biases they demonstrate (Morrison 1988: 136).

Black elegies, white elegies: Prescriptive gestures

Ramazani (1994) makes frequent references to Black women's work, though some of these references warrant close analysis. The title of Ramazani's book – *Poetry of Mourning* – implies that the contents will provide an overview of poetries that express or embody the practice or experience of mourning. The subtitle – *The Modern Elegy from Hardy to Heaney* – suggests a chronology of twentieth-century elegists beginning with Thomas Hardy's elegies in *Poems of 1912-13* and ending with those of Seamus Heaney from the 1960s onwards. In other words, based on the title alone, a reader might expect broad and inclusive coverage of elegies from that time period. However, *Poetry of Mourning* is not as broad and inclusive as the book's title implies. Alongside a chapter on Langston Hughes and a section on Michael S. Harper, and in addition to Hardy and Heaney, the book examines Wilfred Owen, Wallace Stevens, W.H. Auden and Sylvia Plath, along with seven other white poets organized under the heading 'American Family Elegy'.

Just as Ramazani's framing of his text as a genealogy implies a survey of the elegiac tradition, many other elegy scholarship texts make explicit claims about their broad scope. For instance, Sacks's book (1987) is described in its blurb as 'an interpretative study of a genre,' while Kennedy's *Elegy* (2007) is described as 'an overview of the history of elegy'. It is only in Zeiger's text, *Beyond Consolation* (1997) that Black women's elegy is given substantial critical space in her engagement with Lorde's breast cancer poems. However, as Morrison points out, 'invisible things are not necessarily "not-there"' (1988: 136). In other words, this broad lack of acknowledgement within elegy discourse does not signify that Black women have not written elegies.

While Ramazani does – importantly – dedicate critical space to Black women's elegy, this largely takes place within a chapter which examines the work of Langston Hughes.[1] Ramazani describes Hughes's work as bringing into elegiac poetry a 'scorned world' of Black poverty, in which 'death is no abstract possibility but an omnipresent and everyday reality,' and suggests that in doing so, he 'mak[es] it easier for a poet like Gwendolyn Brooks to write extensively about the death-haunted lives of the black urban poor' (1994: 157).

This description of poor Black lives as a 'scorned world' presents Black poverty as something contemptible or despised: the word 'scorned' – which denotes something mocked, disdained, or rejected – is a derisive choice of wording for the form of marginalization he is indicating (Ramazani 1994: 157). Further, by describing these lives as a 'world,' he presents them as self-contained and separate from – rather than a condition of – society, which subtly operates as an othering gesture that does not acknowledge that Black urban poverty is a product of systemic racial inequality *within* capitalist society. Importantly, his assertion implicitly makes Brooks's work contingent upon the work of Hughes. We might read this as signposting Hughes's influence on poets who came after him (including Brooks); or that Hughes paved the way for other Black poets to be published. But it is nonetheless a genealogical gesture. The description of her poetry as 'extensively about the death-haunted lives of the black urban poor,' reduces her nuanced and complex work to a singular facet that can be traced easily and exclusively back to Hughes (Ramazani 1994: 157). We might also note that Ramazani refers to 'a poet *like* Gwendolyn Brooks,' rather than to Brooks specifically (1994: 157; emphasis mine). By implying that a poet *like* Brooks was able to write because Hughes did so first presents a literary lineage which elides issues of gender that existed both within and outside of the literary milieu within which Brooks was writing.

Ramazani's broader discussion of Hughes's work appears to distinguish the work of Black elegists as intrinsically different from those written by white elegists. His chapter on Hughes begins with the suggestion that the phrase 'African-American elegy' might 'seem to be a contradiction in terms or a redundancy': a 'contradiction' because elegy has been 'defined as a European form, inherited from the Alexandrian Greeks, and passed on via Spenser and Milton to the English-speaking whites of subsequent periods'; and a 'redundancy' because 'African-American poems' have often been categorized as 'Sorrow Songs' (1994: 135). Ramazani's underlying point appears to be that Black writers have written poems that span a range of different forms and emotional registers, but his framing and phrasing exemplifies the way in which genealogical approaches to elegy enable the marginalization and exclusion of Black writing. The definition of elegy as a 'European form' is presented as unquestionable fact, even though Ramazani notes that Black writing is often understood as elegiac in nature.

Having stated that Black poets have created work that explores a wide range of forms and subjects, he goes on to say that 'they have mastered the elegy,' later referring to the work of Hughes and other Black poets as a 'large achievement' (Ramazani 1994: 135). His use of the word 'master' here implies an act of taking ownership of something that does not already belong to a person; or the acquiring of a skillset that one does not initially possess. Further, while the word 'master' has carried the meaning of a craftsman or skilled person since the late twelfth century, the word cannot be extricated entirely from its legacy as a sixteenth-century legal term for a slave owner. Thus, the word 'master' carries white supremacist implications, albeit perhaps deeply embedded. The depiction of this supposed mastery of the elegy as a 'large achievement' implies that the skillset acquirement is one that does not come naturally; that it required considerable effort to attain (Ramazani 1994: 135). It reflects the way in which a genealogical framework understands elegy as a literary form which integrally belongs to white writers; and moreover, that for Black writers to engage with it requires some kind of exceptional or extraordinary ability.

This implication is reinforced by later assertions that 'African-American elegists have remade the Eurocentric genre *in their own image*,' and that Black elegies are a 'revisionary *appropriation*' (Ramazani 1994: 135–6; emphases mine). Ramazani's discussion of Black elegiac work thus depends on an understanding of the elegiac mode as, first-and-foremost, Eurocentric; the notion of 'revisionary appropriation' implies a primary Eurocentric ownership of elegy as something that has been taken and modified (1994: 135–6). This is also evident in the claim that the 'large achievement' of the so-called mastery of elegy by Black writers is 'diminished when placed in this genealogy [i.e. *Poetry of Mourning*] or in comparable genealogies of such European genres of sonnet and epic' (Ramazani 1994: 135). This seems to suggest that the accomplishment reflected by Black elegies is lessened or devalued when held in comparison with the 'English elegy' and its European legacies. It is only in a 'dual context of African-American and European forms of poetic lament' that Hughes's work can be 'properly appreciated,' according to Ramazani (1994: 135). This reflects and reinforces the idea that elegy is a mode that intrinsically belongs to Europeans, and to those of European descent. In other words, it demonstrates the way in which genealogical conceptions of elegy inevitably lead to equivocations about who can and cannot be included within it.

Later in the text, Ramazani discusses elegies that were written by Black poets following the death of Malcolm X, and in doing so claims that some of these poems – those by Amiri Baraka and Margaret Walker in particular – were written 'in a collective, eulogistic mode less functional for contemporary white Americans' (1994: 174). This assertion suggests explicitly that they are not as useful to white readers as they are to Black readers. His reasoning is that they constitute a 'representative response, articulating "our" loss on behalf of other members of "our" community' (1994: 174). This relies upon an assumption that elegy might have a particular function that can only be experienced within racial categories. Specifically, it implies that white readers have nothing to gain from engaging with the loss of Malcolm X through perspectives articulated by Black writers. The use of quotation marks around the words 'our' serves to emphasize a sense of separateness and exclusion; Ramazani appears to imply that Baraka and Walker's poems are 'less functional' because they are not explicitly addressed to non-Black readers (1994: 174).

As Sonia Sanchez recounts in an interview with Eisa Davis and Lucille Clifton, the perception of Malcolm X as a figure of no interest beyond the Black community is a revisionist one: '[p]eople don't understand that whites, blacks, everybody loved Malcolm. […] they stood up and clapped and stamped their feet for this man' (Davis 2002: 1055). We might also argue – to borrow from Michael Awkward's examination of minority studies – that elegies like those for Malcolm X, 'represent sophisticated traditions of thought that can effectively illuminate the political, cultural, and economic history of non-European and/ or non-white male descendants in America' (1995: 80). In other words, white readers have plenty to gain from reading articulations of loss outside of those written by white writers or those addressed to white readers, particularly when these articulations specifically address events that took place within an important political and cultural context. We might thus read Ramazani's assertion as potentially reinforcing what bell hooks refers to as 'assumptions that cultural productions by black people can only have "authentic" significance and meaning for a black audience' (1990: 110).

This argument leads Ramazani to the conclusion that the 'subjective ambivalence,' and 'anti-eulogistic poetics of white American poets' (such as Sylvia Plath, Robert Lowell and John Berryman), is 'in part, ethnically based'; a claim that implies a distinction between a white elegiac aesthetic and a Black one (1994: 174). This raises a number of problematic issues. To begin with, if there are arguments to be made for such a distinction, they would certainly require significant further analysis to substantiate them. To simply demarcate the two aesthetics as 'eulogistic,' on the one hand, and 'anti-eulogistic' on the other, is a considerable oversimplification. For instance, if – as it would seem – Ramazani uses the elegies for Malcolm X as representative of *all* Black elegies, he consequently overlooks that many Black elegists have written work that incorporates 'subjective ambivalence'; while many white elegists have adopted a eulogistic – and indeed a collective – mode (1994: 174).

Further, such a demarcation draws comparisons with the complex and contentious notion of a Black Aesthetic. Though many theorists have drawn upon this notion – particularly in relation to poetry written during the Black Power and Black Arts Movements – many Black writers themselves have articulated ambivalence towards the term. Gwendolyn Brooks, for instance, has stated that she was 'so sick and tired of hearing about the "Black aesthetic,"' and further that she was, 'glad of [its] loss,' after the 1960s (Tate 1985: 45). Similarly, Nikki Giovanni asserted, when asked if there is a Black Aesthetic: 'I am not interested in defining it. I don't trust people who do,' and further that '[t]hat kind of prescription cuts off the question,' of what Black culture has achieved, 'by defining parameters' (Tate 1985: 63). Ramazani's distinction seems to perform a similarly prescriptive gesture by implying that some Black elegies might be of little use for white readers; and that they might be understood as separate from or subsidiary to a Eurocentric tradition that can equally – according to these demarcations – be reduced to one particular poetic mode. We might understand this delineative gesture, as with any delineation based on racial categories, as constituting what Kutzinski refers to as a 'policing [of] canonical borders,' based on 'problematic assumptions about how authors and texts ought to profess their national, political, or ethnic identities' (1992: 552). By gesturing towards a distinction between poetic modes of Black and white elegy, Ramazani's points maintain a binary that allows for the policing of the ways in which poets of different racial identities articulate grief through poetry. However, as Kutzinski points out – and as can be discerned in the ambivalent assertions of Brooks and Giovanni above – writers themselves frequently regard these kinds of 'critical and cultural systems of classification [...] with some measure of disdain' (1992: 552). Simply put, writers do not always subscribe to the kind of literary policing that such demarcations enact and permit.

To be clear, in my analysis of Ramazani's chapter here, I do not mean to imply that his text exhibits deliberate racial biases, but rather that a racial binary nonetheless underlies some of the statements made within it. In some ways the focus on Ramazani's text in particular is unfair since, as I have outlined earlier, many elegy scholarship texts do not critically engage with Black women's elegies – or indeed, Black elegists of any gender – at all.

Safe grief and dangerous grief

bell hooks addresses the issue of Black writers publishing within a hegemonically white industry. She argues that Black writing 'is shaped by a market that reflects white supremacist values and concerns,' and that Black writers trying to publish will usually encounter a 'white hierarchy determining who will edit one's work' (1990: 18, 11). A similar assertion is made by Young, who argues that a 'predominantly white publishing industry reflects and often reinforces the racial divide that has always defined American society' (2010: 4). This context is integral to understanding the intellectual feats that are examined in this chapter, since it is the fundamental backdrop against which such feats take place.

Let us take, for example, the publishing context of Phillis Wheatley's poems. Wheatley was forced to legally defend the authorship of her poetry in court. Her book *Poems on Various Subjects, Religious and Moral* (1773) was prefaced with paratextual material that verified her as its author, written by a number of Boston men of standing including the famous signatory John Hancock, the minister Charles Chauncy and the governor of Massachusetts Thomas Hutchinson. Her access to publication was therefore entirely mediated, controlled and facilitated by her wealthy white owners and their acquaintances. Wheatley was later unable to publish further work, despite making several proposals for a second volume. As Helen M. Burke has suggested, '[w]ithout the aid of her powerful friends in the white establishment, [...] Phillis Wheatley was indeed silent and silenced' (1991: 40).

Gwendolyn Brooks's publications provide another example. Having published with Harper & Row up until the late 1960s, her shift to small and independently run Black presses – Broadside and Third World – was unprecedented. James D. Sullivan suggests that it was a transferral not motivated by economic factors, but rather signifying a move away from a 'mainstream-poetry-buying public,' to a publisher that enabled her to write, publish and distribute her work 'in a black context' (2002: 557; 560). This implicitly presents Harper & Row as a white publishing context from which Brooks actively decided to break. Though her later poems published through Broadside and Third World have received academic attention, many readers outside of an academic context are – according to Young – only familiar with the (now HarperPerennial) *Selected Poems* which, he suggests, 'remains the most widely available venue for casual readers of her work' (2010: 103–4).

Young's analysis of this book's paratextual material is insightful, particularly in relation to the intellectual feats we are seeking to examine here. He cites an afterword by literary critic Hal Hager, which states that 'there is nothing bitter or explicitly vengeful,' about Brooks's work (cited in Young 2010: 104). He also cites an excerpted essay by Harvey Curtis Webster, who claims that Brooks 'is a very good poet [...] compared to other Negro poets or other women poets but to the best of modern poets, she ranks high [*sic*]' (cited in Young 2010: 106). This excerpt continues, seeking to reassure readers that, though her poems explore explicitly racial subject matter – he lists Emmett Till, Little Rock and Dorie Miller, for instance – she nonetheless refuses 'to let Negro-ness limit her humanity' (cited in Young 2010: 106–7). As Young points out, Webster's remarks not only 'implicitly identif[y] the "best of modern poets" as white and male,' but they also approach Brooks's work entirely through 'racialist discourse' (2010: 107). Similarly, Hagar's remark depends upon racist assumptions in its implication that, as a Black woman poet, she might be *assumed* to be bitter or explicitly vengeful.

Tellingly, Webster's remarks have been abridged in more recent reprints of the anthology, though surprisingly not removed entirely. The 2006 version included on its back cover only the extracted phrase: 'compared... to the best of modern poets, she ranks high,' in which the ellipsis omits its overtly racist content (2006: n.p). We can discern similar discourse in another quote on the same 2006 cover, this time from Robert F. Kiernan that reads '[p]robably the finest black poet of the post-Harlem generation' (2006: n.p). This quote explicitly limits the superlative quality of Brooks's work to within a racial category of poets and qualifies its assertion with a conditional. In other words, for Kiernan, Brooks is not 'the' finest poet, but 'probably' the finest one 'of the post-Harlem generation'. Moreover, given that the Harlem Renaissance – to which Kiernan's 'post-Harlem generation' comment is referring – was a Black cultural and artistic movement, it is doubly strange that he chooses to further include the word 'black'. This has the effect of gesturing towards her Blackness twice, both implicitly and explicitly, perhaps in order to be unequivocal – for the sake of white readers – in his classification of Brooks as a Black writer. His description of Brooks, not as the finest poet of the post-Harlem generation but 'probably' the finest 'black' one, implies the possibility that there are other, non-Black post-Harlem poets who are perhaps better. Thus, though Kiernan's quote might seem – on the face of it – to constitute praise, its heavy reliance on racial discourse also serves to set the book apart from white writing. In Young's view, this kind of 'carefully package[d]' promotion of Brooks's work not only elides most of her later poetry in favour of work published with Harper & Row, but also operates as a means of presenting Brooks as what he calls a '"safe" Black poet' (2010: 104, 107).

What Young's assertion gestures towards here is a binary that underlies promotional descriptions of Brooks's work; that Brooks is a 'safe' Black poet in comparison with others who might, by implication, be considered 'unsafe' or 'dangerous'. We can see another example of this binary at work in Allison Cummings's description of how a 'largely white critical establishment' praised Brooks's early work in part for its '"transcendence" of racial themes' (2005: 7). This implies a trend for white critics to consider racial themes unworthy of praise. We can also see it at work in Sullivan's citing of a review of Brooks's *Selected Poems* by Louis Simpson published in *Book Week*. The review questions whether it is 'possible for a Negro to write well without making us aware he is a Negro,' and further that 'if being a Negro is the only subject, the writing is not important' (cited in Sullivan 2002: 559). For Simpson, then, racial themes were not only considered unworthy of praise but irrelevant for critics and readers and thus not worthy of critical attention at all. We might identify a similar binary underlying C.D.B Bryan's *New York Times* review of Toni Cade Bambara's collection of short stories, *Gorilla, My Love*. In it, he states: 'I am so tired of being shouted at, patronized, bullied, and antagonized by black writers,' and further 'I dislike being told I'm an insensitive, arrogant honky who won't listen' (cited in Tate 1985: 26). He praises Bambara for her 'quiet, proud, silly, tender, hip, acute, loving' writing that explores themes of love to which he feels he can relate (cited in Tate 1985: 26). Here, Bryan's conception of a 'safe' Black writer is one who does not antagonize white readers or address them *as* white with any contempt or criticism, but is instead unobtrusive (quiet), dignified (proud), unserious (silly), affectionate (tender, loving) and cool (hip) in their writing. Within this binary, then, 'safe' might be understood as applying to work that does not engage with issues of race, that does not draw attention to racial experiences, and that does not antagonize white readers. 'Unsafe' or 'dangerous' work, on the other hand, would apply to work that is overtly or deliberately resisting white authority; that is perceived by white readers as bitter or vengeful in tone; or that adopts a rhetorical stance that makes white readers uncomfortable.

Alicia Ostriker's article on Lucille Clifton's poetry in *The American Poetry Review* (1993) provides a further example of how this binary operates as an intellectual feat enabling the tacit dismissal of Black women's poetry. Ostriker begins her review by describing Clifton's work as 'deceptively simple,' and 'declarative and direct,' adopting a 'smooth mix of standard English with varying styles and degrees of black vernacular' (1993: 41). Denoting Clifton as a 'mimimalist artist,' Ostriker claims that her poetry urges readers to 'take [their] humble places with a sense of balance and belonging instead of the anxiety and alienation promoted by more conspicuously sublime and ambitious artistries' (1993: 41).

This is a description that, on the face of it – like Kiernan's quote on the back cover of Brooks's *Selected Poems* – appears to constitute praise. However, a closer reading reveals ways in which the language used is codedly or obliquely disparaging. By depicting Clifton's work as 'simple,' 'mimimalist,' and as encouraging readers to 'take [their] humble places,' Ostriker repeatedly associates it with modesty (1993: 41). The word 'simple' implies unpretentiousness but also artlessness or lack of sophistication; an insinuation reinforced by her distinction between Clifton's work and that which is 'more conspicuously sublime and ambitious' (1993: 41). This delineation implies that Clifton's simplicity reflects passivity or a lack of visible assertiveness. Rather than reading Clifton's minimalism as precision or exactitude, she understands it as something less ambitious than poetry that is more linguistically elaborate. By describing it as less sublime than other artistries, she designates it as inferior in terms of expressing noble ideas; exploring higher spheres of thought or spirituality; achieving transcendence; or inspiring awe and extreme emotion. Thus, Clifton's work is distinguished from 'more ambitious artistries' which might be understood as striving towards a higher poetic endeavour. The explicit distinction between '*standard* English' and a 'black vernacular' implies that the latter should be understood in contradistinction to – rather than a part of – the former; it is *other*, existing outside the realms of so-called standard English (1993: 41; emphasis mine). For Ostriker, one of the positive qualities of Clifton's work is its ability to combine these two forms of articulation in a 'smooth' way; in other words, in a way that is not jarring for white readers, who may not be familiar with colloquialisms and idioms of a 'black vernacular' (1993: 41). Thus, for Ostriker, Clifton's work incorporates the 'other,' but not in such a way as to be alienating; it signifies difference, but in a way that remains relatable and familiar to white readers.

While Ostriker's description of Clifton's work may not explicitly incorporate discourses of race, Ostriker shifts tone midway through the review to address what she terms, 'the shadow' of race 'that is inseparable from the pleasure' she takes in Clifton's poetry (1993: 44). Read through the lens of this latter part of the review, the earlier description is inflected by implicit racial coding. Ostriker's analysis of Clifton's work is underscored by this conception of race as a 'shadow'; a blot or apparition that is indivisible from the perceived pleasurable qualities in Clifton's work.

For Ostriker, 'Black writers commonly appeal [...] to white readers,' by 'pull[ing] *us* out of *ourselves* into the condition of the Other, while their power and courage – as writers, as humans – empowers and encourages *us*' (1993: 44–5; emphases mine). This statement highlights that the focus of her concern is centred on the ways Clifton's work might be of interest for white readers. The use of words like 'us,' and 'ourselves,' is inherently racial; it implicitly assumes that the reader is white. Moreover, Black writers, according to the statement, inherently occupy a condition of 'the Other'. This condition is, in Ostriker's view, the source of Black writing's appeal. By 'pulling' white readers out of themselves, it enables them to experience difference conceptually and in an entirely abstract way. The 'power and courage' that Ostriker praises in the statement is qualified by the subsequent clause: 'as writers, as humans' (1993: 44–5). This statement performs a double movement: on the one hand, it praises Black writing for its ability to enable white readers to experience 'the Other'. However, it flattens out that difference in the qualification that it is 'as humans and writers' that Black writing 'empowers and encourages' (1993: 44–5). Thus, the possibility of its 'power and courage' deriving specifically from Clifton's identity as a Black writer is elided (1993: 44–5). We might understand this double movement in relation to bell hooks's description of an 'Otherness' that 're-inscribes patterns of colonial domination, where the "Other" is always made object, appropriated, interpreted, taken over by those in power, by those who dominate' (1990: 125). For hooks, this kind of othering gesture 'annihilates' and 'erases' the poet's voice by claiming '[n]o need to hear your voice when I can talk about you better than you can speak about yourself' (1990: 152). In other words, by evaluating Clifton's work in this way, Ostriker demonstrates a tendency for white readers to re-inscribe work with meaning according to their own hegemonic lens; to commodify the work's perceived 'Otherness' in order that it serve their own hermeneutic purposes. For Ostriker, Clifton's work has value because it permits white readers to experience 'the Other,' but within the same sentence, she denies the possibility of that value deriving from that very same 'Otherness'.

Ostriker recounts how she has seen 'a whole classroom of white undergraduates break into smiles,' reading Clifton's work because its 'self-affirmation was contagious' (1993: 44). This anecdotal example underscores a broader problem. In a discussion of teaching, bell hooks states, 'when I enter a classroom to teach about people of colour and the students present are nearly all white, I recognize this to be a risky situation' (1990: 132). hooks questions whether teaching in such a context might amount to 'serving as a collaborator with a racist structure'; a structure that systemically prevents Black students from accessing higher education (1990: 132). If Ostriker is aware of such a risk, she does not articulate it; the fact that her 'whole classroom' is made up of white undergraduates is a detail that goes unaddressed (1993: 44). Or rather, Clifton's poetic value is measured by the reactions of her white students; it has merit *because* it is relatable to them. In this way, Ostriker's anecdote is underpinned by an assumption that whiteness is the universal condition; a standard by which everything is measured.

By stating that she can 'identify with Clifton's voice, presence and power despite [her] whiteness and [Clifton's] blackness,' Ostriker claims a readerly ability to transcend racial binaries (1993: 44). In her view, Clifton's work does not incorporate what she terms 'militant rhetoric,' though it does incorporate what she refers to as 'bitterness' (1993: 44–5). We might compare this to Hal Hager's paratextual comments on Brooks's anthology, which claim 'there is nothing bitter or explicitly vengeful' about Brooks's work (cited in Young 2010: 104). In Ostriker's review, the word 'bitter' is made contiguous with, and compared to, a 'militant rhetoric,' as in Hager's comments it is made contiguous with vengefulness (1993: 44–5). It signifies acrimony, disagreeableness or hostility. For Ostriker, the 'pride and anger' in Clifton's work can only be experienced 'vicariously,' and she therefore concludes that Clifton's work 'targets' her whiteness, 'draw[ing] a circle in the sand' from which she 'stand[s] hurt, outside' (1993: 44–5). This undermines the earlier claim that she can 'identify' with Clifton's work 'despite [her] whiteness and [Clifton's] blackness' (1993: 44). Indeed, this conclusion explicitly expresses an inability to relate fully to Clifton's poetic anger, or even read it as part of what she terms a 'condition of the Other' (1993: 44–5). Specifically, it is Clifton's perceived mockery of white bodies in the poem 'my dream about being white' that particularly 'grieves' Ostriker (1993: 46). She laments that Clifton's poetry has the power to exclude white readers in its address. However, the interpretation of this poetic mocking as a direct criticism of the reader relies on the assumption that, to borrow again from bell hooks, the 'first people' that Black writers are addressing 'are privileged white readers' (1990: 11). It is the refusal in Clifton's poetry to be wholly and unquestionably relatable to white readers which amounts, for Ostriker, to the action of 'drawing a circle in the sand'.

We have seen how Ostriker derives value from Black poetry's appeal to white readers, who expect Black poetry to articulate experiences relatable to them. A deviation from that expectation represents, for Ostriker, a boundary or limit that Clifton has crossed. It is important to note that the 'circle in the sand' is not Clifton's own construction; it is one that Ostriker perceives in her work. Clifton has transgressed the parameters of a value-framework for what Ostriker believes Black poetry should be. The 'circle' metaphor signifies Ostriker's boundary of a perceived white literary authority; a boundary which her critique seeks to police. The shifting of responsibility for the 'circle' to Clifton fails to acknowledge Ostriker's own participation in a racialized hermeneutic dynamic. Her rhetorical appeal to Clifton – 'I don't demonize you, so don't demonize me' – further simplifies this dynamic to a Black writer–white reader dichotomy of the white imaginary; an ahistorical, reciprocal exchange between individuals who operate on a level playing field (1993: 46). But this dialogue is neither equal nor reciprocal, even in Ostriker's critique. Her assertion that Black writers 'pull' white readers 'into a condition of the Other,' is not a dynamic that works both ways (1993: 44–5). It is Clifton's ability to make Ostriker feel 'Other' – excluded outside of the so-called 'circle' – that she criticizes. She desires to be 'loved back' by the poetry and is unable to reconcile that her whiteness excludes her from such a possibility (1993: 46). Consequently, while Ostriker reads Clifton's work according to racial binaries, the perception of a racial discourse within Clifton's work is read as alienating to white readers and characterized as a 'shadow' within it.

Ostriker attempts to reconcile this conflict in her reading by rationalizing Clifton's anger. She argues that 'if whites actually tried to imagine being black,' they would 'go mad with pain and rage' (1993: 45). She describes 'being black' as living 'in a pool of hatred'; as being 'despised' while at the same time 'unconsciously envied'; and as a condition in which 'your boys and men can be killed,' while 'your women are just brown sugar' (1993: 45). This provides a distorted, one-dimensional representation of Blackness focused entirely on negative racialized and gendered tropes. She goes on to suggest that 'white people's ways' represent an 'abuse of power which black people would/will abuse too when they have equal opportunity,' and that 'all peoples are racist' (1993: 46). These phrases operate as a means of justifying white privilege by shifting focus towards what oppressed minorities 'would/will' do if social and racial hierarchies were reversed (1993: 46). In other words, they reflect anxieties of the white supremacist imaginary: that oppressed minorities must be 'kept under control' lest the balance of power be reversed. As Mbembe terms it, '[t]he white fears me not at all because of what I have done to it or of what I have given it to see, but owing to what he has done to me and thinks that I could do to him in return' (2019: 133).

Ostriker's imagined subversion of racial power structures also reflects a white liberal desire – and failure to – appropriate Black experience. Ostriker is grieved because she perceives herself to be excluded from the 'circle' of Black subjectivity. Imagining a reversal of the dynamics of racial oppression is a means of attempting to draw a fictional circle of one's own. 'If only the situation were reversed,' this fiction implies, 'I too might have my own circle from which I could exclude you'. That the majority of white poetry already operates as exclusionary to Black readers by assuming a supposedly universal white readership does not occur to Ostriker within her critique. Nor does the exclusion of Black students from academic spaces, as reflected in her description of the all-white classroom. Her focus is instead on Clifton's ability to exclude white readers. But, by prioritizing white responses to Clifton's work, she excludes Black readers from her own review.

This examination of Ostriker's article demonstrates how a rhetorical binary of the 'safe' Black poet vs. the 'unsafe' or 'dangerous' one is – intentionally or unintentionally – put to work as an intellectual feat that enables the disparagement of Black women's poetry. For Ostriker, Clifton's poetry is 'safe' when its simplicity and perceived lack of ambition is unthreatening; and when it enables white readers to engage with Otherness from a locus of abstraction and poetic detachment. It may, in other words, engage in racial discourse – such as the use of a Black vernacular – but not in a way that makes white readers feel uncomfortable or alienated. But Black poetry does not necessarily need to be 'militant' (i.e. overtly aggressive or antagonistic towards white readers) in order to be implicitly interpreted by white critics as 'dangerous'. It simply needs to transgress the boundaries of white expectation by either speaking from a position of Black subjectivity or speaking directly to a Black readership.

Militant grief and the Black Aesthetic

This 'safe' vs 'dangerous' binary is just one example of a racial framework that enables the marginalization and exclusion of Black women's poetic work. We might also consider as another example the framework of a Black Aesthetic. Formulations of a Black Aesthetic arose out of the Black Arts Movement (BAM) as a direct response to critical dismissals of Black writing by white scholars. These formulations were meant, in part, as a means of providing new ways for Black critics to approach Black literary work. However, many of these formulations simply subverted white hegemonic critical binaries. Thus, for instance, whereas in Ostriker's review a '*militant* rhetoric' is presented as a negative quality in Clifton's work, Cummings describes how, in accordance with a BAM Black Aesthetic, Gwendolyn Brooks's post-Harper & Row poetry was celebrated for its 'racial themes, violence, [and] *militancy*' (Cummings 2005: 7; emphases mine;

Ostriker 1993: 44–5). As we have seen, the term Black Aesthetic is one about which Brooks – among other writers – has articulated ambivalence. bell hooks, for instance, describes the BAM Black Aesthetic as 'fundamentally essentialist' in its approach (1990: 107).

The term might broadly be defined as describing work that aimed to be 'accessible to ordinary readers,' through 'recognizable, coherent, empowering representations of race, gender, and class' (Cummings 2005: 14). It has been used to designate work that sought to 'turn [...] away from a white audience [...] to construct works addressed to a specifically black audience' (Hoyt W. Fuller, cited in Sullivan 2002: 559). And it was used to encompass work that focused on 'black identity, black solidarity, black self-possession and self-address' (Brooks, cited in Jackson Ford 2010: 388). Arising out of a need 'to struggle collectively against [...] white hegemony's devaluative figurations of blackness in order to maintain a positive self and group image,' it sought to address itself solely to Black readers, incorporating accessible language and unified representations of Blackness (Awkward 1995: 26).

Nikki Giovanni's description of Black Aesthetic criticism as 'a kind of prescription' that 'defines parameters,' gestures towards some of the issues that arose from reading Black writing through this lens (Tate 1985: 63). Firstly, the BAM Black Aesthetic derived in large part from the Black Power Movement, which bell hooks describes as characterized by an '[i]nsistence on patriarchal values, on equating black liberation with black men gaining access to male privilege that would enable them to assert power over black women' (1990: 16). This clearly problematizes it as a framework for reading Black women's work, especially if that work sought to challenge those same patriarchal values. Secondly, the framework of a BAM Black Aesthetic enabled Black writing to be read according to the extent to which it conformed to its principles. Cummings notes that between the 1970s and 1990s, Black poets faced a 'conflict in literary expectations,' whereby work that was 'difficult and writerly in both canonical and experimental ways,' might be critically dismissed or disparaged as counter to the Movement because it was not accessible enough (Cummings 2005: 4; 15). In a similar way, writing that dealt with complex and nuanced Black identities, as opposed to those that were strictly positive, were dismissed as counter revolutionary. As bell hooks has argued, the insistence that writing focus solely on positive or empowering images, 'effectively silenced more complex critical dialogue,' that transgressed a 'dualistic model of good and bad,' or 'did not conform to movement criteria' (1990: 5; 8; 107–8). As a result, work that presented a 'multiple black experience or the complexity of black life,' was overlooked or dismissed (hooks 1990: 107–8). In this sense, the criteria of a BAM Black Aesthetic represent another example of an intellectual feat that enabled the critical dismissal of Black women's writing. Work considered to transgress these boundaries was disparaged on the basis that it adhered to white traditions, conventions or aesthetics; and thus, might be considered 'not Black enough'.

The Black Aesthetic framework is, perhaps unsurprisingly, not one that appears within mainstream elegy scholarship texts, given their tendency to focus on the 'English elegy' and its European and Anglo-American legacies. It has nonetheless been applied to Black women elegists more broadly. Angelene Jamison describes Wheatley as 'a poet [...] who *happened* to be Black' (1974: 408; emphasis mine). She asserts that 'the first comment of most students is that [Wheatley] *was not Black enough* and of course they are correct,' and suggests that it is 'a mistake to refer to her as a Black poet,' as 'her poetry is a *product of a white mind*' (1974: 411, 415; emphases mine). This argument is based, in large part, on the belief that Wheatley 'did not address herself in any significant degree to the plight of her people' (1974: 408). Similarly, Eleanor Smith refers to Wheatley as a 'white mind,' with a 'white orientation,' who 'was not sensitive enough to the needs of her own people' (1974: 403). Later criticism of Wheatley's work vehemently argues the contrary.[2] For these later critics, Wheatley was a radical of her time. What these conflicting viewpoints highlight is that the act of reading Wheatley solely through the framework of a BAM Black Aesthetic enables her poetic agency, and any subtle subversion within the work, to be dismissed as inadequate.

Critical responses to Gwendolyn Brooks's work raise related issues. We have already seen how critics often separate Brooks's poetry into that which was published at Harper & Row and that which was later published by independent Black presses. Cummings highlights how this later work – though often admired by critics for its 'political engagement' – is dismissed by others for being 'insufficiently revolutionary' (2005: 8). She notes how some Black Arts writers – such as Amiri Baraka – 'found her work rather pale [...] which is to say, not revolutionary or black enough' (2005: 8). Annette Debo argues that this division of Brooks's work has been reinforced by some critics who 'call her early poetry "traditional," "accommodationist," or "white"' (2005: 143). Similarly, Lesley Wheeler draws attention to the way in which critics 'ally themselves with one Brooks or the other, arguing either that her early work transcends race or betrays her Blackness, [or] that her late work either fails aesthetically or finally breaks through its bondage to white forms' (2001: 229). These statements highlight two ways in which Brooks's poems have been critically read: either according to a white hegemonic binary that privileges her 'safe' earlier work; or according to a BAM Black Aesthetic that perceives her later work to be more political and therefore superior. This creates a critical space in which some part of her work must always be read negatively, according to a racial binary.

Cummings also highlights the ways in which this division encourages readers to 'discern more radical shifts than her work necessarily displays' (2005: 12). This is not to say that Brooks's work is not radical, but rather that radical elements exist throughout her entire body of work and that shifts taking place after 1967 were perhaps more to do with addressing herself solely to a Black readership than a modification of poetic themes and forms. Likewise, Wheeler argues that 'to draw too dramatic a contrast between the early and later works is to misread them,' particularly given that Brooks's description of her practice as writing about 'what confronts' her remained consistent throughout her career (2001: 229). What these conflicting arguments emphasize is that to read Brooks's work according to this binary not only allows for a critical factionalism that necessitates part of her work always be dismissed on racial terms, but also that to do so enables connective through-lines in her body of work to be overlooked.

A similar framework has been adopted in critical responses to Giovanni's poetry. Jennifer Walters has described how Giovanni's work and personal life were derided by principal members of the Black Arts and Black Power Movements because of her decision to explore what they considered to be 'non-revolutionary subjects' (2000: 211). Her exploration of supposed 'personal issues' within her poetry prompted accusations of 'selling out,' and elicited critics to suggest 'her words lacked substance, style and maturity' (Walters 2000: 212–13). These 'non-revolutionary subjects' included sexism within the Black Power Movement itself. In Walters's view Giovanni's decision to speak out against this sexism 'cost her the acceptance of leaders and critics across the country' (Walters 2000: 211).

These examples underscore ways in which the BAM Black Aesthetic was used by some as a means of silencing criticism of the Black Power Movement, specifically the voices of women who criticized its patriarchal values. These values are visible in the critical approaches of some writers within, and influenced by, the BAM. For example, poet and publisher Haki Madhubuti's paratextual description of Mari Evans's *I Am a Black Woman* describes her work as 'feminine waves,' and 'softly feminine [...] blackwoman movements,' which are 'strong and angular like Mari herself' (1970: n.p). This description relies on gendered tropes of femininity as 'soft' and 'unstable,' and compares this visual analogy of the poetry with Evans's own physical body. Kalamu ya Salaam, a poet and critic for

Black World, responded to themes of loneliness and single motherhood in Nikki Giovanni's work by asserting, 'I betcha Nikki wanted to be married' (cited in Fowler 1992: 15). In doing so, he ascribes it with heteronormative, patriarchal values that it is explicitly rejecting. In an essay titled 'Love and Liberation' he describes Sonia Sanchez's work as demonstrating staying power 'with a minimum of whining,' and a 'feistiness inversely proportioned to her diminutive body build' (2016: para 2). Like Madhubuti's description of Evans's work, Salaam draws comparisons between Sanchez's work and her physical body. His use of the implicitly feminized word 'feistiness' – which is typically attributed to women who are small but perceived as aggressive or touchy – serves as a means of figuratively belittling her work and diminishing the energy within it. Further, the assertion that it constitutes 'a minimum of whining' operates as a backhanded compliment that relies on misogynistic perceptions of women's work as complaint. The categorization of complaint has often been applied to women's elegiac poetry as a means of degrading it to an overblown grievance, or – in Schiesari's terms – 'mere chatter' (1992: 55). Salaam later suggests that to 'really consider what [Sanchez] is saying requires an acceptance of woman as mind, not only woman as fine (fine as in physically alluring, as in beautiful body)' (2016: para 8). This relies on the idea that an acknowledgement or recognition of 'woman as mind' is not the norm, but rather something unusual required in order to read the work properly. It implies that the standard reader is male, and that to understand Sanchez's work necessitates the effort of considering her a thinking human rather than a beautiful object. This is underscored further by the explicit definition of 'fine' as referring to physical beauty; Salaam is unequivocal so as to ensure that no reader interprets 'fine' simply as meaning acceptable, adequate or sufficient.

What each of these examples emphasize is a tendency for Black women's work to be critically approached within a rhetorical dynamic of heterosexual male desire, in which the poetry and the objectified gendered body of the poet are conflated. In several of the examples, the poet is judged on the way their corporeal form adheres to heteropatriarchal parameters of what women should look and sound like, and the discussion of their poetry is framed within this judgement. Presented in the form of praise, these critiques operate as coded dismissals in which both poet and poetry are demeaned.

Within the context of elegy more specifically, William Grier and Price M. Cobbs's book *Black Rage* provides a further example of how principles of a BAM Black Aesthetic framework have been applied to poetic articulations of grief and loss. Aida Hussen discusses how this text endorsed a binary of Black grief responses comprised of, on the one hand 'a defensive, paranoiac, retaliatory posture' towards white hegemony, and on the other a '"masochistic" […] "cultural depression" characterized by sorrow, injury, and ambivalence' (2013: 304–5). Working against the '"waves of hopelessness" that assault[ed] Black communities across the nation,' Grier and Cobbs sought to imagine a way in which 'black suffering' might be transformed into 'militant black power' and 'aggression' (Hussen 2013: 305). However, though Grier and Cobbs's model offered an alternative to the Freudian binary of mourning/melancholia, its binary structure enabled certain types of grieving to be illegitimized. As Hussen points out, their formulation 'erases other interpretive possibilities for grief,' particularly those that incorporate 'affective uncertainty or ambivalence within African American communities,' dismissing them as 'slavish false consciousness' (2013: 213). As a result, Hussen argues, 'the psychic discomfort of ambivalent mourning is overwritten by black nationalists' claim to a fully conscious politics of grief' (2013: 306).

Simply put, the model expects Black mourners to transform their grief into militancy and aggression, while any mourning that falls outside of these parameters is disparaged as submissive, mindless, inauthentic, and/or reflective of a refusal or inability to acknowledge Black oppression and racial inequality. Citing Baraka's description of this kind of grief as '[u]seless pain,' Hussen argues that it is 'disavowed' not only as false consciousness, but also as 'traitorousness and racial inauthenticity' (2013: 306). Thus, ambivalent mourning is illegitimized on the basis that it is a betrayal of both community and identity. Grier and Cobbs's binary therefore constructs a semantic space in which some elegies – in this case, those that are ambivalent – are read as useless, inadequate, duplicitous, treacherous, or false. It is a binary similar to the one adopted by Ramazani in his examination of Langston Hughes's elegies; one that presupposes 'subjective ambivalence' is a mode which is inherent to 'white American poets' (1994: 174). We have already seen how the racial categorization of elegiac modes operates as what Kutzinski refers to as a 'policing [of] canonical borders' (1992: 552). Grier and Cobbs's binary, which seeks to demarcate mourning responses, similarly polices the borders of grief protocols based on assumptions about how mourners ought to articulate their grief experiences.

In summary, then, we have discussed a white hegemonic critical framework that reflects – to borrow from Charles W. Mills – a '"white racial frame" through which to (mis) apprehend the world' (2013: 36). And we have discussed how a BAM Black Aesthetic, subverting the binaries of white hegemony, created a critical space in which Black writing that deviated from its criteria – particularly women's writing that sought to challenge its patriarchal principles – was derided, demeaned or dismissed. Both frameworks depend on binaries that subscribe to essentialist principles, and as such we might read them as reflecting and sustaining notions of what Awkward terms 'monolithic black subjectivity'; the idea that Black writing can or should represent a singular 'universal' Black experience (1995: 65). He signposts the way in which white critics have created for Black American writers 'an untenable position of striving to tell the truth of blackness when there is no single, unitary truth to tell' (Awkward 1995: 66). In a similar way, Young argues that a predominantly white publishing industry reinforces such racial divisions by 'representing "blackness" as a one-dimensional cultural experience' (2010: 4). He asserts that within this context, texts by Black writers undergo editing and promotion that represents a mythologized and '"particular" Black experience to a "universal," implicitly white [...] audience' (Young 2010: 4).

In this chapter, we have seen some examples of these essentialist principles at work. In Ostriker's review of Clifton's poetry, the work is praised for its simplicity, modesty and 'Otherness,' while at the same time derided both for its refusal to address itself – first and foremost – to a white readership and for its perceived potential to alienate that readership by transgressing parameters of white subjective experience. We have seen notions of a 'monolithic black subjectivity' arising out of the framework of a BAM Black Aesthetic, specifically in its insistence that work employ accessible language, positive representations, and unilaterally transform suffering into aggression and militancy (Awkward 1995: 65). And we have seen how these binaries can lead to categorizations that seek to distinguish aesthetically between Black elegies and white ones. Realistically, however, there can be no singular, monolithic Black response to grief just as there can be no singular, monolithic white one. That these binary formations can lead to such generalizing conclusions should call into serious question their use as a means of reading elegiac work.

Radical Black women's elegy: Wheatley, Brooks, Clifton

So far, this chapter has focused on the critical reception of Black women's elegies, exploring some of the intellectual feats by which such work has been marginalized and excluded by and from genealogical approaches to elegy. Within their poetic work, many of the elegists discussed – Wheatley, Brooks, Clifton, Giovanni, Sanchez – challenge principles of whiteness and patriarchy upon which genealogical constructions of elegy are based. Having investigated the reception of their work, we will now focus on individual elegies by some of these writers, so as to critically engage with their work in ways that existing genealogies of elegy have not. These elegies by Wheatley, Brooks and Clifton are radical in important ways: Wheatley's elegy in its subtle anti-British and anti-slavery sentiment and its subversive transformation of George Whitefield into a figure of progress and hope; and Brooks and Clifton in their commemoration of the lives of working-class Black women.

The question of why to focus on these writers – and not others – must also be addressed. This is, as we have seen in the Introduction, what genealogical formations elide: that the choices made about whose work to include necessarily preclude those made about that which is not included. It is for this reason that the chapter ends with a gesture towards some (and only some; there will inevitably be writers overlooked within it) of the other possible choices that might have been made: an incomplete list of elegies by Black, African American, multiracial and biracial women writers. This list may also provide some partial further guidance for readers who want to engage further with Black women's elegies beyond what is critically examined here.

As Antonio Bly notes, over half of Wheatley's thirty-nine published poems – and a quarter of her unpublished ones – were elegies (1999: 10). Printed in 1770, her first poem which acquired international attention was an elegy for the Anglican evangelist George Whitefield. Wheatley wrote the elegy at the age of seventeen after being in America for nine years, and the poem was reprinted after its initial publication 'at least five times' (Richards 1992: 188 n. 4). Whitefield was an English cleric who came to prominence because of his prolific and dramatically delivered sermons across the colonies. On the issue of slavery, he was an ambivalent figure: while his evangelical preaching was considered radical for its inclusion of slaves within its doctrine, he was himself a slave-owner who campaigned enthusiastically in support of slavery in Georgia (Willard 1995: 255 n. 27).

Based on Wheatley's choice of elegiac subject, it is perhaps not difficult to see why Jamison and Smith, reading her work through a BAM Black Aesthetic lens, concluded that her work does not 'address itself to a significant degree to the plight of her people,' or 'was not sensitive enough' to their needs (Jamison 1974: 408; Smith 1974: 403). However, other critics have argued against this way of reading her work. Sondra O'Neale highlights how, in using the 'language and doctrine' of evangelical Christianity, Wheatley offered a challenge to 'conventional colonial assumptions about race' (1986: 144–5). Her elegy for

Whitefield reminded readers that his sermons included slaves within a rhetoric of redemption and Jeffrey Bilbro argues that the praise in her elegy is based on Whitefield's helping to 'lay the theological and rhetorical groundwork for the evangelical abolition movement' (2012: 571). He goes on to claim that Wheatley's poetry had a considerable influence on Whitefield's friends, the minister John Newton (who wrote the hymn 'Amazing Grace') and the poet William Cowper, both of whom went on to become advocates of slavery's abolition.

Carla Willard offers a more radical reading of Wheatley's praise in the poem. She suggests that her choice of elegiac subject is not an 'attempt to give a "true" picture of the hero at all,' but rather to present him as a hero 'praised into performing liberating acts which greatly contrast with [his] acts in life' (1995: 239). According to Willard, Wheatley's Whitefield figure serves to 'remind the majority of [her] readers, both royalist and patriot, that they were, in fact or in sympathy, a slave-owning audience – a fact they would have preferred to forget' (1995: 239). She 'makes him over in the interest of [her] own agenda,' by depicting him as a man who sermonized upon 'an earthly equality of the whole human race' and an equality in the afterlife (Willard 1995: 243–4; 245). Her depiction of Whitefield, Willard maintains, 'points implicitly [...] to a classist and race-divided society' (1995: 246). In so doing, Wheatley's poem emphasizes the 'intrinsic lie, of the Jeffersonian premise' which maintained that Africans were, by nature, inferior (Willard 1995: 247).

Certainly, it is difficult to reconcile Wheatley's description of Whitefield as a 'happy saint' with his slave-ownership and his advocacy for slavery during his lifetime (Wheatley 2001: 113; 115). Willard's reading is also in keeping with Carretta's historical account of Wheatley, in which she met with the abolitionist Granville Sharp during her visit to England in 1773, prior to being freed upon her return to America later that year (2001: xxvi). In Carretta's view, Wheatley 'appropriates the persona of authority or power normally associated with men and social superiors,' in poems that 'exploit the rhetorical possibilities that ambivalence and ambiguity offered her' (Carretta 2001: xxi; xxxi). He argues that her inclusion of the African-born Roman poet Terence in her book's opening poem 'Maecenas' emphasized not only her own position within Western literary tradition, but that Western literary tradition 'has included Africans since its beginning' (Carretta 2001: xx).

The version of the elegy which appeared in Wheatley's *Poems on Various Subjects, Religious and Moral* (1773) differs from versions published in October 1770 broadsides (Wheatley 2001: 113; 115). Significantly, what is missing from the former is a sequence of lines describing America, specifically New England.

Brought to America at the age of seven, Wheatley was purchased by John and Susanna Wheatley who were prominent members of the evangelical community. While some of Wheatley's other poems, such as 'On Being Brought from Africa to America' – which Henry Louis Gates, Jr. describes as 'the most reviled poem in African American literature' – describe America in glowing terms, her elegy for Whitefield is much less flattering (Gates 2003: 71). She describes it as a 'distress'd abode' whose streets are 'crimson'd' with 'guiltless gore' (Wheatley 2001: 113–14; 116–17). In contrast to the idyllic descriptions of Whitefield's apotheosis – such as his 'immortal throne'; his journey towards 'Heav'n's unmeasur'd height'; and his visibility in 'yon azure skies' – America is presented as both reddened with a blood that has been shed in carnage and afflicted with pain and suffering (Wheatley 2001: 113–14; 115–16).

That the blood which colours the streets is described as 'guiltless' may be read in two ways: as innocent (i.e. free from guilt) or as callous and cold-hearted (i.e. remorseless) (Wheatley 2001: 113; 116). Wheatley seems to suggest the 'burden'd' Americans in the poem cannot be held responsible for the brutality and violence that reddens their streets (Wheatley 2001: 113; 116). This may be an allusion to the colonial wars and territorial disputes that took place between North America and Europe prior to the Great Rebellion in 1776, or to various territorial disputes between New England and other colonies that took place during that time. In any case, the poem depicts America as violent, barbaric, cruel and unchristian prior to Whitefield's arrival. It is a place of anguish, violence and cruelty. The absence of this section of the poem from Wheatley's book, which was published in England, may be due to the fact that her 'arguably anti-British poems [...] are not included in the 1773 collection published against a background of rapidly growing tensions between Britain and its North American colonies' (Carretta 2001: xix). This would suggest that Wheatley's depiction of violence in American streets implicitly lays blame for this blood and 'gore' upon the British (Wheatley 2001: 113; 116).

Wheatley has been an ambivalent poetic figure for some readers, as we have seen with Jamison and Smith. However, others such as R. Lynn Matson argue that a Black nationalist stance 'would have been impossible considering the time and her position' (1972: 223). Similarly, John C. Shields argues that Wheatley's work often incorporates subtle subversion that enables her to 'levy sometimes severe censure, particularly of the institution of slavery, under the guise of an innocuous purveyor of the status quo' (1994: 633). We have seen the potential for reading some of this kind of subversion in her elegy to Whitefield. While we cannot always easily categorize the subject matter of her poetic work as subversive or radical, Shields reminds us that Wheatley rejected the 'Christianity of her white oppressors,' in her last known poem, 'An Elegy on Leaving _____,' written months before her death (1994: 646).

Perhaps, however, what is most radical about Wheatley's elegies is their very existence. Hortense J. Spillers describes slavery as a 'hostile and compulsory patriarchal order, bound and determined to destroy' enslaved Black people (1987: 75). Wheatley's poetic work embodies – to paraphrase Spillers again – 'a degree of courage and will to survive that startles the imagination even now' (1987: 75). If, as Mbembe – citing Paul Gilroy and Susan Buck-Morss – suggests, '[s]lave life […] is a form of death-in-life,' in which communication is characterized as 'anti-discursive and extralinguistic,' then Wheatley's poetry operates as a radical 'exercise of the power of speech and thought,' within a context structured to erase and destroy any trace of her subjectivity (2019: 75).

Writing nearly two hundred years later, Gwendolyn Brooks was a highly celebrated poet who held the position of Poet Laureate Consultant in Poetry to the Library of Congress and garnered numerous honours for her poetic work. Many of her poems have an elegiac tone, including 'Of De Witt Williams on his Way to Lincoln Cemetery' and 'Malcolm X'. Her elegiac Petrarchan sonnet, 'the rites for Cousin Vit,' was originally published in *Annie Allen* in 1949 – a collection for which she won the Pulitzer Prize – and later appears in her *Selected Poems* (2006).

The sonnet begins with several subjectless lines within the poem's sestet. Vit – whose name implies *vit*ality but also display (as in *vit*rine) and disgrace (as in *vit*uperate) – is introduced as a compliant or acquiescent body in transit, borne by unidentified mourners (2006: 58). In the second subjectless line, however, a sense of defiance is implied: the action of kicking away the funeral bier suggests a refusal of, or rebellion against, death. This act of kicking both reminds us that Vit is dead – since to 'kick it' means to die – and provides an image of negation or denial of death (as a 'kicking against'). Vit, the poem tells us, cannot be held by the coffin in which she has been placed. The coffin's accessories – its padding and its glossy fabric lining – are unable to contain and constrain her (2006: 58). Such is her vitality that even the coffin lid – which, it is implied, represents remorse, repentance or sadness – cannot contain her. Vit, it would seem, is altogether too alive for death.

The poem's fifth line expands on this refusal of containment in the phrase, 'Oh oh. Too much. Too much' (2006: 58). The articulatory phoneme 'Oh' (as distinguished from 'O,' which would preface a vocative phrase) is an exclamatory utterance that is extra-lexical, functioning as sound rather than language. It operates as a form of vocal interruption signifying astonishment, revelation, vexation, pain, distress, yearning or grief. But it also implies zero or nothing. In addition to expressing deep emotion, the phrase places nothingness or non-being in contiguity with excess or superfluity (2006: 58). This echoes the idea, expressed in the opening lines, that Vit cannot be contained by death. But it also implies, conversely, that the coffin's material ornamentation outlined in the opening lines – its lustrous fabric, padding and fasteners – represent an excess that is incompatible with Vit's own style. The comfort, extravagance and materiality they represent, the poem suggests, are 'too much' (2006: 58).

This fifth line also provides a voltaic shift in the poem's focus, from the funeral parlour to spaces of memory and speculation. Unlike the surety with which Wheatley imagines a metaphorical ascension for Whitefield, Vit's is one which we are explicitly asked to imagine or hypothesize (2006: 58). The sixth line is the first point in the poem that Vit is an active subject; before this she has been a passive object who is moved and enclosed without agency (as borne, held and enfolded). In the ascension which we are asked to imagine, however, Vit is instead vital, lively and unstoppable. And unlike the divine idyll to which Whitefield ascends, Vit returns to locations she occupied in life: public houses, drinking establishments and secluded spaces of desire. While it is unclear whether the 'love-rooms' in the poem refer specifically to brothels, the poem's positioning of Vit in 'repose,' within these spaces implies, if not sex work, then sex as leisure (2006: 58). The ascension we are asked to imagine, then, is not the ascendant movement usually associated with apotheosis, but one that leads back to earthly spaces of life, drinking, dancing and sex.

Vit is depicted as dancing – the poem references a blues dance made famous by Earl Tucker in Harlem in the 1920s – and she does not seem to care when she spills cheap wine on the fabric of her dress (2006: 58). It is at this point that we encounter one of the most ambiguous phrases in the poem. In addition to the spaces of drinking and desire, Vit is also described as returning to 'the things in people's eyes' (2006: 58). This implies a vision clouded by commodities or material objects. As inanimate objects without life, these 'things' present a contrast to the energy and vitality of Vit (2006: 58). Like the material trappings of the coffin in the opening lines, they are incompatible with her character. The spaces which she occupied in life are therefore subtly associated with commodity fetishism, in which perceptions are focused on the exchange of objects rather than social relationships between people. We might also infer, then, that they are spaces in which Vit herself was objectified. Though they are depicted as spaces of vitality and pleasure for Vit in life, this line adds complexity to that pleasure.

They are, in other words, not only spaces of pleasure for Vit, but spaces in which she is perceived as existing for the gratification of others.

In the ninth line, the poem returns to subjectless phrases. Something, we are told, is more alive than these spaces allow for (2006: 58). While this may apply to Vit, since the poem has already depicted her as a person whom death cannot contain, the lack of subject implies that things are not that simple. As with the lines that imply that Vit is 'too much,' for death, this subjectless line suggests that Vit is so alive that she cannot be contained even by the pronoun 'she'; Vit is, in other words, too alive for language to contain. This excess in the ninth line is also connected with the adjective 'squeaking,' which implies a shrill noise often associated with animals or birds; a narrow escape (to 'squeak through') or to barely survive (to 'squeak by') (2006: 58). Thus, the earthly spaces to which Vit has returned, like the space of the coffin in the opening lines, are unable to contain her, just as the poem itself struggles to contain her. And while they may be spaces in which she derived pleasure in life, they are nonetheless spaces that constrain her vitality. The subjectless imperative to 'emerge,' articulates an urgent necessity to come forth from these spaces of containment – the coffin, the spaces she occupied in life, the space of the poem – in order to transcend what is earthly and material (2006: 58).

Repetition of the phrase 'even now,' in lines five and ten serves to complicate the temporality of this imagined ascension. On the one hand, it implies presence – it is 'at this moment' or 'as we speak' or 'even in death' – that Vit is dancing and drinking in these spaces (2006: 58). On the other hand, this phrase suggests 'in spite of all this,' or 'even in our imagination'. It is, after all, the phrase which prefaces that we must *imagine* Vit's ascension. This temporal complication creates an ambiguity: we cannot be sure if Vit's drinking and dancing is an embodiment of her excess of vitality, or whether there is a subtle reprimand within the poem for the failure of our own imagination. Perhaps, in other words, it is we as readers who are failing to imagine Vit as anything other than someone who dances and drinks in these spaces of commodity fetishism and objectification. Perhaps the subjectless imperative to 'emerge,' is urging us to think beyond these limiting and constraining ways of perceiving her (2006: 58).

The poem ends with Vit as an active subject walking through both open and secluded public spaces. The singular, subjectless and capitalized one-word sentence, 'Is,' at the poem's end suggests a coming into existence, resolving the earlier imperative demand that someone or something 'emerge' (2006: 58). Both life and death, the poem implies, are processes of transformation, like pupal stages out of which one must unfold in order to truly 'be'. This ontological emergence takes place liminally; Vit moves from open and secluded public spaces to the threshold of two potential emotional registers: one which implies contentment and the other, uncontrollable laughter or weeping (2006: 58). It is uncertain, the poem implies, at which of these emotions Vit arrives; or rather, it implies that she accidentally arrives at both without falling firmly within either. The space in which she comes into being – the space in which she 'Is' – exists at the margin of these two affective responses; she is neither entirely happy nor entirely hysterical, but on the threshold of both (2006: 58). Vit's transcendence or ascension, then, is uncertain, haphazard and occupies a marginal space of emotional ambivalence. Unlike Wheatley's elegy, which describes an ascendancy for Whitefield that is idyllic and certain, Brooks's poem imagines a contingent and ambiguous transcendence for a working-class Black woman whose life and vitality cannot be contained adequately either in language, in the spaces she occupied in life, or in death. The ambivalent complexity of her life as characterized by both pleasure and objectification is reflected in the ambivalent complexity of her ascension, and it is within this complexity that she truly exists or 'Is' (2006: 58).

Born nineteen years later than Brooks, Clifton wrote numerous elegies, including 'malcolm' (for Malcolm X); 'In the same week' (for her brother Sammy); 'Here' (for Nkosi Johnson, a South African child who publicly criticized President Mbeki for his negligent handling of the HIV epidemic and who died of AIDS aged 12); and 'poem on my fortieth birthday to my mother who died young'. Clifton's elegy 'here rests,' was published in *The New Yorker* in 2001 and is addressed to her sister Josephine, who was older than Clifton and the daughter of their father's first wife, Edna Bell Sayles. The six-stanza poem was written fifteen years after Josephine's death.

The title of the poem is an ancient funerary phrase commonly used on epitaphs or memorial stones. As such, it recalls the epitaph at the end of Thomas Gray's 'Elegy Written in a Country Churchyard' (1751): '[h]ere rests his head upon the lap of Earth / A youth to Fortune and to Fame unknown' (T. Gray 1981: 21–5). Gray's poem, often included in genealogies of elegy, meditates upon the way in which some people are not recognized for their actions in life and how their potential remains unfulfilled. The grave upon which Gray's poem focuses is revealed, in the final epitaph, to belong to an unknown poet. Based on this epitaphic allusion, the title of Clifton's poem implies it is an elegy that acknowledges her sister's unrecognized potential. But while the phrase 'here rests' would ordinarily function – as in Gray's poem – as an inscription on a tombstone, here it designates the poem itself as a textual marker memorializing its subject, implying that Josephine has been 'laid to rest' within the poem itself.

Like Cousin Vit in Brooks's poem, Josephine is a figure of ambiguous complexity: a pious, literate and compassionate sex worker who – as 'most wanted' – is either a fugitive from the law or a woman who is highly desired or in great demand (Clifton 2012: 589). Her pimp, Diamond Dick, is a similarly complex figure. He joins Josephine in reading biblical passages aloud; a gesture that operates, in the poem, as one of tenderness and care, in contrast with the ostentatious masculinity implied by his name. The poem's reference to the Book of Job also echoes this complex ambiguity. It is a story about how human suffering and loss are part of a larger plan of which humans have no knowledge, or as Michael V. Fox puts it, a story which signifies 'inevitable ignorance of vast realms of facts and processes' (2018: 12). Stefano Perfetti describes this larger plan as a 'divine providence [that] rules a myriad of natural processes outside our competence and ability to judge' (2018: 85). He describes exegeses of the text, following Gregory the Great, as outlining a 'model of perseverance in affliction and patience rewarded' (2018: 82). Similarly, Fox suggests that one of the key themes of the text is to 'recognize God's beneficence and to remain loyal to him, even in affliction […] in other words, […] to maintain *faith*, a trust in God not based on knowledge' (2018: 8).

The poem's reference to the Book of Job comes from Josephine herself who, when expressing certainty that Clifton will write a poem about the care they are providing for their dying father, explicitly tells her to remember it (2012: 589). This instruction implies that the impending death of their father, a man 'who sexually abused his children,' ought to be accepted as part of a larger design whose purpose cannot fully be known (Wall 1999: 566). But it also implies Clifton's claiming of the knowledge necessary for authorship. As Edward Whitley suggests, Clifton also invokes Job in her memoir *Generations* as a means of asserting 'the right and authority to tell a story' (2001: 56).

By opening with the modal verb 'may,' the final lines are articulated in the form of a wish or blessing that the afterlife be populated with 'literate men' who treat Josephine 'with respect' (2012: 589). On the one hand, Clifton's image of a heaven in which sex is an integral part operates as a radical rejection of the Christian idea that sex – and by extension sex work – is a mortal sin that would be punished in the afterlife. Indeed, it turns on its head the idea of sex as sinful, by portraying it as an activity that takes place in heaven. Moreover, in wishing this afterlife for her sister, Clifton depicts Josephine as a woman who takes pleasure in sex and has agency over her own sexuality and desire.

On the other hand, however, Clifton's final lines may be read as implying that, in death, Josephine does not so much rest as continue with the sex work she undertook in life. This might operate as a playful mocking of Josephine's belief in blind faith or divine moral justice; there is an irony in the suggestion that in heaven she would be rewarded with respectful sexual partners rather than a reprieve from sex altogether, which in life – it is implied – operated for Josephine as a form of labour. This is also complicated by the final lines' adherence to Jezebel stereotypes, in which Black women are represented as hypersexualized or objectified in an explicitly sexualized way. The poem represents Josephine as having a complex identity in life, and yet in death these other facets are flattened out in the poem's final wish, and she is instead represented only by her sexualized body. It is significant, for instance, that the poem depicts Josephine as an avid reader and lover of books, but in death this is reflected in the literacy of the men with which heaven is filled, rather than, say, by a greater access to books or more leisure time to read them. It is also significant that the sexual dynamic is presented as the men 'bedding' Josephine and not the other way around. This troubles a reading of the final stanza as the depiction of a woman with total agency over her own sexuality. While the lines articulate a wish that they do so 'with respect,' there is within them a certain implied inevitability to the 'bedding' relationship, as if heaven – for Josephine – could never be anything different (2012: 589). In this way, the 'rest' offered in the poem's title is implicitly undermined (Clifton 2012: 589). Josephine does not so much rest at the poem's end as appear to continue the work she undertook in life. It is possible to read this as reflecting an anger – much like Job's – at a patriarchal God, for the suffering that women endure within patriarchal social structures. Intentionally or not, Clifton's final lines gesture towards the inescapability, even in death, of the sexualization of Black women.

Like Brooks's elegy then, Clifton's poem retains at its end an ambiguous complexity that cannot easily be resolved. More significantly, this irresolvability also reflects the system of moral justice depicted within the Book of Job, in which God is portrayed as violating standards of moral justice for 'reasons beyond human comprehension' (Fox 2018: 10). Divine justice is, Fox argues, necessarily 'incomplete,' in order that 'human righteousness [...] be pure' (2018: 10). In other words, God cannot reward for virtue systematically, since humans might be motivated to be good only in the 'expectation of a payoff' (Fox 2018: 10). Divine justice, according to the Book of Job, is not a straightforward transaction that correlates with one's actions in life. In a similar way, the poem maintains within it a sense of incompleteness; a lack of neat resolution – or 'payoff' for Josephine. Her ascension – like Cousin Vit's in Brooks's poem – is contingent. Unlike Whitefield in Wheatley's poem, it is not an ascension to divine status, but a continuation of Josephine's circumstances of life. Clifton eschews the elegiac trope of an easy and straightforward transcendence for reasons which the poem does not provide. It is, simply put, beyond our capacity – as reader – to fully understand.

Like the elegies by Wheatley and Brooks, Clifton's poem challenges the normative frame of elegy as presented by genealogical formulations. While all three poems destabilize the characterization of elegy as the domain of European and Anglo-American white men, Brooks and Clifton's poems further undermine the genealogical model of white male poets mourning other white men by commemorating the lives of working-class Black women and, further, by retaining within their poems the complexities of these women's lives. Both poems trouble and complicate elegiac tropes, firstly of straightforward apotheosis – the 'elevation of the soul [...] and its entry into a spiritually raised [...] natural world' – and, secondly, of the 'transcendental consolation' that often characterizes canonical elegies (Ramazani 1994: 295; Sacks 1987: 114).

The next chapter will further explore work by both Brooks and Clifton, as well as elegies by Sanchez and Giovanni, Audre Lorde, June Jordan and Danez Smith. For readers who want to engage further with elegies by Black, African American and multiracial women writers, what follows is a list of examples that may be of interest. It should be noted that this list does not represent a genealogy or a complete survey of Black women's elegiac work in its entirety; such an exhaustive list is beyond the scope of this chapter. However, some useful examples include, for instance, Ann Plato's 'Reflections, Written on Visiting the Grave of a Venerated Friend' (1840); Charlotte Forten Grimke's 'Charles Sumner' (c. 1874); Mary Weston Fordham's 'In Memoriam Alphonse Campbell Fordham' (1897); Henrietta Cordelia Ray's 'Lincoln,' Robert G. Shaw,' and 'To My Father' (1876; 1910; 1910); Angelina Weld Grimke's 'To Joseph Lee' and 'To Keep the Memory of Charlotte Forten Grimke' (1908; 1915); Georgia Douglas Johnson's 'Motherhood' (1922); Gwendolyn Bennett's 'Epitaph' and 'Lines Written at the Grave of Alexandre Dumas' (1924; 1926); Margaret Walker's 'For Malcolm X,' 'Elegy,' and 'Epitaph for My Father' (1970; 1970; 1975); Maya Angelou's 'Mourning Grace,' Elegy' and 'Remembrance' (1971; 1975; 1978); Audre Lorde's 'The Day They Eulogized Mahalia,' 'Eulogy for Alvin Frost' and 'There Are No Honest Poems About Dead Women' (1973; 1978; 1986); Alice Walker's 'Good Night Willie Lee, I'll See You in the Morning' (1975); Ntozake Shange's 'Dark Phrases' (from *For Colored Girls Who Have Considered Suicide When The Rainbow is Enuf*), 'With No Immediate Cause' and 'for all my dead & loved ones' (1976; 1978; 1978); Mari Evans's 'On the death of Boochie by starvation', 'Eulogy for all our murdered children' and 'Eulogy for a child whose parents prate of love' (1979; 1981; 1992); Rita Dove's 'Your Death,' 'The Wake' and 'Canary' (for Billie Holiday) (all 1989); Colleen McElroy's 'For Want of a Male a Shoe Was Lost' (1990); Naomi Long Madgett's 'Echoes' (for Duke Ellington) (1996); Elizabeth Alexander's 'Five Elegies' (2005); Natasha Trethewey's *Native Guard* and 'Elegy ["I think by now the river must be thick"] (2006; 2012); Thylias Moss's *Tokyo Butter* (on death of her cousin Deirdre) (2006); Patricia Smith's "Buried," "Elegy" and "Black, Poured Directly into the Wound" (2008; 2015; 2017); Toi Derricotte's 'For my unnamed brother (1943–1943),' 'I see my father after his death' and 'Elegy for my husband' (all 2011); Camille Dungy's *Smith Blue* (2011); Nikky Finney's 'Left' (a poem written after Hurricane Katrina) (2011); Tracy K Smith's *Life on Mars* (an elegy for her father who died in 2008) (2011); Wanda Coleman's *The World Falls Away* (2011); Evie Shockley's *The new black* (2012); Patricia Spears Jones' 'Failed Ghazal' (an elegy for friend Peter Dee) (2015); and Erica Hunt's 'Mourning Birds' (2016). Readers interested in elegiac work by African writers may be interested in Nana Asma'u's elegies or the Akan funeral dirges outlined by Ruth Finnegan in *Oral Literature in Africa* (2014). For work by Black and Caribbean British women poets, see, for instance, Grace Nichols's 'Praise Song for My Mother' (1984); SuAndi's *The Story of M* (1995); Dorothea Smartt's *Lancaster Keys* and *Samboo's Grave/Bilal's Grave* (2001; 2008); Jackie Kay's 'Brendan Gallacher' (2007) and Karen McCarthy-Woolf's *An Aviary of Small Birds* (2014).

Notes

1   There are other instances in which Black women elegists are mentioned within Ramazani's text: Gwendolyn Brooks's 'Of De Witt Williams on his way to Lincoln Cemetery' is given as an example of how 'African-American poets conduct funerals in a style of spare simplicity'; Phillis Wheatley and Mary Weston Fordham are noted as 'channel[ing] much of their poetic output into the elegiac genre'; and Henrietta Cordelia Ray is acknowledged among a list of women who have 'written hundreds of professional elegies for fellow poets and political leaders' (1994: 17; 295; 297).

2   See Burke (1991: 33; 38); O'Neale (1986: 144–5); Shields (1994: 632–3); Matson (1972: 223); and Will Harris (2008: 36–8).

2

Resisting necrophilous white patriarchy: Elegies about racial injustice

While genealogical approaches in elegy scholarship have sometimes included references to work by writers who are *not* white men, this work is often defined and measured in accordance with principles upon which genealogical models are based: namely whiteness, patriarchy and heteronormativity. And this inclusion creates a paradox in which work that is defined as 'other' by the genealogical formulations themselves is included within them on the basis of a perceived difference that is then flattened out. This chapter takes a closer look at questions raised by the act of subsuming and assimilating within existing Eurocentric genealogical frameworks elegies by writers which those very same genealogies designate as 'other'. To put it differently, this chapter considers how elegy scholars might acknowledge difference without understanding it only in relation to the Eurocentric standards of the genealogical model.

We have seen, in the previous chapter, Ramazani's suggestion that elegies by Langston Hughes might only be 'properly appreciated' in the 'dual context of African-American and European forms of poetic lament' (1994: 135). This implies that elegies by Black writers might be considered both in relation to a European genealogy and – at the same time – as part of a separate genealogy of Black elegies. There is a problem with this approach: namely it would require the assumption – to borrow from Kutzinski – that it is possible for Black elegies 'to violate the rules of canonical propriety by existing in more than one defining location at the same time' (1992: 551). More importantly, because it requires that Black elegiac writing be read in relation to two genealogical frameworks – while white elegiac writing is read only in relation to one – it reinforces white Eurocentric genealogical structures as the 'zero point of orientation' for elegy scholarship (Mbembe 2019: 122). In other words, it frames white Eurocentric elegy as the standard against which all elegiac writing must be measured.

The question of how to re-evaluate literary canons without flattening out difference is not a new one. In her essay, 'American Literary History as Spatial Practice,' Kutzinski asks a similar question: how to 'rescind all borders and boundaries' of a literary canon without, as she puts it, 'submerging diversity' (1992: 555). How, in other words, to 'change the ways in which we traverse textual and other cultural territory' without performing a 'rhetorical levelling' of difference (1992: 556).

Toni Morrison describes this kind of 'levelling' as both a 'neutralization' of difference 'designed and constituted to elevate and maintain hegemony' and a restriction of the work to 'a mere reaction to or denial of' conventions according to 'Eurocentric criteria' (1988: 134). That is to say: differences are flattened out as either conforming to, or deviating from, the aesthetic and formal standards of the canon. Morrison likens the former to a 'gathering of a culture's difference into the skirts of the Queen,' and the latter to a 'reaction to or denial of the Queen,' a comparison which highlights a widespread colonialist tendency to assimilate all literary work within, and measure it according to, Eurocentric ideals understood as 'universal' (1988: 134). How, then, might elegy scholarship attend to and address this issue?

The limits of elegiac genealogy

While Ramazani's suggestion that the elegies of Hughes can only be 'properly appreciated' in a 'dual context' explicitly maintains the primacy of a Eurocentric framework, it may be that underlying this assertion is an important point (1994: 135). After all, as bell hooks has highlighted, Black women's work is often influenced by 'generations of black ancestors whose ways of thinking [...] have been globally shaped in the African diaspora and informed by the experience of exile and domination' (1990: 111). Perhaps Ramazani means to highlight the point that to subsume elegies by Black writers under the rubric of a singular genealogical framework would overlook – because of that framework's Eurocentric emphasis – the African diasporic cultural influences upon the work and the important historical contexts within which that work was written.

Describing the origins of a Black American engagement with literary traditions from a historical perspective, Awkward cites Henry Gates Jr.'s assertion that early Black American writers were responding directly 'to extant racialist incredulity about black people's ability to reason' (1995: 27). We have seen examples of such incredulity in Jefferson's response to Wheatley's poetry. Awkward also signposts a late nineteenth-century notion – deriving from writers such as Frederick Douglass – that a 'mastery of the tropes of literary expression' operated as a 'means of gaining [...] liberation from the debilitating tenets of white hegemony' (1995: 26). In other words, for some early Black American writers, engagement with European literary traditions was motivated, at least in part, by a desire to dispel racist and essentialist notions about Black people's capacity for rational thought and artistic expression. These essentialist notions – as Awkward's citation of Douglass emphasizes – operated as a form of social control. Employing the tropes of Eurocentric literature within their writing therefore offered a potential means of challenging and resisting white supremacist ideas.

Awkward also cites Donald Wesling, who argues that language – or 'the word' – operates as the 'vehicle through which human identity is said to be achieved in the logocentric West,' and that a refusal to allow Black people an opportunity to engage with literacy enabled white authority to 'believe and create in others the perception of an absent black subjectivity' (1995: 71). In this way, white supremacist attempts to inhibit and prevent Black literacy operated as a systemic means of denying Black people subjecthood. Ramazani's suggestion of a 'dual context' for reading Hughes's work may be highlighting – despite its problematic framing – that a subsumption of Black elegies into a Eurocentric genealogical framework would elide these sociohistorical and contextual factors (1994: 135). The key problem, then, is that the colonial and white supremacist suppression of Black literacy and the elision of Black writers from genealogies of elegy cannot simply be retrospectively redressed by constructing a revised singular genealogy that overlooks or omits that suppression and elision having taken place. It is not enough, in other words, to symbolically address the marginalization and exclusion of Black elegiac writing by retroactively including it within a genealogy from which it has historically been excluded, and which has historically been defined by principles of whiteness and patriarchy. A gesture of such symbolic literary restitution would be a form of colonialist violence; a drawing of Black writing 'into the skirts of the Queen,' to return to Morrison's phrase (1988: 134).

As we have seen, genealogical frameworks of elegy are based upon value systems of whiteness, patriarchy and heteronormative binaries of gender. As such, they do not acknowledge the contexts of white supremacy, patriarchy and social inequality about which – and in resistance to which – Black elegiac work is often writing. As June Jordan writes, Black poets 'seldom pen a poem about wild geese flying over Prague, or grizzlies at the rain barrel under the dwarf willow trees,' but will instead be likely to address 'the terror and the hungering and the quandaries of [...] African lives on this North American soil' (2004: 178). This means that there is a considerable disconnect between the privileged white contexts from which European canonical elegies emerged – such as Milton's 'Lycidas,' or Arnold's 'Thyrsis' – and what bell hooks calls the 'cultural context of white supremacy,' within which Black elegies are written (1990: 124). To ignore that disconnect operates as a rhetorical revision of Black work.

Is it possible, then, to abandon Eurocentric genealogical frameworks altogether? Such an approach would follow bell hooks's emphasis on the necessity for 'dispel[ling] the notion that white western culture is "the" location where a discussion of aesthetics emerged,' in favour of an understanding of it as '*only one* location' (1990: 109–10; emphasis mine). As long as elegy is understood according to a linear chronological narrative – beginning with the Greek pastoral and followed by the 'English elegy,' which is rooted in hetero-patriarchal colonialist ideologies – it cannot contain both the elegies imbued with these principles and those by writers subjected to that same hetero-patriarchal colonial oppression. What, then, might an anti-genealogical approach to elegy look like? While there is no straightforward answer to this question, the remainder of this book explores and investigates possibilities for new ways of understanding elegy beyond genealogical frames.

To begin with, this chapter examines a range of elegies by Black and African American women and non-binary writers that arise from – and write in resistance to – racial injustice, white violence and oppression. There is no attempt, in these analyses, to establish a genealogy of Black women's and/or non-binary elegy. Rather, the aim is to read these elegies in ways that acknowledge the 'cultural context of white supremacy,' within which they were written, without seeking to totalize them as a 'reaction to [...] Eurocentric criteria' (hooks 1990: 124; Morrison 1988: 134). The elegies examined point towards formulations of a necrophilous white masculinity whose maintenance depends on violence to Black bodies in exchange for, and in protection of, an ideological construction of white feminine purity. As such, they offer radical resistances to the principles of whiteness and patriarchy upon which genealogical frameworks are based. And, in mourning Black lives lost to white supremacist violence, they undermine this necropoetic system of principles, whose purpose is to give primacy to the public grieving of white lives.

Red ooze, severed gaze and the maintenance of white masculinity: Elegies for Emmett Till

In a discussion of Black elegies written about, and in response to, racial injustice, there is good reason to begin with elegies written about the murder of Emmett Till. Many theorists, including Clenora Hudson-Weems (1988), Shawn Michelle Smith (2015), Terry Wagner (2010), Harold K. Bush (2013) and Teri A. McMurtry-Chubb (2017) have described Till's murder as the 'catalyst', 'spark' or 'beginning' of the Civil Rights Movement.[1] Christopher Metress describes how Till's murder is 'woven [...] intimately into the fabric,' of the work of Black writers and how Till's image has 'emerged as one of the most powerful and haunting reminders of racial injustice in America' (2003: 89). Moreover, Angela Onwuachi-Willig has signposted how 'the same race-based forces,' and 'racist tropes,' that characterized Till's murder and its treatment by white systems of authority 'are still operating in today's society,' and 'remain quite ordinary today' (2016–2017: 1119). Thus, an examination of elegies for Emmett Till provides us with insight into the legacies of white supremacy that persist in contemporary discourse.

Till was a fourteen-year-old from Chicago who, in 1955, went to visit relatives in Mississippi. On 24 August 1955, he visited Bryant's Grocery and Meat Market just outside of Money – a small cotton mill community – along with a group of friends and relatives. Here, Till encountered Carolyn Bryant, the 21-year-old wife of the grocery store's owner, Roy Bryant. Details of what exactly took place during their encounter remain, as Wagner indicates, 'a point of fierce contention,' due to various conflicting accounts from witnesses and the fact that Till spent a short period of time alone with Carolyn in the store (2010: 190). She later 'testified under oath that Till put his arms around her, held her by the waist and propositioned her' (Tell 2017: 121). Other witnesses, however, 'claimed that nothing noteworthy occurred,' and that 'Till never came onto, accosted, or assaulted' her (Onwuachi-Willig 2016–2017: 1130). One key detail that accounts appear to agree on is that Till whistled when he left the store, an act which is read in many of the witness accounts as a wolf-whistle, a 'dangerous breach of Mississippi racial etiquette,' during the Jim Crow era of segregation in the South (Wagner 2010: 188).

On 28 August, Roy Bryant and his half-brother J.W. Milam went to the home of Till's aunt and uncle where he was staying during his trip. They kidnapped him, beat him, shot him, tied a large cotton-gin fan around his neck with barbed wire and threw him into the river. His mutilated body was found three days later. Till's mother, Mamie Till-Bradley, upon receiving her son's casket in Chicago, defied pressure from the Mississippi authorities that the casket be kept sealed and insisted on an open-casket funeral stating that 'the world [had to] see what they did to [her] boy' (Till-Bradley cited in Onwuachi-Willig 2016–2017: 1132). She held a 'four-day, open-casket memorial,' attended by 100,000 people, including members of the Black press who published photographs of the mutilated body (Onwuachi-Willig 2016–2017: 1132). The media circulation of these photographs caused a national public outcry, which was exacerbated when, on 5 September 1955, Milam and Bryant were acquitted of murder by an all-white male jury (Onwuachi-Willig 2016–2017: 1133).

There are several elegiac poems written about Till's murder, among them Wanda Coleman's 'Emmett Till' (1986); Marilyn Nelson's *A Wreath for Emmett Till* (2005); and Patricia Smith's 'Black, Poured Directly into the Wound' (2017). This chapter focuses on two interconnected elegiac poems for Till by Gwendolyn Brooks (1960) and one by Audre Lorde written over twenty years later (1981). These three poems, though connected by their elegiac subject, each approach the murder of Till from different angles: one with a focus on Carolyn Bryant, one with a focus on Mamie Till-Bradley and one from the personal perspective of the writer-speaker.

Brooks's two connected 1960 elegiac poems 'A Bronzeville Mother Loiters in Mississippi. Meanwhile, A Mississippi Mother Burns Bacon,' and 'The Last Quatrain of the Ballad of Emmett Till,' approach the horror of Till's murder from the perspectives of Carolyn Bryant and Mamie Till-Bradley, respectively. The poems are interlinked in that the latter operates as a separate – or disconnected – final quatrain of the former, despite significant formal differences in both poems. The former poem's title gestures towards both Till-Bradley (as the 'Bronzeville Mother') and Bryant (as the 'Mississippi Mother') though the poem focuses exclusively on Bryant, with Till-Bradley not mentioned until the 'Last Quatrain'.

That Brooks presents both women as mothers in the title draws a connection between them as maternal figures, and it is through Bryant's role as a mother in the poem that she is forced to confront the horror of Till's murder. However, this framing also gestures towards the media coverage of the murder in 1955. As Davis W. Houck points out, 'very early in the reporting of the case, Bryant's wife doesn't have a name, nor an age, nor a description' (2005: 232). Later, she was referred to by the press as '*very much a mother* to two young boys' (Houck 2005: 236; emphasis mine). In a similar way, McMurtry-Chubb argues, it was 'as *a mother*' that Till-Bradley 'appealed to the nation' after the death of her son, and it was 'as *a mother*' that 'the nation heard her' (2017: 642–3; emphasis mine). Thus, Black press in the north and white press in the South characterized both women through their maternal roles; a rhetorical strategy designed to elicit sympathy from the public during the trial, both for the prosecution and for the defense.

However, the poem's title presents some subtle differences between them. Till-Bradley is presented as 'A Bronzeville Mother' in Mississippi: an out-of-place outsider or interloper loitering in a location rhetorically presented as strange to her. This is despite the fact that Till-Bradley was born in Mississippi and returned to Chicago after the trial – when the poem is set – suffering from 'nervous exhaustion' (Houck 2005: 254). On the other hand, Bryant is a 'Mississippi Mother'; her identity is explicitly linked with the location of the poem and as such, she is presented as a local or a resident of the poem's setting. This discrepancy suggests that Brooks is drawing readers' attention to the racially divisive rhetoric of the Southern press preceding, during, and after, the trial of Bryant and Milam.[2]

Though both of Brooks's poems employ a distinctly elegiac mode, they also engage formally and stylistically with that of the ballad. 'The Last Quatrain' adheres to its four-line structure and ABAB rhyme scheme – even though each of the four lines of the quatrain is cut in two by its line breaks – while 'A Bronzeville Mother' explores the ballad's conventions and tropes despite its free-verse structure. The latter poem draws attention to this from the outset, describing the events leading up to Till's murder as 'like a Ballad' (Brooks 2006: 75). Bryant sees herself as the 'milk-white maid' in a heroic love story, in which Roy is a 'Fine Prince,' who rescues her from Till's 'Dark Villain' (Brooks 2006: 75). From the poem's opening, then, Brooks establishes Bryant as characterized by delusion and fantasy. Her initial understanding of events is presented according to a pattern of mythic tropes of chivalry and fairytale. As the poem progresses, these tropes gradually disintegrate to reveal the mythos of toxic white masculinity underpinning them.

In the poem, Bryant makes breakfast for her family: bacon, eggs, sour-milk biscuits and a homemade preserve. Breakfast, here, operates as a symbol of the 1950s all-American nuclear family and of the maternal role of nurture and care codified within that symbol. When Bryant burns bacon and hides the evidence – by discarding it and cooking more – we are alerted to a symbolic failure in the performance of that idyllic role. In this way, the burning of bacon symbolizes a glitch in the perfect all-American-happy-family mythos; a glitch which Bryant tries to conceal. It is, in other words, an irregularity in the surface of an idyllic image that Bryant seeks to maintain. This brief and concealed moment of failure echoes the failure of the psychic rationalizations she uses to justify Till's murder. And, after burning the bacon, her chivalric fantasy begins to unravel as we observe numerous further glitches in the symbolic myths she has created. The image of Till as a child refuses to cohere with the archetypal 'Dark Villain' of her constructed fantasy (Brooks 2006: 75). She is struck by the ridiculousness of the image of Roy Bryant as a 'Fine Prince' on a horse chasing down a child (Brooks 2006: 75). No longer able to remember what Till had done to warrant such an attack, her chivalric illusions fracture in ways that she cannot repair; there are multiple breaks or tears within them and she cannot think of any 'thread capable' of sewing them back together (2006: 77). Once again, the maternal ideals of nurture and care reach a point of failure: 'sew-work' gestures towards an all-American mother figure as a mender and seamstress patching up holes in her family's clothes (2006: 77). This maternal ideal refuses to sustain itself under the strain of her psychic rationalizations; facing the horrific truth and senseless violence of Till's murder, she is unable to hold together her self-image as a perfect mother in a perfect all-American family.

In stanza seven, the Bryant children are made to sit in designated seats at the breakfast table while Carolyn calls her husband to breakfast. Roy is designated in the poem as 'Him,' as if she cannot bear to speak his name (2006: 77). The image of children sitting 'in their places,' evokes the rigid hierarchy of the nuclear family (2006: 77). We might draw parallels between this hierarchy and the racial hierarchy in the South in 1955. In 1956, Milam gave a paid interview to William Bradford Huie for *Look* magazine after he and Bryant were acquitted of Till's murder. In it, as Onwuachi-Willig points out, he complains 'over and over that Till simply refused to capitulate to the understood racial hierarchy of Mississippi society' (2016–2017: 1144). The mythos of white masculinity – both in the context of the nuclear family and in the context of the Jim Crow laws of the South – depends on an inflexible hierarchization of power within social roles, with the white male at the top and everyone else underneath. The capitalization of 'Him' in the poem emphasizes this self-imposed position of hierarchical dominance (Brooks 2006: 77).

Carolyn's own place within the hierarchy is more complex and less secure. Before she calls her husband down to breakfast, she hurries to the mirror to apply lipstick and comb her hair because, we are told, she sometimes imagines he looks at her like he is '[m]easuring her,' in order to weigh up whether 'she had been worth It' (the pronoun 'It' is capitalized as if she cannot bear to articulate Till's murder, just as she cannot bear to speak her husband's name) (Brooks 2006: 77). As Dave Tell points out, Carolyn was '[t]he winner of two white beauty pageants,' a fact which Milam and Bryant's legal defense team put to use in order to emphasize Till's supposed wrongdoing: he had, according to them, 'physically assaulted "the fairest flower of Southern womanhood"' (Timothy Tyson cited in Tell 2017: 121). In addition – according to Houck's analysis of press surrounding the trial – in every story, newspapers described Bryant in terms that made reference to her looks. For instance, she is described as 'comely'; as a 'pretty brunette wife'; or as 'Bryant's attractive wife,' to such an extent that '[i]t was as if a salutary adjective had replaced Carolyn as her first name' (2005: 236–44). Her attractiveness, in Houck's view, operates as a means of assisting 'white Southern men' in their vigorous defense of 'Southern womanhood' (2005: 239). Thus, Bryant's physical beauty characterizes her place within a rigid Southern hierarchy: as the 'milk-white maid' of the chivalric fantasy, she is a trophy for which the 'Fine Prince' battles (Brooks 2006: 75).

However, it is upon this beauty that her place in the rigid hierarchy depends, as a treasured symbol of preserved white femininity. Her notion of her husband's 'measuring her,' and the perceived question of whether she had been 'worth It,' both imply an economy of exchange in which the protection of an imagined white feminine purity is paid for with violence against Till's Black body (2006: 77). Moreover, this exchange depends on the configuration of Till as 'Dark Villain,' even when the reality does not cohere with that configuration (2006: 75). Bryant imagines her husband overcome by Till's 'little-boyness,' during the murder and concludes that she must maintain her beauty so that he never determines, in his measuring of her, that 'she had not been worth It' (2006: 77). In other words, she implicitly understands the maintenance of her physical beauty as a necessary part of the construction of the myth of white masculinity: her husband must never have cause to feel as if the price he paid for her supposed 'purity' is too high. Thus, the exchange of racial violence for imagined white feminine purity – in order that white masculinity is asserted and maintained – requires the constant preservation of all the mythic constructions that sustain it. If the reality of Till as a fourteen-year-old boy does not uphold the required features of the 'Dark Villain,' then Bryant must work even harder to uphold the features of imagined white femininity through the safeguarding of a pristine image as a beautiful, pure and wholesome wife and an all-American mother, in order that the figurative exchange does not collapse altogether (Brooks 2006: 75).

The smooth preservation of this economy as a 'Happiness-Ever-After' for Carolyn also requires upholding an image of Roy Bryant as a noble hero within a chivalric fantasy (2006: 75). But as the poem progresses, Carolyn becomes increasingly aware of her husband's murderous, violent and monstrous qualities. When he slaps one of the children across the face for throwing a pitcher at his sibling, she imagines that the child's cheek has been replaced by 'a heaviness,' and an endless 'lengthening red' (2006: 79). Later, when he embraces her, it is with a sense of proprietary ownership and she cannot escape the image of a 'red ooze' soaking over everything, including her own body (2006: 79). Finally, when he kisses her, his 'very, very, very red' mouth seems to engulf or overwhelm her own (2006: 80).[3] In this way, her husband transforms in her imagination from a 'Fine Prince' into an all-consuming, bleeding wound (2006: 75). Beneath the illusory veneer of white masculine desire, configured as chivalric fantasy, is a reality underpinned by an overwhelming, life-draining violence that spreads across everything, from her child's face to the entire world and its closest planetary neighbour, Mars.

Throughout this transformation from fantasy to reality, Brooks repeatedly draws our attention to Carolyn's silence: she does not respond when her husband slaps the child, nor when she leaves the table; and when she is confronted with the full collapse of her ideological fantasy, she 'did not scream' (2006: 80). She is both imprisoned and smothered by the horror of its underlying reality, with her fear and her memories of the trial compared to iron restraints and to an overbearing wall respectively. In this way, the poem imagines for Bryant an inescapable incarceration of her own making; a prison which inverts the role she played in Till's murder. As the propagator of a fictionalized account of the events that resulted in Till's killing, Bryant inhabits – in the poem – a role where her own fiction both confines and silences her; while at the same time it constantly torments her with the reality it conceals.

The horror of Carolyn's imprisonment within the rigid structure of Southern white patriarchy reaches its culmination in the penultimate stanza, in which her hatred of Roy blooms 'into glorious flower,' that is '[b]igger than all magnolias' (Brooks 2006: 80). The floral metaphor of this blossoming hate recalls the depiction of Carolyn, in media coverage of the trial, as 'the fairest flower of Southern womanhood' (Timothy Tyson cited in Tell 2017: 121). Magnolias are the official state flower of Mississippi and a symbol of bridal purity in Southern weddings. They signify white feminine purity as it exists in the patriarchal construction of white masculinity; a construction which, as we have seen, depends on violence against Black bodies to sustain itself. In its violent burst into flower, Carolyn's hatred of her husband is greater than this mythic construction; it is greater than all the symbols of white feminine purity that may be used to uphold manufactured ideals of white masculinity, rigid racial and patriarchal hierarchies, and the image of an all-American family as a 'Happiness-Ever-After' (Brooks 2006: 80; 75).

The ending of 'A Bronzeville Mother' directs us to Brooks's second – and related – poem about Till's murder, 'The Last Quatrain Of The Ballad Of Emmett Till,' which is described in the final stanza as 'the last bleak news of the ballad,' and 'the rest of the rugged music' (2006: 80). As 'bleak' and 'rugged,' the poem signposts the 'Last Quatrain' as bare, cold, cheerless, broken, rocky and austere. What these two poems signify collectively is a ballad that has been broken in two; severed from its final stanza and, by consequence, any potential arc of resolution. Brooks's two poems embody a symbolic rupture of the balladic form – a form that is understood, in genealogical formations, as Anglo-European in origin – emphasizing its inability to contain the weight of the account of Till's murder.[4]

Comprising ten lines (a quatrain broken into eight lines; plus two introductory lines), the poem is briefer and starker than 'A Bronzeville Mother'. It is sparse and understated, employing short, unembellished sentences in contrast with the syntactical complexity of the preceding poem. In short, it marks a distinct shift in tone from fantasy to reality. The poem begins with two parenthetical lines which explicitly situate the poem in a temporal context after Till's murder and memorial. In contrast with the opening of 'A Bronzeville Mother,' which begins by exploring the imaginary past of Bryant's chivalric delusions, these parenthetical lines in 'The Last Quatrain' ground the poem in a particular temporal moment; one which implicitly foregrounds the killing of Till and his funeral.

Having situated the temporality of the poem, the quatrain shifts its focus to Till-Bradley for the remaining eight lines. These lines construct an image of her as an objectified commodity, similar to the way in which Carolyn is depicted as a figure of white feminine beauty in 'A Bronzeville Mother' (Brooks 2006: 81). This passive, objectified image of Till-Bradley operates in direct contrast with scholarly descriptions of her, such as Bush's account of her 'heroism, wisdom and faith […] driven by a belief in moral justice'; or Myisha Priest's account of her creating 'a community of hearers to give ear to her complicated articulation of grief and grievance' (Bush 2013: 13; Priest 2010: 15). Instead of the brave, defiant, galvanizing picture painted by these accounts of her participation in the Civil Rights Movement, Brooks's poem focuses on her attractiveness and her colouring. This disparity is striking, but the poem is likely gesturing towards depictions of Till-Bradley in the Southern print media. In Houck's analysis of press surrounding the trial, he points out that '[w]riters were eager to comment on [Till-Bradley's] appearance,' describing her as '[a] small neat woman,' and outlining in detail her clothing and jewellery (2005: 245–6). In other words,

Brooks's depiction may rely on a certain amount of irony. The passive, objectified depiction of Till-Bradly in the poem is significantly out of keeping with that in the 'sophisticated and nationally respectable black press,' with which she had established an important 'alliance' (Bush 2013: 12–13). Rather, it is more in line with the objectifying and trivializing rhetoric of the Southern press during the trial.

Similarly, Brooks's depiction of Till-Bradley as a woman sitting passively contrasts starkly with the image of an emotional Till-Bradley who fell to her knees at the arrival of her son's casket in Chicago; or who repeatedly 'invoked the metaphor of her son as "my heart buried in a pine box underneath glass"' (Metress 2003: 90; Priest 2010: 15). The only emotion she explicitly exhibits in the poem is remorse or regret which seems, in contrast with these critical accounts of her, a significant understatement. It also differs starkly from Carolyn's hyper-romanticized fantasies in 'A Bronzeville Mother'. But by portraying Till-Bradley's grief in understated terms, Brooks rejects the kind of poetic hyperbole that enables and sustains Carolyn's balladic delusions. She refuses to dramatize Till's murder as a heroic ballad narrative because to do so would subscribe to similarly constructed fictions. The 'Last Quatrain,' then, operates not only as a symbolic rupture of the ballad form, but also of its tropes and narrative conventions.

The poem is significant in its use of colour. The coffee Till-Bradley drinks, the room in which she sits, the landscape in the final lines – even Till-Bradley herself – are defined in terms of their colour. Everything in the poem, in other words, is characterized by its colour except for Till, who is characterized instead by his having been murdered (Brooks 2006: 81). While the poem's reds and greys echo the violence and bleak desolation of his murder, Till is the only element of the poem not defined by colour, since it is colour that defined his killing.

The 'grays' of the final lines imply the colour of ash; that which remains after something has been burned (2006: 81). These 'grays' are nebulous; they have no substance, order or solidity and they move through the landscape like turbulent ghosts (2006: 81). Since they follow directly from the understated depiction of Till-Bradley's emotions, these 'grays' operate as a potential manifestation of her internal and private experience of grief as she sits passively within a room (2006: 81). Their 'chaos' implies confusion and upheaval, while the adjective 'windy' implies volatility and tempestuousness (2006: 81). And they contrast with the red in the poem's earlier lines, signifying both despair and violence (2006: 81). The poem therefore implies that while externally she is composed and contained (both within the room and in her demeanour), internally Till-Bradley's emotions are kinetic, wild and uncontrolled.

The 'grays' also signpost the colour that results when black and white are mixed together (2006: 81). In this way, they reflect the volatile, racially charged atmosphere surrounding Till's murder and the inflammatory rhetoric used by the Southern press during the trial. As Houck points out, Till's murder took place against the backdrop of the Supreme Court's *Brown v. Board of Education* school integration case, which caused racial violence to flare in the Mississippi Delta (2005: 229–31). 'Racial politics,' he argues, 'were *boiling over* in Mississippi during the summer of 1955' (Houck 2005: 231; emphasis mine). Moreover, Mississippi press reported during the trial that, as a result of national contention, residents in the state were 'facing a *loaded and cocked pistol* of racial strife' (*Clarion-Ledger* cited in Houck 2005: 239; emphasis mine). The poem's 'grays' point towards the aftermath – the remains – of this combustible atmosphere, much like the ashy remains left behind after a fire (2006: 81).

It is also worth acknowledging that 'gray' is a disparaging term for a white person, as well as a historical metonym for Confederate soldiers in the American Civil War (because of their grey uniform).[5] Thus, the 'grays' in the final lines also gesture towards Mississippi's failure to convict Milam and Bryant of a racially motivated murder that upheld Confederate values (Brooks 2006: 81). As one northern Delta newspaper stated at the time of the murder investigation, if a conviction could not be secured, then 'Mississippi may as well burn all its law books and close its courts,' as it would no longer be 'a self-governing state capable of making and enforcing its own laws' (*Clarksdale Press Register* cited in Houck 2005: 233). And twenty-two days after this newspaper statement was made, an all-white male Mississippi jury acquitted Milam and Bryant in just 67 minutes (Bush 2013: 9). The poem's 'chaos' of 'grays' highlights this catastrophic failure of law which the acquittal represented in the South, and the violent, vainglorious and bombastic rhetoric used by the trial and the press to achieve it (Brooks 2006: 81).

The red landscape of the final line echoes the colour of the room in which Till-Bradley sits in the poem's opening. Both of these red spaces – one contained and one unbounded, one interior and one exterior – symbolize the volatile emotional matrix of rage and anger which the murder of Till represented, as well as a reference to the horrific violence of the murder itself. They also echo the growing and expanding 'red ooze' in 'A Bronzeville Mother'; the depiction of Southern white masculinity as a leaking, bleeding redness that consumes everything around it (Brooks 2006: 79). This seeping red ooze extends beyond the confines of Bryant's post-trial kitchen in 'A Bronzeville Mother' and permeates the spaces of 'The Last Quatrain' (2006: 81). Thus, Bryant's sense, in the former poem, that her husband is a red ooze 'seeping, spreading' over everything is brought to a stark conclusion as it infuses both the interior and exterior landscapes of the 'Last Quatrain' (2006: 79).

In contrast with Brooks's two elegiac ballads, Audre Lorde's 1981 poem 'Afterimages' explores the horror of Till's murder from the poet's own perspective as a young writer. Indeed, perspective is a key theme in the poem, which continuously returns to the eye as organ of perception; and to the ways in which horrific events alter the way in which the world is seen. The poem begins with a description of how some images – such as the newspaper picture of Till's mutilated body – become imprinted on one's mind. In the poem, Lorde describes her eyes as caves in which fish evolve, specifically 'dragonfish,' an American fish that lives in mud and sand; a scavenger often marketed by pet shops for its aggressive nature, when in fact it is docile, with very poor eyesight (2000: 339). In the poem, these figurative fish are 'always hungry' but, like extremophiles, they are 'learning to survive' in an environment without food (Lorde 2000: 339). In this way, Lorde characterizes her eyes as desiring of a visual nourishment that she is unable to find. They have a curiosity for the world that is never quite satisfied. In the context of this desirous curiosity, the image of Till's mutilated body is one which 'enters,' and whose 'force remains' (2000: 339). It is 'etched' and 'fused' to her way of seeing; melted or engraved permanently within the mind's eye (2000: 339).

Lorde's focus on the eye as an organ of looking can be understood in relation to what bell hooks calls the 'oppositional gaze,' which 'interrogate[s] the gaze of the Other, but also look[s] back,' in order to name what is seen (1992: 116). It is a resistant and critical gaze whose function is to 'document' (1992: 116). The permanent damage of 'etching' and 'fusing,' which Till's image effects upon the speaker's eye in the poem represents what hooks – following Manthia Diawara – describes as a 'rupture,' that defines a relation between Black spectator and image (1992: 116). Lorde's eye, then, is an interrogating eye, but one which, in its looking, experiences a 'material and physical' violence (Teresa de Lauretis cited in hooks 1992: 118; 120). Speaking specifically about cinema, hooks states that '[f]or black female spectators who have "looked too deep" the encounter with the screen hurt' (1992: 121). For Lorde, it is not an encounter with a screen but an encounter with a newspaper image that causes this visual harm.

In part III of the poem, Lorde describes the photograph of Till's body as an 'afterimage' that characterizes her '21st year,' despite attempts to avert her eyes from its ubiquity in the news media (2000: 340). She draws attention to the spectacle into which the figure of Till's body is transformed by the press, the sensationalism used to report it, and the way in which it was consumed by the public. Using phrases like 'secret relish,' and 'savored violence,' in relation to media reportage, she implies that the press and the public derived from their 'avid insistence of detail' a pleasure and satisfaction such as one might experience when dwelling upon something eaten (2000: 341). We might compare this to Butler's description of how photographers of war torture '*feasted* on [a] sadistic scene' (2016: 82; emphasis mine). In both examples, the act of viewing or looking is likened to the act of eating, specifically in a voracious fashion.

The consequence of this sensationalizing of Till's image, particularly the ubiquity and frequency with which the image of his mutilation is presented, creates an effect of desensitization. As Butler asserts in relation to photographs of war, an image may 'overwhelm and numb its viewers' (2016: 68). When people are 'bombarded with sensationalist photography,' they argue, a 'capacity for ethical responsiveness' is 'diminished' (2016: 68). Lorde registers this diminished capacity in her description of the way in which the image is 'used, crumpled, and discarded' (Lorde 2000: 341). The frequency with which the image is encountered normalizes Till's mutilated body and its consumption by those who are situated in the position of spectator. For many people, it has become nothing more than a disposable commodity. Lorde, on the other hand, is haunted by the image. This haunting may be due, if we follow Butler, to a photograph's capacity to 'act on us in part through outliving the life it documents' (2016: 98). 'If we can be haunted,' by an image, Butler argues, 'then we can acknowledge that there has been a loss and hence that there has been a life' (2016: 98). But it may also be because, as Butler suggests, a photograph does not simply depict an event but 'becomes crucial to its production, its legibility, its illegibility, and its very status as reality' (2016: 82). In other words, the image of Till's body is haunting precisely because it plays a role in how Till's murder is deciphered and understood (and, equally, made indecipherable and incomprehensible).

In her description of the press's gleeful focus on detail, Lorde includes reference to the way in which Till's eyes were mutilated or 'gouged out' (2000: 340). Till-Bradley's (by this point, Till-Mobley) autobiography, in giving account of identifying her son's body, describes 'an eyeball hanging down, resting on [his] cheek' (Till-Mobley cited in Onwuachi-Willig 2016–2017: 1128). That

Lorde extends this violence to both of Till's eyes draws explicit attention to their sightlessness. Thus, she emphasizes how the violence committed upon his body involves the removal of his perspective. While his body is the subject of the national gaze, his own has been 'sewed shut' (Lorde 2000: 340). There is, therefore, no reciprocal gaze with which viewers of the image might find themselves gazed upon in return. Without this reciprocal gaze, Till's image is rendered pure spectacle; a thing to be looked at. According to Butler, Susan Sontag suggests this is characteristic of photographs of the dead. '[T]he dead do not care whether we see or not,' they suggest; they are 'profoundly uninterested in us – they do not seek our gaze' (2016: 100). However, as Butler acknowledges, this raises issues for 'our inability to see what we see' (2016: 100). There is something important in the dynamic of being looked back upon within the act of looking, the lack of which is registered in Lorde's description of Till's sightless image. Perhaps it relates to a sense of being caught in the act of looking; one that might potentially interrupt the 'secret relish' with which the image is consumed, or prevent the image from being 'used, crumpled, and discarded' (Lorde 2000: 341). There is, the poem suggests, something dehumanizing in the severance of Till's gaze that makes visual consumption possible.

In addition to the recurring motif of the eye, Lorde's poem is thematically suffused with water. The second part of the poem describes a television report of a 1979 flood in Jackson, Mississippi, in which a 'white woman' is interviewed while leaving her flooded house (2000: 339). It is easy to draw parallels between this woman and Carolyn Bryant in Brooks's 'A Bronzeville Mother'. Both are weighted down by despair and both are silenced by a fear of their abusive husbands. Both survey their ruined lives to measure the damage. The Jackson woman questions what she has paid in order to 'never know' the cost of her 'honor,' just as Brooks's poem questions the exchange whereby Carolyn's imagined white feminine 'purity' is upheld through violences committed upon Till's body (Lorde 2000: 341). In Lorde's poem, Till is not a 'Dark Villain,' but a boy who – by whistling – performed a masculine act that he had been taught, and as a consequence, he was mutilated by 'his teachers' (Brooks 2006: 75; Lorde 2000: 341). Thus, in 'Afterimages,' the exchange of supposed white feminine honour for violence against the Black body is a consequence of Till's perceived transgressive adoption of white masculine codes of behaviour towards white women.

For Lorde, the dynamic upon which white masculinity depends is a 'double ritual of white manhood': the sexual subjugation of women through performances of masculine acts of sexualized violence; and the mutilation of Black bodies in exchange for the ownership of white femininity (2000: 341). Twice in the poem, Lorde compares the mutilated body of Till with images of sexualized violence towards women (2000: 341). These references point towards a collapse of Milam and Bryant's – and by extension, white patriarchy's – 'double ritual' into one singular drive to subjugate through sexual power, in order to maintain a white masculine hierarchy (2000: 341). What underlies Milam and Bryant's – and by extension, white patriarchy's – construction of Till as an imagined sexual threat to white femininity is an anxiety about the loss of white masculine power in the American South. As Mbembe points out, following Fanon, 'a racist society is one that is worried about the question of losing its sexual potential' (2019: 131). In Lorde's poem, Milam and Bryant's celebration of their 'aroused honor' following their murder of Till 'in the name of white womanhood' is configured around the same fictions of desire and morality as Bryant's chivalric fantasy in 'A Bronzeville Mother' (Lorde 2000: 341) It is a celebration of the maintenance of white masculine power, expressed through a hypersexualized performance of virile masculinity.

The parallels between Roy Bryant in Brooks's poem and the Jackson woman's husband in Lorde's remind us that this performance of virile white masculinity is intrinsically linked with violence and death. In Lorde's poem, the man has 'an executioner's face,' his hands are likened to 'ham,' and the words in his mouth are 'rotting meat' (2000: 342; 340). These latter two references draw an implicit connection between the husband in 'Afterimages' and Bryant, who was the owner of the Grocery and Meat Market where Till encountered Carolyn. But while Roy in 'A Bronzeville Mother' is an all-consuming, bleeding wound, Lorde's Bryant figure's very words are decaying flesh and death. Thus, both figures of white masculinity in the poems are associated with carnage, bloodshed and slaughter.

Moreover, the hierarchical positions of both these men depend on the silence of their respective wives: in 'A Bronzeville Mother,' reference is repeatedly made to Carolyn's not speaking, while the Jackson woman in 'Afterimages' is 'unvoiced' and 'never allowed her own tongue' (Lorde 2000: 342). Both of these depictions of Carolyn – explicit and implicit – as silenced are significant, since her testimony at the Till trial was crucial for Milam and Bryant's defense, despite it being ruled inadmissible and despite her never naming Till specifically (Houck 2005: 250). Carolyn's role in the court's failure to convict Milam and Bryant relied both upon her ability to speak (in the creation of a fictional story that supported her husband's statements to the police) and upon her silence (as a complicit participant in the murder of Till by neglecting to articulate what had actually happened). It is perhaps no coincidence, then, that both poems deny Bryant her voice. Nor is it a coincidence that both poems imagine for her a nightmarish existence: in Brooks's poem as a prisoner of her own fiction and in Lorde's as a woman whose life is in ruins. Both poems effectively provide for Carolyn a figurative – and poetic – justice. Interestingly, a 2018 article in the *Clarion Ledger* – a daily newspaper in Jackson – describes how at the age of eighty-four, Carolyn had 'said privately that the Emmett Till case has kept her a prisoner' (Anderson 2018: para 72). If this is to be believed, both Brooks's and Lorde's depictions of her were eerily prescient.

The river in Lorde's poem also operates as a force of justice, and one that is explicitly retributory. Lorde depicts the Pearl River near Jackson as the site of the murder, though in actuality Till's body was found in the Tallahatchie River, about 86 miles away. Describing Till's death as a baptism, Lorde reconfigures it as a holy ceremonial purification. This stands in contrast to the 'muddy judgment' the river visits upon the white woman's family, laying waste to her home and livelihood through flooding (Lorde 2000: 341). Indeed, Lorde's image of the flooded Jackson houses genuflecting 'like sinners,' implies that the flood is a divine punishment visited upon the city because of the state's failure to convict Milam and Bryant (2000: 339). And Till is depicted as riding the crest of the flood wave; a driving force at the forefront of this natural disaster, personally delivering the justice that was denied him in reality. Crucially, by depicting Till as 'whistling' as he rides the wave, Lorde transforms the notorious wolf-whistle – so prominent in the media and legal rhetoric surrounding the murder and trial – from a hypersexualized signifier of Black masculine threat into one of redemptive joy and triumph (2000: 342).

Though the Jackson woman in the poem has lost everything to the flood, Lorde is unequivocal in her lack of sympathy for her loss. By withholding her 'pity' and 'bread,' Lorde refuses any mercy or compassion (2000: 341). A denial of bread is a denial of solidarity and community; the word *companion* derives from the Latin *companionem* meaning 'bread fellow'. While she may be pitiful, the poem implies, she deserves neither pity, nor compassion, nor support. Though Brooks's poems and Lorde's differ in their perspectives, forms and use of images, both poems gesture towards an imagined retribution or reckoning for Carolyn; one that envisages her silent complicity in Till's murder repurposed into a form of wretched and intolerable confinement from which she cannot escape. Perhaps most importantly, both writers use their elegiac poems as a means of highlighting the exchange upon which white masculinity depends: the ownership and protection of an imagined white feminine purity at the cost of violence to the Black body.

Reflections, disintegrations, incendiary materials: Civil Rights elegies

Emmett Till's murder marks one catalyst of the Civil Rights struggles that took place in the 1950s and 1960s. There were, however, other events that caused and exacerbated civil unrest during this time, including the *Brown v. Board of Education* landmark ruling in 1954, anticipation of which helped to create a climate of racial tensions in Mississippi in 1955. Rosa Parks's refusal to give up her seat on a segregated bus in Montgomery, Alabama in 1955 – the same year Till was killed – is another. Her arrest for violating Jim Crow segregation laws precipitated a thirteen-month boycott of buses in Montgomery, which was headed by the city's new minister, Martin Luther King, Jr.

Most timelines mark the end of the Civil Rights Movement in 1968, following the assassination of King and the consequent passing of the Civil Rights Act, which was expedited by riots that took place following King's murder. Nonetheless, race-related civil unrest continued into the early 1970s.[6] There are countless instances of horrific racial injustice that took place prior to, and during, 1968. Among these, the most well-known include the obstruction of the Little Rock Nine from entering their recently desegregated Central High School in 1957; the repeated mob attacks on Freedom Riders who challenged failures to desegregate buses in the South in 1961; innumerable instances of police brutality during Civil Rights protests, particularly – though not limited to – protests in the South; the bombing of the Sixteenth Street Baptist Church in 1963, in which four young girls were killed; the murder of James Chaney, Andrew Goodman and Michael Schwerner, three Civil Rights activists who sought to register Black voters in Mississippi; the assassination of NAACP Mississippi field secretary Medgar Evers in 1963; the assassination of Malcolm X in 1965; and the assassination of King in 1968. Many of these events are the subject of elegies: notable examples include Audre Lorde's 'Suffer the Children' (1964; about the children killed in the Sixteenth Street Baptist Church bombing); Margaret Walker's 'For Andy Goodman, Michael Schwerner, and James Chaney' (1970), 'Micah' (1970; about Medgar Evers) and 'For Malcolm X' (1970); Gwendolyn Brooks's 'Medgar Evers (For Charles Evers)' (1968) and 'Malcolm X (for Dudley Randall)' (1968); Sonia Sanchez's 'Malcolm' (1978); and Lucille Clifton's 'malcolm' (1972) and 'the meeting after the savior gone 4/4/68' (1969). It is beyond the scope of this chapter to encapsulate the full breadth and variety of elegiac poems about instances of racial injustice that took place during the Civil Rights struggles. However, to make space for this important poetic work, and to avoid flattening out the vastly different poetics of these various writers, this section examines two elegiac poems written following the assassination of Martin Luther King, Jr.: 'Reflections on April 4, 1968' by Nikki Giovanni (1968); and 'In Memoriam: Martin Luther King, Jr.' by June Jordan (1968).

Giovanni's poem was written in 1968, originally appearing in her self-published second volume *Black Judgement* (1970), and available in *The Collected Poetry of Nikki Giovanni 1968-1998* (2007). Designating the poem as 'reflections,' the title implies a quiet thinking through – or a recollection and remembrance of – the assassination of King. However, the poem's tone is at odds with this implication, and it is likely that the title carries a strong degree of irony. It is therefore useful to consider some of the other semantic possibilities that the word 'reflection' implies. For instance, it can signify the action of a mirror reflecting an image; an instance of being driven back after an impact; the action of bending or folding back upon oneself; or the turning back from a point of progression. Each of these might aptly describe the movement of Giovanni's poem. In its fierce call to arms, the poem 'reflects back' the state-sanctioned violence against Civil Rights protesters that culminated in King's assassination. Equally, King's murder led to violent nationwide riots of 'epidemic proportions,' and the poem registers the 'reflection' – the affective impact of King's death – that galvanized these instances of violent protest (Spilerman 1970: 632). In its explicitly violent tone, the poem is a 'reflection' – or a folding-back-upon – the non-violent protest strategies for which King advocated. And, despite King's assassination precipitating the passing by Congress of the Civil Rights Bill 1968, his death, as Minchin and Salmond argue, 'left an enormous vacuum in the civil rights movement, especially as there was no longer a charismatic figurehead for the media to focus on' (2011: 59). In this way, the poem also registers the death as a 'reflection' – a turning back from – the point of progress which the Civil Rights Movement had so far reached.

Giovanni's poem has been described as 'violent'; as having a 'militant thrust'; and as what 'many readers could consider the epitome of bitterness and hatred as expressed in its violent and dramatic calls for punishments of whites for King's assassination' (Holladay 2004: 21; Lordi 2018: para 3; Harris 2014: 74). We have seen, in Chapter 1, the ways in which words like 'militancy' and 'bitterness' are often utilized as coded critical dismissals of Black women's poetry. Here, these two terms are used to euphemistically highlight the violence in Giovanni's poem, which is explicit from the outset. The poem begins with Giovanni asking what she can do as 'a poor Black woman, […] to destroy america,' to which the poem gives three answer: she can either 'kill,' 'protect those who kill' or 'encourage others to kill' (2007: 49) Trudier Harris suggests that this violent rhetoric is out of keeping with Giovanni's stance in reality, given that she has responded to critics' perceptions of her as 'bitter and full of hate,' by asserting, '[n]othing could be further from the truth' (Giovanni cited in Harris 2014: 74). Harris reflects on this discrepancy by suggesting that, rather than reflecting Giovanni's own position, the poem captures 'the spirit of the times, the intense sense of loss and anger that King's death engendered' (2014: 75). That Giovanni's poem is a rhetorical call to arms is without question. It certainly incorporates within it calls for retaliation in response to King's murder. But perhaps understanding it simply as capturing the 'loss and anger' at the time oversimplifies some of its complexities (Harris 2014: 75). Reading the poem through the lens of key speeches from the Civil Rights movement – by Malcolm X ('The Ballot or the Bullet,' 1964), Stokely Carmichael ('Black Power,' 1966) and King ('The Other America,' 1968b) – enables an unpacking of that complexity.

Malcolm X's speech, delivered in 1964, principally argued in favour of Black sovereignty – as opposed to white governmental control – over the politics and economies of Black communities. It highlighted the failure of American politicians to deliver on promises made to Black communities about Civil Rights legislation, particularly in relation to voting rights. His approach to violence is ambivalent: he advocated for non-violence in the face of non-violence, but for violence 'when the enemy gets violent,' stating that 'where the government has proven itself either unwilling or unable to defend the lives and the property' of the Black community, that community is justified in defending themselves (1964: para 57; para 60).

Carmichael's speech, which was originally delivered in Greenwood, Mississippi, in 1966 during the March Against Fear demonstration (and later at the University of California, Berkeley), contended that 'every time black people move in this country, they're forced to defend their position,' and, moreover, it is time for white people 'to start defending themselves as to why they have oppressed and exploited [Black people]' (1966: para 17). Asserting that 'white society' has failed 'to make nonviolence work,' he suggested that Black people 'have already been nonviolent too many years,' and that it is white communities – unable 'to deal with their own problems inside their own communities,' and who 'beat up black people every day' – who needed to learn non-violence (1966: para 42; para 11; para 57). Moreover, asserting that Black communities 'are on the move for […] liberation,' he stated that, if white people refused to allow for that liberation, there was 'no choice but to say very clearly, "Move over, or we're gonna move on over you"' (1966: para 61).

King's speech, delivered at Grosse Pointe High School in 1968, described how '[t]here are two Americas': one, for white people 'who have food and material necessities for their bodies, culture and education for their minds, [and] freedom and human dignity for their spirits'; and another of 'sub-standard housing conditions,' inadequate, overcrowded schools, low-income, low-quality jobs and high unemployment (1968b: para 3). King attributed the 'despair and bitterness' that arose from Black communities 'perishing on a lonely island of poverty in the midst of a vast ocean of material prosperity' as the cause for riots that took place across the United States (1968b: para 5). Explicitly restating his commitment to 'militant, powerful, massive, non-violence,' he condemned the 'contingent, intolerable conditions' that had precipitated riots by causing 'individuals to feel that they have no other alternative than to engage in violent rebellions' (1968b: para 7).

What each of these speeches gestures towards is an untenable position into which Civil Rights protestors had been forced: when Black non-violence is confronted relentlessly and remorselessly by white homicidal violence, there is no choice but to retaliate or risk annihilation. Giovanni stated in a 1982 interview that the shooting of King was 'so unnecessary,' and the riots that it precipitated were a 'perfectly logical response'; an 'answer' to the 'message' that the shooting of King sent (Elder 1982: 70). This 'answer' she refers to is the Holy Week Uprising, the 'greatest wave of social unrest since the Civil War,' in which 'looting, arson, or sniper fire occurred in 196 cities in thirty-six states plus the District of Columbia' (Levy 2018: 153). In the poem, Giovanni's answer is simpler: 'I can kill,' the poem suggests in its opening, '[t]here are no other ways' (2007: 49). By stating that Lyndon B. Johnson had 'declared war on Black people,' and by asserting that white people 'shoot at the wind,' Giovanni highlights white America's propensity for senseless murder and destruction (2007: 49). Johnson is explicitly depicted as a necropolitical figure whose presidency is wholly defined – and will continue to be defined – by death (2007: 50). Her assertion that the 'first step toward peace,' is the amputation of 'two fingers' – the means for firing a gun – from white people's hands explicitly holds white people accountable not only for the assassination of King, but for all of the violence and unrest in the country (2007: 49). Thus, according to the poem, non-violence and peace cannot be achieved as long as white people have access to guns.

We might compare these statements in the poem to Malcolm X's assertion, in 'The Ballot or the Bullet,' that 'Uncle Sam's hands are dripping with [...] the blood of the black man' (1964: para 36). Equally, we might read Giovanni's description of King's assassination as an 'act of war,' as an echo of Carmichael's televised statement that 'white America [had] declared war on black America' and that, since there is 'no alternative to retribution [...] Black people have to survive, and the only way they will survive is by getting guns' (Giovanni 2007: 49; Carmichael cited in Franklin 1968: para 21). So, we can read the opening of Giovanni's poem at face value, as a straightforward call for the destruction of what Carmichael refers to as the 'clearly racist' institutions of white America (1966: para 5). But we might also read it as expressing an incredulous irony: '[w]hat can I, a poor Black woman, do to destroy america,' when America is already founded on such widespread white destruction and violence? (Giovanni 2007: 49) The assertion, then, that '[t]here are no other ways,' but to kill operates as a lament for the failure of strategic non-violence in the face of unremitting and indiscriminate violence against Black people (Giovanni 2007: 49). To be clear, this reading is not an attempt to neutralize the ferocity of Giovanni's articulation. Its intent is, rather, to suggest that the unmistakable violence of the poem's language might additionally be understood as a means of turning back upon itself – or 'reflecting' – the violence of white America.

Later in the poem, Giovanni condemns white critique of the Holy Week Uprising that followed the assassination of King. The poem responds to the poetic figure of 'some honkie' criticizing the unrest with disbelief that Black people are being told 'how to mourn' (Giovanni 2007: 49). While it is likely an address, in general terms, to all white people, the figure of 'some honkie' may also be read as a reference to Johnson who, immediately after King's assassination, 'went on national radio and television [...] asking Americans to pray for peace and to end "lawlessness and divisiveness" in the land' (Johnson cited in Goldzwig 2003: 37). According to Goldzwig, in the days following the murder, Johnson 'tried desperately to find words to help quell the civil disturbances,' and 'called upon Americans to "deny violence its victory"' (Johnson cited in Goldzwig 2003: 37). Subverting the famous title of Malcolm X's speech, he stressed that 'America shall not be ruled by the bullet, but only by the ballot of free and just men' (Johnson cited in Goldzwig 2003: 40). Alternatively, it may be read as a reference to white liberal politicians like Robert F. Kennedy, who spoke against what he termed the 'mindless menace of violence,' in a speech given in Cleveland, Ohio, on 5 April 1968, the day after King's assassination (1968: para 1). Or, equally, it could refer to white figures of authority like Mayor Richard Daley of Chicago, who 'pleaded for peace on TV after King's murder,' and later issued to Chicago police a shoot-to-kill order for arsonists and a shoot-to-maim order for looters (Newsweek Archives 2017: para 18).

In any case, the sentiment is the same for Giovanni: critique of the riots as a reaction to King's assassination amounts to an attempt to police the grief of the Black community. According to Hussen's analysis of Grier and Cobb's book *Black Rage*, we might understand the post-assassination riots as 'a necessary affirmation of black humanity and a compelling reanimation of black political potential under tremendously hostile sociopolitical circumstances' (2013: 307). It is a grief response that 'wards off the debilitating, defeatist alternative of black despair' (Hussen 2013: 307). Configuring King as her 'beloved', Giovanni incredulously questions the gesture to 'determine and qualify' her – and others' – grief responses (2007: 49). And in doing so, she emphasizes the hypocrisy of white America's urging for non-violent expressions of grief, given that King himself was a victim of the same pervasive white violence against Black communities that she outlines earlier in the poem. The riots, as she points out, represent a 'fire' that white people have themselves started, by filling 'a room with combustible materials' and closing it 'up tight' (Giovanni 2007: 50).

In the fourth stanza, Giovanni creates a complex metaphor which expresses the wish that King's blood 'choke the life from ten hundred million whites' (2007: 49). This might be read simply as a desire for all white people to suffocate in the violent aftermath of King's assassination. But since 'blood' also implies ties of family and lineage, the phrase also carries within it a hope that future Black generations will continue the violent struggle against oppression and exploitation. Moreover, it also operates as a corruption of the eucharist, implying that King's blood – or, figuratively, his murder – is consumed by white people in a grisly subversion of the sacrament. This gesture not only subtly transforms King into a Christ-like figure of sacrifice but also presents white people as ghoulish, cannibalistic consumers of the spectacle of King's murder.

Later in the poem, Giovanni configures King as a 'Black Madonna' figure who has fought a symbolic battle with Zeus and lost (2007: 50). Here, Zeus operates as an image of American patriarchal power: one of Zeus's symbols is the eagle, an icon shared by the US National Emblem (Becker 2000: 57). Originating as part of a device for the Great Seal for the United States, Congress decided in 1782 on a design that incorporated an 'American (the bald-headed) eagle,' because of its 'ancient mode of bearing,' as an 'imperial' symbol of 'supreme power and authority' (Journals of Congress cited in Hamilton 1853: 99–103). Zeus, as the god of lightning and thunder, is also a symbol of punishment and division; as Douglas Taylor notes, Zeus 'punished humans for their insolence by splitting them in two' (2010: 89). On a more subtle level, the figure of Zeus gestures towards the co-opting of symbols relating to European lightning gods by white supremacist and white power groups, such as the double-lightning bolts of the Nazi Schutz Staffel adopted by the American Nazi Party and the Aryan Brotherhood (Etter 2001: 62; 68). Conversely, Black Madonnas, according to Jude Morton, have 'historically and perennially served as icons of liberation,' representing marginalization and 'rebellious, [...] defiant characteristics,' as well as 'the concrete struggles of quotidian existence' (2013: 108; 106). Thus, as a representative of disempowerment and disenfranchisement defying patriarchal power, King – Giovanni suggests – has wrestled with the force of a racially divided nation and lost.

The end of Giovanni's poem is suffused with further biblical allusions and references. The penultimate stanza demands that America be baptized in fire, which references Matthew 3:11 or Luke 3:16 (KJV 2001: 620; 661). This reference implies that the post-assassination riots of the Holy Week Uprising might be understood as a force of divine 'judgment and punishment' or 'destruction' that represents the wrath of God; or a 'purification, cleansing, purging, or sanctification of the believer' (Nel 2017: 168; 170; 171).

In the final stanza, Giovanni echoes King's 'I've Been to the Mountaintop' speech – delivered in Memphis, Tennessee, the day before his assassination – by referring to America as 'the promised land' (Giovanni 2007: 50). The title of King's speech is a reference to Deuteronomy 34: 1–4, in which Moses climbs Mount Nebo in order to be shown the promised land before he dies (KJV 2001: 157). In his speech, King speaks of how he would like to have seen the Israelites escaping 'across the Red Sea, through the wilderness on toward the promised land' (1968a: para 2). At the speech's conclusion, he goes on: 'I've seen the Promised Land. I may not get there with you. But I want you to know tonight, that we, as a people, will get to the promised land' (1968a: para 53).

In making this reference, King draws upon a long tradition within Black Christian culture of analogizing Black suffering and slavery with that of the Israelite slaves of the Bible. For instance, Civil War soldier and Baptist minister George Washington Williams, in a speech in Cincinnati in 1876 stated, 'let us press forward to the promised land' (Williams cited in Bigham 2005: 228). Renford Reese, arguing that Canada represented the 'promised land' for US slaves after its abolishment of slavery in 1834, describes how '[m]any of the common slave hymns told stories of a heavenly journey to the land of Canaan' (2011: 210). Herbert Robinson Marbury outlines how the poet Frances Ellen Watkins Harper draws upon this comparison in her 1869 epic poem 'Moses: Story of the Nile'; and how Zora Neale Hurston references the exodus story in her 1939 novel *Moses, Man of the Mountain* (2015: 53–82; 107–32). Moreover, in *The Souls of*

Black Folk, W.E.B DuBois states that many slaves believed, '[e]mancipation was the key to a promised land of sweeter beauty than ever stretched before the eyes of wearied Israelites'; and yet still, some forty years after abolition, 'the freedman has not yet found in freedom his promised land' (2007: 10).

Giovanni's poem explicitly takes issue with the way in which white America has appropriated this analogy. For Giovanni, as for King and DuBois, it is Black people who are 'God's chosen people,' and they hold this status because they have 'always had to suffer' (Giovanni 2007: 50). In the poem – as for Harper in 'Moses: Story of the Nile,' and for King in his 'I've been to the Mountaintop' speech – the promised land is a place not yet reached. And, according to the poem, there is only one way that this may be addressed: through the sharing of suffering with others.

The ambiguity and ambivalence of this idea of shared suffering – perhaps deliberately – invites multiple readings and interpretations. On the one hand, in light of the poem's earlier calls to violence, it operates as a straightforward call for retaliation; one which relies on a biblical formation to lend it rhetorical weight. Vengeance through violence, the line implies, is sanctioned by God. This is the most literal reading, but nevertheless the most ambivalent. Earlier, the poem states that killing one white man in response to King's murder would not allow Black people to prevail over white violence; it is no more effective, the poem implies, than worshipping skin-lightening creams (2007: 50). Moreover, vengeance as sanctioned by God is explicitly censured in the Bible, in passages that either state that vengeance belongs only to God and/or that people should eschew vengeance in favour of loving their neighbour.[7] It seems unusual, in a poem explicitly lamenting the murder of King – and in which he is rendered poetically as both a Christ-figure and the Black Madonna – that Giovanni would undermine biblical scripture in this way.

But this subversion may equally represent a psychical sublimation of emotion. In the poem's final line, Giovanni makes a reference to King's favourite gospel song, 'Take My Hand, Precious Lord,' which Mahalia Jackson sang at his funeral at his request (2007: 50). The song, which was written by Reverend Thomas A. Dorsey as an expression of his inconsolable grief at the death of his wife and child in 1932, operates both as a symbol of desolate sorrow and loss, and as a form of prayer for guidance and leadership during times of suffering. In the poem, Giovanni modifies the song's title, and in doing so, speaks for a collective grief at the loss of a social and spiritual leader. The preceding lines about sharing suffering, whose implications deviate not only from the teachings of biblical verses but also from King's own stance of strategic non-violence, might therefore be read as an uninhibited expression of grief as pure rage; a frank and unrestrained articulation of a desire for retribution for the devastating loss felt both by Giovanni and by the Black community more broadly, regardless of what the Bible says about vengeance belonging only to God. If read in this way, the claim that suffering should be shared might be understood as a forthright expression of anger that is deliberately tempered and rendered ambiguous by the poem's final line, which appears to ask both God, and King, for guidance on how to proceed.

It should be noted, however, that neither of these readings of the final stanza is neat, since the poem does not allow for neat and easy interpretation. Such is the nature of grief; it is not neat nor orderly, and Giovanni's poem is full of complex emotions and articulations that cannot be reduced to clear-cut and uncomplicated explication. We cannot straightforwardly assume, for instance, that the poem's intentions are what the poem itself states them to be. Or that the emotions expressed by the poem's speaker are directly analogous with the sentiments of the writer. In a 1982 interview, Giovanni asserted that she did not believe in a single poem's capacity to effect universal change; she stated, '[t]here will never be the poem that will free mankind. We would be fools... anybody that thinks that is a fool' (Elder 1982: 69–70). This troubles our ability to read it as a straightforward call to arms designed to effect lasting change. And if, as Harris suggests, Giovanni was a poet 'who mostly disagreed with King,' our reading is further complicated, since the poem may be deliberately working against his position on strategic non-violence, while at the same time lamenting his death and condemning the white violence responsible for it (Harris 2014: 75).

June Jordan's 'In Memoriam: Martin Luther King Jr.' is a very different type of elegy from Giovanni's. Similarly written following King's assassination in 1968, the poem was first published in *Some Changes* in 1971 and later in *Directed by Desire: The Collected Poems of June Jordan* (2007). In contrast with Giovanni's rhetorical directness and emotional candor, Jordan's poem reflects a language in disarray; an articulation subjected to disintegration, broken up into fragments and dispersed without logical order. The poem opens – just as Giovanni's ends – with a reference to King's 'I've Been to the Mountaintop' speech. However, Jordan's reference is more oblique, with images of the Promised Land – both the biblical land of milk and honey and the metaphorical image of America as prosperous and abundant – undergoing linguistic mutilation. Jordan's fragmented syntax refuses straightforward interpretation, implying that, just as there is no rational way to articulate the senseless loss felt in response to the murder of King, there is also no easy way to understand it.

We might read the word 'honey,' in the opening lines, for instance, as an affectionate term of address (as if the speaker is directing the poem to a specific reader), though it is perhaps more plausible to read 'honey' and 'people' together as a compound noun which operates as the subject of the first line (Jordan 2007: 29). 'Honey people,' then – those who 'murder mercy' – would be those for whom America is already a land of pleasure and wholesomeness; in other words: white people (2007: 29). As Albert J. Raboteau points out, 'Americans have always thought of themselves as a chosen people, specially blessed by freedom, liberty and prosperity' (1994: 8). Interestingly, American regional slang of the 1960s also links the word 'honey' with manure or faeces. Jordan may well be playing on these multiple meanings to signpost white America as both privileged and putrescent.

The 'milkland' of the second line associates the 'U.S.A' of the poem with notions of whiteness, infancy, nourishment and compassionate humanity (as in the milk of human kindness) (Jordan 2007: 29). But crucially, it is a land that turns people 'to monsters'; in that it teaches people to 'kill,' 'violate' and 'destroy' (2007: 29). Thus, Jordan's opening lines ironically subvert white America's perception of the United States as a 'Promised Land' by signposting a fractured and polluted reality where the potential represented by King's 'I've Been to the Mountaintop' speech is both corrupted and corrupting. By instructing only violence and destruction, the 'U.S.A' of the poem suffocates any potential for freedom before it can be realized (2007: 29). The first and second stanzas of the poem are separated by the single-word line, 'America,' which operates as a means of dividing them like a linguistic barrier (2007: 29). In this way, Jordan destabilizes America as a signifier; one which traditionally projects ideological notions of commonality, togetherness and shared values. Instead, it functions as a means of *dis*unity in the poem, operating as a textual partition on the page. Like its metonym, the 'Promised Land' of the white imaginary in the first stanza, the symbolic concept of 'America' – as one representing unity – is undermined.

The second stanza begins with temporal uncertainty; future and past are collapsed such that temporalities refuse to have distinct meanings (Jordan 2007: 29). This temporal flattening denies the reader possibility for hope of any change to the circumstances the poem has so far presented. And, in the second stanza, these circumstances become bleaker. The stanza is composed largely of violent active verbs, often disconnected from their subject and object. This accumulation of verbs has the effect of creating a sense of continuous, intensifying violent action without any specific perpetrator or victim; an endless forceful aggression linguistically detached from humanity. As the stanza progresses in fragments, it builds a picture of nature disrupted and driven out; of forms of protest distorted; and of the circumscription of emptiness or nothingness. It also depicts the violent burning of body parts, specifically those that signify maternal care and emotion, the articulation of progressive ideas, and the act of supplication (2007: 29). These fragments not only undermine America as a symbol of unity, but present it as always having been, and always going to be, a continuously intensifying process of senseless, dehumanized violence that destroys both people and environment, precluding the possibility of insurrection or demonstration, and creating boundaries where there is nothing to demarcate.

The stanza's final lines highlight this intensification through the inclusion of both internal and end rhymes. These loosely dactylic lines – echoing the dactylic hexameter of classical Greek elegiac poetry – create a sense of escalation as the stanza reaches its climactic end in a violent subversion of the pastoral notion of a 'rising springtime'. Rather than denoting a fresh and vital new beginning, Jordan's springtime is full of terror, torment and intimidation: in which people must strengthen or secure themselves like bullets; and/or in which bullets enable a frenzied and delirious greed to thrive and prosper (2007: 29). In other words, there is no possibility of renewal, rebirth or revitalization; the springtime in the poem signifies only a return to the atemporal cycle of dehumanized violence and destruction.

This is not to say that there is no possibility offered within the poem for an interruption to this intensifying cycle, though the means by which it is offered is a paradoxical one. The final lines of the poem's first part signify an inescapability from this cyclical process of violence. But they also operate as a forceful imperative demand for its end, marked by the word 'STOP' (2007: 29). In other words, at the same time as expressing that no one can bring an end to the escalating cycle of death, Jordan also ends the first section of her poem with a command for its cessation (2007: 29). The word 'STOP', capitalized and standing alone in the final line is a performative textual blockade, just as the word 'America' earlier in the poem functioned as a textual partition (2007: 29). Both words operate as a textual boundary that encloses the ever-increasing cycle of destruction, though one ('America') is the means by which we enter it, and the other ('STOP') is the means by which we find a way out (2007: 29). The word 'STOP' thus operates as a performative stemming or closing of the wounds inflicted by the cycle of violence (2007: 29). In other words, though Jordan's poem implies that there is no hope of ending this cycle, the placement of the word 'STOP' resists this articulation; it refuses to accept its own message by attempting to perform, textually, the very thing it suggests cannot be done.

Unlike the disjointed phrases of the first section, whose obfuscated semantic meanings reflect the senselessness of the destruction they describe, the opening of section II adheres to more recognizable syntax patterns. 'They sleep,' we are told, whose home, status, or location; vitality, energy or life force; epoch, season or flow of time; and/or outlook or climate is in some way controlled or governed (Jordan 2007: 30). This suspension of consciousness may, on the one hand, signify rest and respite, or it may, conversely, signify passivity, inactivity or a figurative death. Moreover, it is a condition of sleep that operates in accordance with some predetermined pattern or 'stage direction' (2007: 30). This gestures towards an inevitability; a widespread and general tendency or pattern, but one which is managed or administered by a supervisory force – a 'stage director' – whose controlling power is clearly apparent. The simile 'like shorewashed shells,' calls back to the 'tide' of the opening lines, likening this supervisory force to the power of the flowing and swelling of the sea (2007: 30). We might draw a parallel here between the inevitable force of this imposed pattern and the inevitability of the escalating cycle of violence in the poem's first section. In other words, Jordan offers here a corresponding, but slightly different, image of America, as one that is carefully controlled – and pacified – by hegemonic powers.

The second stanza of section II begins with another syntactically coherent line before once again deteriorating into disconnected fragments. The last poetic moment of coherence, before the poem's syntax breaks down into subjectless and objectless verbs and detached nouns, is a shared 'afternoon of mourning'; a moment of grief and common humanity in response to the assassination of King (2007: 30). The line which follows returns the poem to an atemporality like the collapsed past and future in section I, stanza 2. The moment of mourning is therefore situated within a liminal space of future uncertainty where nothing can be predicted. However, it also – like much of the rest of the poem – signposts temporal confusion since the word 'mourning' implies its homophone 'morning'. Thus, this shared moment of grief carries within it a sense of the times of the day upturned or subverted.

The poem's fragmented final lines signify, among other things, rebellion, irregularity and tumult; relapse and change; the practice or anticipation of death; a ceremonial observance, or a compulsive routine of fear and madness; and lamentable, hopeless failure or abandonment. We might interpret this as an inevitable return to the cyclical and escalating violence articulated in the poem's first section, particularly given that the poem's final words indicate a sense of accumulation and escalation (2007: 30). However, there are two elements that enable us to discern a possibility of hope in the poem's ending. Firstly, there are gestures in the syntactically disintegrated final lines that are not present in those at the end of the poem's first section. While the broken phrases imply violence, degeneration, regression and uncertainty, they also imply a future that is not set; the possibility of rebellion; a potential change in the course of action; or a sudden forward movement. In other words, they offer the possibility of active resistance, in contrast to the passivity and inaction depicted by the 'sleep' of the second stanza's opening lines (2007: 30). Instead of a straightforward return to the cycle of violence depicted in the poem's first section, we might understand the poem's final lines as a move towards meeting and challenging that cycle through struggle and confrontation.

Secondly, the return to a broken syntax allows us to understand the shared 'afternoon of mourning' as a pause in the poem like that offered by the capitalized 'STOP' at the end of the first section (Jordan 2007: 29–30). Both enable a moment of hiatus that operates as a point of possible healing, not only from the wounds that the cycle of violence enacts, but also from the collapse of meaning that the cycle imposes upon language. To put it differently, the cycle of violence articulated in the poem corresponds with a disintegration of language, in which syntactical connections are broken down and meaning begins to collapse. The capitalized 'STOP' of the first section's final lines operates as an interruption of that linguistic disintegration; and what follows is the opening of the second stanza, which brings a more coherent shift in the poem's syntax (2007: 29). Like the shared 'afternoon of mourning,' it also provides an interval of clarity or a moment of rest in which temporalities are upturned or subverted (2007: 30). From this perspective, the 'sleep' of the second section's opening lines no longer necessarily signposts passivity and inaction, but repose, peace and calm (2007: 30). Thus, both the 'STOP' and the shared 'afternoon of mourning' offer a potential moment of stillness in an ongoing cycle of agitation and aggression (2007: 29–30).

Though both poems share a deep, resonant sense of grief and loss, Giovanni's poem and Jordan's offer two very different poetic responses to King's assassination. In contrast with Ramazani's suggestion – outlined in Chapter 1 – that 'subjective ambivalence' might belong to the poetics of 'white American' writers, both Jordan and Giovanni's elegies articulate emotional contradiction and irresolution (1994: 174). Despite its explicit call for violent retaliation, the final lines of Giovanni's poem are tempered such that the end of the poem gestures towards the kind of leadership that King provided; one that was explicitly and strategically non-violent in its approach. Jordan's poem, on the other hand, occupies an ambivalent space between hope and despair; inevitability and resistance. Her poem documents the breakdown of language that results from an endless cycle of violence. The griefs each of the poems articulate are too complex to enable the possibility of straightforward and clear-cut readings that can be homogeneously understood as 'eulogistic', and they articulate such nuances of affect that it seems like a considerable oversimplification to argue that they might be read as 'representative' of, or 'articulating [...] on behalf of' the Black community as a whole (Ramazani 1994: 174). Indeed, close analyses of these poems clearly indicate that these kinds of monolithic statements about elegies flatten out the manifold intricacies, subtleties and particularities of grief, sorrow, anger, desolation, hopelessness and hope in these very different poetic expressions of loss.

Necrophilous white state violence: Post-Civil Rights elegies

The final section of this chapter examines three elegies written in a post-1968 context: one from 1970 (two years after the assassination of King and Johnson's signing of the Civil Rights Act 1968); one from 1987; and one from 2014 (one year after the beginning of the Black Lives Matter movement following the acquittal of George Zimmerman in the shooting of Trayvon Martin). Each of these poems articulates a particular kind of institutional social injustice so far unaddressed in this chapter, and the purpose of these analyses is not to draw a totalizing equivalence between them. The sociopolitical contexts they reflect are too nuanced to warrant such connections, and to do so would amount to no more than a sweeping generalization. As I hope this chapter has already gone some way towards demonstrating, a tradition of elegy cannot be understood as fixed, monolithic or genealogical; it has many overlapping strands and cannot be represented by a singular or arboreal chronological mapping.

Lucille Clifton's poem, 'after kent state,' was first published in her second volume of poetry *Good News about the Earth* in 1972, and later in *The Collected Poems 1965-2010* (2012). The poem is written in response to events that took place at Kent State University, Ohio, on 4 May 1970, during which four students were shot and killed by National Guardsmen. According to Ronald L. Hatzenbuehler, the university had 'experienced a measure of turmoil on campus in the late 1960s,' though nothing that compared with some of the larger protests at other universities in the state, or in the country more broadly (1996: 214–15). However, following demonstrations protesting the US invasion of Cambodia on 1 and 2 May – during which some localized violence and vandalism took place in the town's main street and the Reserve Officer's Training Corps building was burned – 'Mayor Leroy Satrom [...] called the Guard to Kent based upon his fear that the disorder [...] would escalate dramatically' (Hatzenbuehler 1996: 211–12). On 4 May, students gathered on the campus Commons at 11am despite an order banning large gatherings. Approximately one hour later, the Ohio National Guard fired tear gas canisters into the crowd and, in response, some of the students threw rocks at the guardsmen. According to Christina R. Steidl, there followed a 'standoff during which several guardsmen knelt and aimed their guns but did not fire' (2013: 749). However, after retreating up the hill away from the student protesters, '28 guardsmen turned, knelt, and fired' their guns (Steidl 2013: 749). Students Allison Krause, Jeffrey Miller, Sandra Scheuer and William Schroeder were killed, and nine others were wounded. President Nixon's response to the massacre 'argued that the guardsmen were justified in using force to control protesters' (Steidl 2013: 750). The Ohio Guardsmen were eventually acquitted in a 'short criminal trial' in 1974, though a later civil suit was settled in 1979, 'offering monetary compensation and a statement of regret from state officials' (Hatzenbuehler 1996: 213). In 2007, an audio recording of the shootings revealed 'the voices of Ohio National Guard leaders ordering troops to fire into [the] crowd' (Maag 2007: para 1).

It is important to situate this violent event within a broader context. As Broadhurst points out, university protests in response to the Cambodian invasion happened in nearly 1,350 campuses across America, during which 'thirty-five thousand National Guardsmen were called to quell riots at twenty-one universities' (2010: 289). Ronald Reagan – then governor of California – shut down the state's campuses, while Stanford, Columbia, Princeton, Notre Dame and University of Pennsylvania all experienced significant forms of protest, either via strike or violent riot (Broadhurst 2010: 289). In other words, the Kent State protests were not an isolated event; similar student demonstrations were happening across the country in response to the US invasion.

While the Kent State shootings were not explicitly racially motivated – in the sense that, unlike the murders of Till and King, they did not obviously demonstrate white violence against Black bodies in clear-cut ways – Clifton's poem reads the event as reflecting the broader racialized violence of a necrophilous white patriarchy. The poem is extremely stark and sparing at just eleven lines, some of which consist of only one or two words. The opening five lines gesture towards urban crises of the 1960s and 1970s. The reference to the killing of cities in the third line may indicate, for instance, what Gioielli terms the 'decline of the urban environment' in the 1970s, demonstrated by 'garbage-strewn streets, gray smoggy skies, and creaky, dilapidated apartment buildings' (Gioielli 2015: 38). In Cleveland in 1965, for example, Black residents carried 'rats and roaches caught in decaying apartments, torn clothes, and old furniture,' from poor areas to City Hall to protest living conditions; while around the same time, garbage protests took place in Black communities in Brooklyn to protest the 'daily piles in many densely packed ghetto neighbourhoods' (Gioielli 2015: 33; 35). This urban decline, Gioielli argues, was a consequence of the 'transfer of capital, jobs, and population' from cities to suburbs which, he suggests 'was the result of a series of conscious decisions made by governments, private institutions, and individuals' (2015: 41). Such decisions, he contends, included 'governmental policies that subsidized the growth of suburban areas, making them extremely attractive to both large corporations and individual consumers' (2015: 41). As a result of what he terms 'America's antiurban, pro-suburban policies,' many US '[c]ities were torn apart or left to rot, sometimes both' (Gioielli: 1).

Clifton's fourth line about the killing of trees might be understood as an elaboration upon this point. As Gioielli points out, the development of cities in the 1950s and 1960s involved the construction of urban highways, which led to 'the destruction of local parks and natural areas' (Gioielli 2015: 74). However, we might also read this line specifically in relation to the Vietnam War. In his study of environmental history in Vietnam, David Biggs describes how the fighting inflicted 'unprecedented levels of destruction' upon hills west of the city of Huế through 'saturation bombing, chemical defoliation, napalm drops, and base construction' (2018: 1053). The war, he argues, 'cleared several million hectares of land' (Biggs 2018: 1054).

Clifton's fifth line, about the killing of children, potentially serves the double function of gesturing both towards the victims of the Kent State massacre and towards casualties of the Vietnam War. By 1970, there were approximately 40,000 fatalities among US servicemen, 90 per cent of whom were aged between 18 and 26 (National Council on Family Relations 1970: 197). Initially, men were drafted according to an order set by the president, 'with highest priority for "delinquents," second priority for volunteers, and third priority for non-volunteers between the ages of 19 and 25, in order of their dates of birth' (Card and Lemieux 2001: 97). From December 1969 onward, however, men were drafted according to a randomized lottery system 'for males born between 1944 and 1950,' i.e. 19–25-year-olds (Bergan 2009: 381). In summary then, though Clifton's opening five lines appear to refer to generalized patriarchal violence, they can also be understood as highlighting specific forms and instances of violence that relate both to the Kent State shootings and the Vietnam War, which the students were protesting.

Each of the forms of destruction described – urban, ecological and filicidal – is presented by Clifton as a means of maintaining or protecting anxieties. An undesignated possessive masculine pronoun ('his') functions throughout the poem as a metonym for all patriarchal systems; this metonymic 'he' operates as a potential stand-in for the administrations of Kennedy, Johnson and Nixon, which were each responsible either for instigating or perpetuating the war (Clifton 2012: 77). It also stands in for military officials such as General William Westmoreland – whose aggressive war of attrition strategy vastly underestimated the National Liberation Front and led to a major increase in additional US troops sent into conflict – and General Creighton Abrams, who oversaw 'intensive bombing of the countryside' which caused 'heavy casualties among civilians' (Daddis 2013: 360–1). And it stands in for instrumental figures in the Kent State shootings: Mayor Leroy Satrom, who called in the National Guard; Captain James Snyder, who ordered the National Guardsmen to load their weapons; and Brigadier General Robert Canterbury, who 'directed the troops to advance on the crowd with M-1 rifles locked and loaded, bayonets fixed' (Hatzenbuehler 1996: 212; Maag 2007: para 14). Clifton's list of destructive acts – killing cities, trees and children – are thus presented as a means for men such as these to maintain, abide by, protect or retain a vague sense of anxiety about future danger or evil that is designated, by the poem, as small in value; trivial or small-minded.

Importantly, the fifth line also includes the word 'oh,' a word which is separated from the rest of the text by a significant amount of space (Clifton 2012: 77). As we have seen in the earlier analysis of Brooks's poem 'the rites for Cousin Vit,' the word 'oh' is an extra-lexical utterance; it is a means of both exclaiming and interrupting. As in Brooks's poem, the 'oh' provides a shift in the poem's emotional register. The list of forms of destruction in the poem's first five lines accumulate towards the 'oh,' which operates as a climactic utterance of grief. The intensity of this utterance is enhanced by its disconnection from the other words in the poem. Situated on the right-hand side of the page, the exclamation operates as an emotional aside that momentarily takes readers out of the space of the poem and into one of pure affect; an inarticulate anguish. At the same time, it operates as the beginning of the subsequent clause that constitutes the final lines of the poem. In this way, the 'oh' is also a vocative expression directed towards society or humanity as a whole. These final lines, like the final lines of Giovanni's elegy for King, gesture towards biblical passages;

in the case of Clifton's poem, specifically towards Proverbs 14: 12 and 16: 25: 'There is a way which seemeth right unto a man, but the end thereof are the ways of death' (KJV 2001: 437; 438). What these Bible passages signpost is the danger of believing oneself to be righteous and virtuous when in fact one's behaviour leads to destruction. Clifton designates the actions of white power and authority – i.e. urban and ecological devastation and war – as necrophilous and leading towards death, thus emphatically warning readers that to follow systems and structures of white power and authority (governmental, industrial and military) will lead to destruction and ruin.

These forms of white power and authority are presented in the poem as 'ways': as metaphorical paths; as directions of travel; or as courses of action (Clifton 2012: 77). In other words, they appear to offer various means of advancing or moving forward. Clifton, however, highlights that this appearance is a pretence; while they may seem multiple, they are in fact singular, and they do not lead anywhere except towards devastation. As an alternative to these 'ways,' Clifton invites the reader into 'the Black,' which is presented, conversely, as a space of vitality (2012: 77).[8] Unlike the systems of kinetic progression and necrophilous momentum of the white imaginary, 'the Black' appears in contrast as a static and stable locus, as if to offer a dwelling place or a means of shelter (Clifton 2012: 77). And rather than a movement towards death, it represents life: survival, creation, productive activity, energy and vitality. In this way, Clifton's poem echoes W.E.B DuBois's depiction of Blackness as 'the sole oasis of simple faith and reverence in a dusty desert of dollars and smartness' (2007: 14). Clifton's 'white ways' resemble DuBois's configuration of whiteness as 'brutal dyspeptic blundering,' and 'coarse and cruel wit,' in comparison with 'light-hearted,' 'determined,' 'loving' and 'jovial' Black ideals (Clifton 2012: 77; DuBois 2007: 14).

There are also potential connections to be made between Clifton's description of 'white ways' and Fanon's description of the colonizer in *The Wretched of the Earth* (Clifton 2012: 77). Fanon describes how in the colonized world, the 'spokesperson for the colonizer and the regime of oppression, is the police officer or the soldier' (2004: 3). These agents of government use 'a language of pure violence,' and their work is to ensure the 'colonized are kept under close scrutiny, and contained by rifle butts and napalm' (Fanon 2004: 4). As in Fanon's description of the colonized world, Clifton's poem about the Kent State massacre depicts a world that is 'divided in two,' where the border is 'represented by the barracks and the police stations' (2004: 3). And Clifton's depiction of 'white ways' leading towards death echoes Fanon's description of colonizer values (in particular, Christianity and individualism) as 'parasites, carriers of disease' to be 'vomited up'; or as 'pale, *lifeless* trinkets,' and a 'jumble of *dead* words' (Clifton 2012: 77; Fanon 2004: 7–8; 11; emphases mine). For Fanon, then, as for Clifton, 'white ways,' represent a movement towards death (2012: 77).

In a similar way, Clifton's invitation into 'the Black' not only associates Blackness with life – in opposition to whiteness and death – but also with community and solidarity (2012: 77). This positioning of 'the Black' as a communal space of unity and collective interest undermines what Fanon describes as a white colonialist mentality of 'thinking my brother is my wallet and my comrade, my scheming' (Clifton 2012: 77; Fanon 2004: 11–12). Thus, Clifton's contrast between a vital Black space of unity and commonality and a white individualist and capitalist progression towards death echoes Fanon's description of the colonial world as a 'petrified' one, in contrast to the 'dreams of action, dreams of aggressive vitality' of the colonial subject (2004: 15).

The title of Clifton's poem provides a contextual lens through which we can better understand what might seem, upon a first reading, like a string of general statements about the consequences of white patriarchal violence. The poem's non-specific opening lines about killing cities, trees and children condense and compress the emotional overwhelm experienced by witnessing both the destruction of urban communities and the news of countless fatalities in the Vietnam War. The Kent State shootings referred to in the title thus operate both metonymically as an event that represents white patriarchal violence and destruction, and as the apotheosis of that destruction.

We can see a similar critique of urban destruction, militarized forms of policing, and the state-endorsed killing of children explored in Sonia Sanchez's poem, 'elegy (for MOVE and Philadelphia),' published in her collection *Under a Soprano Sky* (1987). Sanchez's poem focuses on the 1985 police bombing of a Black commune in west Philadelphia that killed eleven people – including six children – and levelled three city blocks.

Variously described by newspapers and scholarly articles as a 'religious movement'; a 'primitivist group'; a 'radical, cult-like black group'; and a 'Black revolutionary organization,' MOVE occupied 'three adjacent row houses' in a quiet Philadelphia neighbourhood (Hunter-Young 2018: 43; Persons 1987: 249; Quinn 1986: 1; Sanders and Jeffries 2013: 568; Shipley and Taylor 2019: 26). Shipley and Taylor describe the group as advocating a 'radical, back-to-nature, antimodern philosophy,' while Quinn describes the group as 'against machinery, cooked food, education, utility charges, clothing and soap,' and Sanders and Jeffries outline how they 'demonstrated at zoos, pet stores, political rallies, and other public spaces' (Quinn 1986: 458; Sanders and Jeffries 2013: 568; Shipley and Taylor 2019: 33). The MOVE movement was founded by John Africa (born Vincent Leapheart) whose radical utopian vision involved 'a natural, harmonious way of living in which reciprocity, not competition, defines everyday interactions,' and advocated 'the base sovereignty of each being: plant, animal, and human' (Shipley and Taylor 2019: 27; 28).

The 1985 bombing was not the first instance of conflict between MOVE and the Philadelphia police. In 1978, a siege of MOVE's previous premises took place that lasted fifty-five days, which included the use of 'high-pressure water hoses, a battering ram, bulldozers and automatic weapons,' followed by a shootout during which an officer was fatally shot (though some witnesses believe he was killed by police firepower) (Sanders and Jeffries 2013: 568–9). Nine members of MOVE were arrested and charged with 'thirty to one hundred years each' (Quinn 1986: 459). In 1985, following neighbourhood complaints about the lifestyle of those occupying the MOVE premises on Osage Avenue, police obtained a warrant to search the house and arrest several members on charges relating to possession of firearms, health code violations and unpaid utility bills (Sanders and Jeffries 2013: 567). What ensued was a stand-off in which 10,000 rounds were fired into the premises, as well as 'tear gas and high-powered fire hoses' (Sanders and Jeffries 2013: 567). This was followed by the dropping of a bomb – or, in the parlance of the police and the mayor, an 'entry device' – resulting in the deaths of several MOVE members, six children and 'the destruction of 61 homes in a middle-class black neighborhood' (Persons 1987: 249; Quinn 1986: 459).

Sanchez's 'elegy (for MOVE and Philadelphia)' makes several intertextual references to versions of poems by Christopher Okigbo, specifically 'Lament of the Silent Sisters' (*Transition* 1963) and 'Lament of the Drums' (*Transition* 1965), which together form a larger work titled *Silences*.[9] By drawing on these poems, Sanchez's elegy establishes the MOVE members who died in the bombing – including leader John Africa – as political martyrs. Okigbo was a Modernist Nigerian poet – and a fierce supporter of independence for the Republic of Biafra – who was killed in combat during the Nigerian-Biafran war at the age of thirty-seven. As Abba A. Abba outlines, Okigbo was among a number of Biafrans killed during the conflict who 'were celebrated as heroes and martyrs' (2017: 268).

Abba also highlights that 'Lament of the Silent Sisters' was, according to Okigbo, inspired by the assassination of Patrice Lumumba, the Congolese independence leader who was shot in 1961, and in whose killing Belgian colonial powers played a significant role (2017: 271). Further, Abba suggests that 'Lament of the Drums' was inspired by the arrest and imprisonment of Obafemi Awolowo, a Nigerian political leader and a key figure in the Nigerian independence movement (2017: 72). Thus, both of Okigbo's poems, as well as Okigbo's own death, point towards themes of persecution and martyrdom in the struggle for political revolution. Sanchez's inclusion of these intertextual references allows us to draw comparisons between the unlawful assassination of Lumumba, the political imprisonment of Awolowo, and the self-sacrificing heroism attributed to Okigbo on the one hand; and to the killing of the MOVE members by police in 1985 on the other.[10]

The first, and most prominent, of these intertextual references is in Sanchez's two lines that ask how a person or a city, might 'scream in thunder' (1987: 12; 13). These echo Okigbo's poetic line, 'how does one say no in thunder?' (Echeruo 2004: 20–5). In Okigbo's poem, the line appears three times, at different points, in the 1963 *Transition* and *Poetry* Magazine versions; and twice in the 1971 *Labryrinths* version.[11] According to Romanus N. Egudu, the word 'thunder' in Okigbo's poem signifies 'something evil and dreadful – a socio-political upheaval approximating to the magnitude and terror of a war' (2003: 30). It is a 'force to be resisted and opposed' (Egudu 2003: 30).[12] Sanchez's versions of the line each form one-line stanzas; the first following stanza two, which critiques the responses of Philadelphia citizens and the press to the MOVE bombing; and the second following stanza four, which depicts the police's use of high-pressure hoses and explosives (1987: 12; 13). For Sanchez, then, we might surmise that 'thunder' represents the social regulatory forces of the police, press and public opinion, which MOVE – as a movement – were attempting to resist and oppose. Shipley and Taylor describe how MOVE sought to 'agitate the system – by directly confronting the forces of state oppression,' and that because of this, the movement 'represented an existential threat' to 'the Philadelphia police and American media' (2019: 34; 35). Moreover, Sanders and Jeffries highlight a lack of concern shown by Philadelphia citizens regarding the 'heavy-handed tactics employed by the police,' with many praising law enforcement for its handling of the situation (2013: 567). By echoing Okigbo's line, Sanchez depicts MOVE's struggle against these social forces – the press, the police and the public opinion of Philadelphia citizens – as a form of political warfare.

That Sanchez alters Okigbo's gesture of refusal in her own poem – from the act of saying 'NO' to the act of screaming – shifts the struggle from one in which there is potential to disavow, negate or reject social forces, to one in which there is no potential for verbal expression, only a speechless shout; an inarticulate cry of pain or alarm. One of the reasons for Sanchez's alteration of the line might relate to fact that, in 1985, the act of saying 'NO' would have carried connotations of Nancy Reagan's 'Just Say No' campaign against drug use among young people. As Angela Davis highlights, this campaign 'resulted in an exponential increase in federal prisoners and unprecedented racial disparities in the prison population' (2016: 1065). And, as Shipley and Taylor emphasize, legislation dating back to Johnson's administration 'viewed black urban crime as pathological, locating black bodies as the primary site where the War on Crime would be waged' (2019: 31). If Sanchez were to have incorporated Okigbo's line verbatim, it might have enabled it to be read as a response to Reagan's 'Just Say No' campaign. In other words, Sanchez's choice to change 'say NO' to 'scream' may be in response to the fact that, in 1985, the act of saying 'NO' had been co-opted by a Reaganite agenda (Sanchez 1987: 12; 13).

Sanchez's second intertextual reference to Okigbo is in stanza six, in lines that echo Okigbo's 'deliver us from our nakedness' and 'exile for our laughter' in the 1964 version of 'Lament of the Drums' (Moore and Beier 1998: 240). Dan Izevbaye calls this Okigbo poem a 'divination for a sick country,' while Omolara Leslie calls it an 'agitated poem about deprivation and loss, unavoidable pain and mourning' (Izevbaye 2011: 21; Leslie 1973: 54). In it, the speaker invokes Indigenous West African drums and draws on Igbo drum elegies as a means of lamenting the violence, as well as agricultural and ecological damage, caused by the Nigerian civil war.[13] The opening of the poem, from which Sanchez's lines are borrowed, is an invocation calling upon the drums to take shape from their constituent parts: wood and animal skin. It is to the drums that the lines are addressed; the poem's speaker calls upon them as a means of protection against exposure and vulnerability, while the poem asks the landscape to banish and keep out cheerful affect that would be incompatible with a mode of lament (Moore and Beier 1998: 240).

In Sanchez's poem, instead of to the drums, the lines are directed to God; the exclamatory phrase 'O lord' precedes them (1987: 13). As in Okigbo's poem, Sanchez appears to be calling for a protective and solemn space that would enable a lament to take place. Her subsequent lines echo one from Okigbo's 'Lament of the Drums,' which states that robbers will strip the speaker down to their bodily tissue. This line refers back to the 'nakedness' in the opening of Okigbo's poem; it is protection from these robbers that the speaker seeks (Moore and Beier 1998: 240). In Sanchez's poem, it is protection from a 'seduction' that has a corrosive or abrasive quality, peeling skin 'down to [...] veins' (1987: 13). This 'seduction' may be better understood in the context of the first and last stanzas of the poem, and the depiction of Philadelphia that Sanchez presents therein (1987: 13).

In the opening stanza, Sanchez describes Philadelphia as a city which is concealing its true identity; she implies that it has Southern racist ideologies but is masquerading as a liberal and progressive Northern city. To depict it, she combines clerical and religious images with intellectual, capitalist and military ones, alongside the violent spectacle implied by 'modern gladiators,' and the machismo implied by 'cowboys' (1987: 12). The Philadelphia of the poem, then, is an amalgam of ceremony, pageantry, aggression, transaction and institutional learning. The city's own self-image as The City of Brotherly Love is undermined here both by Sanchez's description and by the MOVE bombing, which is indicated by the 'houses,' which 'burn out of control' at the stanza's end (1987: 12).

In the closing stanza of the poem, Sanchez attempts to move past the city's self-image to a more material reality. As in the opening stanza, the description references the city's religiosity and its tendency for spectacle and pageantry. Philadelphia's self-image as a place of faith, tradition and ceremony is depicted as a superficial pretence and a distraction from reality. The references to 'lobotomies,' 'commandments' and 'mummers' imply confused detachment, the observance of rules and performances of mime (Sanchez 1987: 14). So, to return to her earlier line, we might read the poem's plea to God for respite from a corrosive form of 'seduction' – Sanchez's modification of Okigbo's poetic line – as an appeal for relief from the temptation of spectacle; the 'concerts,' 'football' and 'sequined processionals,' for instance, that distract from the social injustice of the MOVE bombing and the harm it caused to the Black community (1987: 13; 14).

Section two of the poem performs an indictment of the ways in which the MOVE bombing was made into a spectacle for consumption both by Philadelphia citizens and by the press. The poem adopts the persona of a Philadelphia resident encouraging another to participate in the viewing of the bombing as if it were a show or celebration. The lines imply the speaker understands the event as something to be consumed, both in a scopophilic sense – as a spectacle to be watched – and in an oral sense, with the bodies of the bombing victims presented as the culinary focal point of a social event, such as a barbecue. We might read these lines as a critique of the way in which – despite Mayor Wilson Goode's approval of the bombing and his later admission of liability for the events – polls showed that after the bombing, 69 per cent of Philadelphians 'believed that the "mayor did a good or excellent job" handling the MOVE confrontation' (Sanders and Jeffries 2013: 567). For Sanchez, this kind of public sentiment amounts not only to a form of complicity, but to a ghoulish and gleeful participation in the deaths of the MOVE members. Like with the 'modern gladiators,' of the poem's opening, Philadelphia citizens are depicted as occupying a 'delirium of death' in which they revel in the gory spectacle (Sanchez 1987: 12).

For Sanders and Jeffries, this kind of public sentiment among Philadelphians cannot be understood in isolation from the media press coverage of the event, which disproportionately presented MOVE as 'dangerous and deviant', as 'terrorists' and as themselves responsible for the bombing (2013: 574). Sanchez draws a similar connection between public opinion and the media. In the second stanza of the same section, she depicts the press as rendering the city insensible or unconscious through manipulative, dishonest and incriminating language. In other words, the 'delirium of death' exhibited in the preceding stanza is presented as a condition brought about by print and broadcast media (Sanchez 1987: 12).

The poem's title designates the poem as an elegy not just for MOVE, but also for the city itself. In its complicity in the killing of its own citizens, Philadelphia has killed its self-image as a city of progress and liberalism; and as connected to the world and the people within it. Whereas Clifton's poem adopts a tone of distanced generality to mourn the Kent State shootings as part of a larger systemic continuum of necrophilous white patriarchy, Sanchez's poem is one of localized particularity and specificity. She uses intertextual references to Okigbo's poems as a means of anchoring the elegy within a broader history of political violence and resistance.

Moving from the 1980s to more recent history, Danez Smith's poem 'not an elegy for Mike Brown,' was published on the website *Split this Rock* in 2014, and appears in different forms within Smith's publications: as part of 'not an elegy' in *Don't Call Us Dead* (2017) and as part of 'Short Film' in *Black Movie* (2015).[14] Smith's poetry frequently engages with an elegiac mode, and there are numerous other poems that might have been discussed here, such as 'summer, somewhere,' 'Politics of Elegy,' 'elegy with pixels & cum' (for gay porn actor Javier Bravo), 'it won't be a bullet,' 'every day is a funeral & a miracle' or 'dear white america'. I focus on 'not an elegy for Mike Brown,' here because, like Clifton's and Sanchez's elegies, it responds to events that are – by necessity – anchored through a particular historical moment, in this case the shooting of eighteen-year-old Michael Brown in Ferguson, Missouri, by the white police officer Darren Wilson.

Brown was, along with his friend Dorian Johnson, stopped by Officer Wilson on 9 August 2014, for allegedly walking in the middle of a residential road. There are conflicting accounts relating the events that followed. An altercation ensued during which shots were fired. Brown fled on foot, pursued by Wilson. Again, accounts vary in relation to the shooting that followed but, as Ikedi O. Onyemaobim points out, '[w]hat is certain is that Officer Wilson fired ten more rounds at Mr. Brown, six of which struck him' (2016: 161). Johnson's statement claims that Wilson 'shot Brown in the back,' after which Brown 'turned around and, with his hands, showed he was unarmed' (Potterf and Pohl 2018: 422). Wilson claimed that he had 'recognized that Mr. Brown fit the description' of a suspect who had stolen cigarillos in a convenience store about an hour previously (Onyemaobim 2016: 160). He also claimed that he had seen 'Brown reach toward his waistband,' the moment before he fired the fatal shots (Potterf and Pohl 2018: 422).

On 20 August, a grand jury was convened comprising twelve jurors – 'three black [...] and nine white,' meant to reflect the county's demographics but not those of Ferguson ('67 per cent black, 29 per cent white') – which 'refused to indict Officer Darren Wilson' (Kaplan 2014: 52–3). After the shooting, Brown's body lay 'on the asphalt pavement [...] for four and one half hours' (Adamson 2016: 189). His death sparked a series of protests, demonstrations and riots during which the Black Lives Matter movement gained national and international recognition, and during which many protestors adopted the protest chant, 'Hands Up, Don't Shoot' (Adamson 2016: 190).

Just as Clifton's elegy highlights how the Kent State shootings are reflective of a wider necrophilous white patriarchy, Smith's poem points to the way in which the elegiac subject, by the very nature of his death, is forced to stand in for broader, more systemic crises of racist police brutality. While the poem's title negates the moniker of elegy, it nonetheless operates as an elegy in terms of mode. More specifically, it designates that the poem is not an elegy 'for Mike Brown,' because it is unable to understand Brown's death in isolation (Smith 2014: n.p). It cannot be an elegy solely for him, since to mourn his death is also to mourn all the instances in which young Black men and women have been killed at the hands of police officers in the United States. In 2019, an *LA Times* article describes getting killed by police as a 'leading cause of death for young black men in America,' because they are '2.5 times more likely than white men and boys to die during an encounter with cops' (Khan 2019: para 1).[15] And, according to CBS News, US police killed 164 Black people in the first eight months of 2020 (Cohen 2020: para 2). In other words, Smith's poem points out how it is difficult to mourn Brown as an individual – as a particular and unique person – because the way in which he was killed takes up all the semantic space surrounding his death.

This point is also present in the opening lines, which not only acknowledge that Brown's death is part of a larger legacy of police killings of young Black men and women, but also articulate the speaker's deep sense of sorrowful weariness at the task of addressing this subject in poetry. While this abject fatigue is tonally different from Giovanni's violent fury in her elegy for King; or from Sanchez's passionate indictment of the press and Philadelphia's citizens in her elegy for MOVE, this weariness draws our attention to Smith's underlying point: Brown's death is one of many and grief at his death is therefore an accumulated grief. In the same year that Brown was killed, one hundred other unarmed Black men and women were also killed by police, including twelve-year-old Tamir Rice, twenty-five-year-old Ezell Ford and forty-three-year-old Eric Garner (Sinyangwe, McKesson and Elzie 2014: n.p). The comparison that Smith draws between Brown's body and those of others killed in the same way highlights that there is nothing extraordinary about their connection other than that they are Black and that – as one of many having died at the hands of the police – they are dehumanized; they have each been made into an 'ordinary' and 'dead thing' (Smith 2014: n.p).

This sense of ordinary-ness also highlights the extent to which the killing of unarmed Black people has been normalized and has become an everyday occurrence. As Sinyangwe, McKesson and Elzie point out on their database website, as of May 2021, '[t]here have only been 3 days […] where police did not kill someone' (Sinyangwe, McKesson and Elzie 2021: n.p). In their multiplicity, police killings not only take lives; they also erase the particularity of the victim. Such deaths are statisticalized and thus rendered part of a plural mass noun from which they cannot easily be disentangled.

It is this kind of normalization, Smith points out, that precludes the possibility of understanding Brown's killing as a tragedy, in the sense that it cannot be understood as a hero-driven dramatic story with a singular main character. In the second stanza, Smith develops this point by asking the reader to compare the kidnapping of Helen of Troy – which led to the Trojan War – with the shooting of a Black man by police. As the subject of Homeric epic (the *Iliad* and the *Odyssey*); classical drama (Euripides's *Helen*); Elizabethan tragedy (Marlowe's *Dr Faustus*); German tragedy (Goethe's *Faust*); as well as opera, modern poetry, film and TV, Helen of Troy is a tragic, celebrated heroine whose mythical kidnapping led to a nine-year siege and the bloody sacking of Troy. In contrast, Smith's poetic figure of a Black man named 'Troy' is anonymous; he represents a Black everyman figure whose killing is understood as so normal an event that it warrants little remark other than that it 'was Tuesday' when it took place (Smith 2014: n.p). To demonstrate the sheer frequency of police killings of unarmed Black men and women in the United States, Smith's figure would later take on even greater resonance when, a year after the poem was originally published, a thirty-one-year-old man named Troy Robinson was killed by police after an officer 'deployed his Taser, causing [him] to fall from an eight-foot wall' (Sinyangwe, McKesson and Elzie 2015: n.p). Typically, no officers were charged.

There are echoes here of the construction of white masculinity in the elegies of Brooks and Lorde for Emmett Till: as that which depends upon the protection of white feminine purity through violence against Black bodies. In Brooks's poem, Carolyn Bryant is a figure of constructed white feminine purity whose supposed 'honour' must be defended or upheld through violence against Till, configured as a 'Dark Villain' in a chivalric fantasy (Brooks 2006: 75). Tatiana Tsakiropoulou-Summer's description of Helen's 'meticulous care in […] her effort to enhance her beauty' as a means of 'avert[ing] male hostility' in the *Iliad* echoes Brooks's description of Bryant applying lipstick and combing her hair as a means of averting her husband's '[m]easuring' of her (Brooks 2006: 77; Tsakiropoulou-Summer 2013: 38). In Stesichorus's poetry, the Gods replace Helen of Troy with an '*eidolon*, a phantom in her likeness, in order to embroil humans in a destructive war' (Tsakiropoulou-Summers 2013: 41; emphasis author's). We might compare this with Lorde's elegy, in which the supposed preservation of Bryant's white femininity is merely a pretext for violence against Black masculinity; a rationalization masking an underlying anxiety about the loss of white masculine power in the South.

Smith's incorporation of Helen as a mythic and literary trope gestures both towards her symbolic embodiment of white-femininity-as-masculine-property – as that which can be 'stolen,' and must therefore be 'defended' – and as a figurative rationalization for white violence. Tsakiropoulou-Summers argues that Helen is a symbol of the 'stigmatized adulteress,' who 'no one will forget,' because 'her memory is so indelibly ingrained in Western culture' (Tsakiropoulou-Summers 2013: 45). This kind of indelibility, which Smith gestures towards in the poem, is not simply because she is an adulteress but because she represents the loss of white masculine power – a failure to possess white femininity – which requires regaining through siege and violent battle. Black masculine subjectivity, represented by the human figure of Troy in the poem, has no such value within a white supremacist dynamic. Helen is superlative in her beauty; her loss is, in literature, understood in terms of her individuality, particularity and uniqueness. The death of the human figure of Troy in Smith's poem, on the other hand, is mundane and normalized; he is an over-simplified and anonymous figure.

In this way, the figure of Troy operates as a reflection of how the police perceived Michael Brown. As the title and the opening lines of the poem remind us, Brown's death is not permitted space to be mourned in its particularity, individuality and uniqueness. In contrast to the dramatic literary tragedy represented by Helen, Smith's poem points towards a more material tragedy: because the killing of young Black men by police has been normalized to such a degree, Brown's death cannot easily be elegized in its singularity. Thus, Smith's poem highlights the way in which US police violence against Black people embodies what Mbembe terms a 'sacrificial economy' which requires, in order to function, 'a generalized cheapening of the price of life,' and 'a habituation to loss' (2019: 38).

This is not to say that Smith does not resist the dehumanizing normalization of the killing of young Black men in the poem. In the second stanza, Smith calls for a response of Trojan proportions in a line that plays on Christopher Marlowe's famous lines from *Dr Faustus*,

> Was this the face that launched a thousand ships
> And burnt the topless towers of Ilium?
>
> (Marlowe 1993: V. i.91-92 A-Text, 190)

These lines draw a causal connection between Helen's beauty and the destruction of Trojan buildings in the war. By presenting her simply as a 'white girl,' Smith's poem strips away all superlatives from the mythic literary trope of Helen; a gesture that humanizes her by removing the layers of implied male ownership that embed it. And, in insisting upon a similar epic response to Brown's death, Helen, the Black male figure of Troy and, by extension, Brown, are each made equal in their grievability; the loss of each warrants an epic response.

In the poem's implication that any unjust killing warrants a violent reciprocal reply, we might draw a comparison with Giovanni's call to arms in 'Reflections on April 4, 1968,' which calls for vengeful violence in response to the killing of King. As we have seen, Giovanni's poem builds on perspectives like those of King, Malcolm X and Carmichael to outline the untenable position into which Civil Rights activists were forced, in which Black non-violence was met continuously with remorseless and homicidal white violence leaving no choice but retaliation or annihilation. One response to King's killing was the riots of the Holy Week Uprising and we might understand the Ferguson protests as a similar 'answer' to Brown's killing. The protests operated, to use Hussen's terms, as 'a necessary affirmation of black humanity [...] under tremendously hostile sociopolitical circumstances' (2013: 307).

However, the poem also suggests that such a stance is generally or widely understood as immoral. There are comparisons that may be drawn here between Smith's line and Clifton's negation of white violence in 'after kent state'. As we have seen, Clifton's poem draws on passages from Proverbs that argue '[t]here is a way that seems right to a man, but its end is the way of death' (KJV 2001: 437; 438). Clifton's poem operates in resistance to these 'white ways': urban and ecological destruction and war engineered by systems of white power and authority (Clifton 2012: 77). By claiming that the act of burning is 'never the right thing,' Smith's poem suggests that reciprocal violence in response to oppressive violence is often understood in a similar way, as perpetuating a cycle of destructive violence (2014: n.p).

Alternatively, there is potential to read this line in relation to Spike Lee's 1989 film *Do the Right Thing*. Dedicated to the families of police brutality victims, the film focuses on an Italian-American pizzeria in a Black Brooklyn neighbourhood. The plot raises questions about the different perspectives on violence of King and Malcolm X; specifically, the former standpoint as one that claims 'violence destroys the community and does not foster brotherly bonds,' and the latter, which advocates 'utilizing violence in self-defense' (Gibson 2017: 188). The 'right thing' in the film's title gestures towards the point in the plot where Mookie – a pizza delivery man – throws a trash can through the window of the pizzeria where he is employed, inciting a riot. In a scene that mirrors the unrest in Ferguson in 2014, a crowd gathers to protest police brutality after one of the characters, Radio Raheem, is choked to death by white policemen using a similar illegal chokehold to the one that killed Eric Garner in 2014. In addition to Radio Raheem, the crowd cite the 1983 killing of graffiti artist Michael Stewart by New York City Transit Police and the 1984 shooting of Eleanor Bumpurs, a Black woman with disabilities, as evidence that they are not safe from police violence.

Mookie's act of throwing a trash can – and the riot that ensues – has been read differently by viewers. Brenda Cooper's study of the relevance of race in audience responses to the film suggests that white audiences tended to overlook the film's police brutality, instead focusing on the pizzeria proprietor's 'rights of ownership and loss of his pizzeria' (1998: 213). In Lee's own words, many viewers found the film's end 'hard to justify,' because the killing of Radio Raheem is, in some viewer's eyes, 'an event of little consequence, but the burning of Sal's pizzeria is of major consequence' (Lee cited in Cooper 1998: 207). If we read Smith's line as a reference to Lee's film, we might understand it as a critique of the contemporary tendency to value '[p]roperty rights over human rights' (Gibson 2017: 200). Despite Smith's demand for retribution in response to the unlawful killing of Brown, the poem also tells us that insurrectionary acts – like Mookie's throwing of the trash can – are frequently socially understood as not 'the right thing' (Smith 2014: n.p).

Smith's demand for an epic war in response to the police killings of Black men parallels Giovanni's poem, which speaks of war in response to King's murder. However, unlike Giovanni's poem, which understands the killing of King as an act of war on the part of the Johnson administration, Smith's demand is a call back to the earlier poetic reference to Helen. As a violent articulatory response to the killing of Brown – which deliberately echoes the Achaean response of launching ships and burning sacred towers – Smith's demand for war operates as an insurrectionary gesture, much like Mookie's act of throwing a trash can in *Do the Right Thing*. It is a pronunciation intended to incite a violent response to oppression.

According to Potterf and Pohl, the news media also framed the Ferguson protests in terms of war, using phrases like 'press under siege,' and 'war zone,' to describe the militarized police responses to demonstrations (2018: 434). Adamson similarly describes how the TV news media depicted 'the Ferguson police force dressed as if for battle in Iraq, fully camouflaged, protected by armored vehicles carrying officers with weapons drawn,' and as 'an overwhelmingly white, hyper-militarized police force, ready for battle' (2016: 240). He highlights how broadcasters like CNN used diegetic sound, such as 'loud vehicles,' to accompany their news coverage of the protests in order to enhance 'the "war" and "chaos" metaphors' (Adamson 2016: 208). His analysis of media coverage of the protests revealed that '[c]haos and war narratives, implicitly and explicitly marked by race, dominated accounts' of the demonstrations (Adamson 2016: 241). These narratives, he argues, prevented meaningful and progressive discussions about the protestor's legitimate grievances from taking place in the media, with 'issues of justice underlying the protests [...] subsumed under the over-reported narrative of violence' (Adamon 2016: 241; 244). Rather than participating in this media narrative, Smith's demand for war is an insurrectionary utterance that seeks to reclaim it. Since the protests were already framed in terms of war by the news media, Smith's demand operates as a means of refocusing the war narrative back towards its causal event: the killing of Brown (as well as the killings of other Black men to which the poem alludes).

The final line of Smith's second stanza takes different forms in different versions of the poem. In the *Split this Rock* version, the line demands 'a song'; while in *Don't Call Us Dead*, the line demands both 'a song,' and 'a head' (2014: n.p; 2017: 68). In *Black Movie*, the line demands both, but states 'a song will do for now' (2015: 20–31). The difference between these iterations is significant. The former implies that, if not a war, then at least a musical or poetic utterance will be sufficient or adequate. The latter two demand something quite different: the life of another as payment for the life that Brown lost; in *Black Movie,* the demand is temporally suspended with the suggestion that, for the time being, the poem will have to be enough.

What is significant about the various iterations of this line is their instability. Like the poem as a whole, they refuse to settle, resolve or become static. In *Black Movie,* the poem becomes part of 'Short Film,' which includes other sections titled 'not an elegy for Trayvon Martin,' 'not an elegy for Renisha McBride' and 'not an ode for John Crawford (a bop)' (2015: 20–31) In *Don't Call Us Dead,* it becomes part of a poem titled simply 'not an elegy' (2017: 67–71). Thus, as a poem, it is constantly shifting, taking on different shapes and incorporating different losses. In this way, the various iterations of the second stanza's final line perform different affective responses to loss. Read collectively, they perform an unresolvable movement between the two different perspectives on violence attributed to King and Malcolm X, just as Spike Lee's 1989 film raises potentially unresolvable questions about these two perspectives. The demand for 'a head' as payment for Brown's death in *Don't Call Us Dead* represents another insurrectionary gesture that echoes Malcolm X's call to '[l]et [...] dying be reciprocal'; while the demand for a song in the *Split this Rock* version of the poem echoes King's commitment to 'militant, powerful, massive, non-violence' (King 1968b: para 7; Malcolm X 1964: para 32; Smith 2017: 68). The more tempered line in *Black Movie* represents the sentiment of the latter, in which exists also the threat of the former. The line, then, in its various iterations, moves from one point to another; from a tentative position of non-violence towards an unequivocal one of necessary retaliation, and back again.

Here, again, we may draw a connection with Fanon's writing on violence. The insurrectionary gesture – Mookie's throwing of the trashcan in *Do the Right Thing;* Smith's demand for an epic war in response to Brown's killing; and Malcolm X's call to '[l]et [...] dying be reciprocal' – may be understood as reflecting what Fanon describes as 'a violent link in the great chain, in the almighty body of violence rearing up in reaction to the primary violence of the colonizer' (Fanon 2004: 50; Malcolm X 1964: para 32). It is a 'cleansing force,' and an alternative to a 'passive and despairing attitude' (Fanon 2004: 51). Thus, the structural and institutional racism that the killing of Brown demonstrates may be understood, like Fanon's description of colonialism, as representing a 'naked violence [that] only gives in when confronted with naked violence' (2004: 23).

Non-violence, in Fanon's description of colonialism, is an 'attempt to settle the colonial problem [...] before the irreparable is done, before any bloodshed or regrettable act is committed' (2004: 23). While for King, it is an assertive political strategy, for Fanon it is a notion of the 'colonialist bourgeoisie' (2004: 23). And, according to Sartre's preface to Fanon's book, it is also an impossible position. For Sartre, non-violence as a strategy is only feasible if 'exploitation and oppression never existed,' and otherwise represents a 'passiveness [that] serves no other purpose than to put you on the side of the oppressors' (2004: lvii). Smith's variations in the poem's line at the end of the second stanza, then, operate as a shift from a position that might be understood as in line with King's strategic non-violence, towards one that is in line with Malcolm X's – as well as Fanon's and Sartre's – positions. We might understand these latter positions as advocating what Butler terms 'counter-violence': resistant violent responses that arise when one already lives within a 'force field of violence,' because one has no other recourse available to them under such circumstances (Butler 2020; 7–8).[16]

The poem ends with a couplet that evokes the Ferguson protests. We might read these lines as suggesting that the protests are a divine construction; an event created by God. This implication lends them a sense of sacred legitimation; like the riots incited by King's murder in 1968 – known as the Holy Week Uprising – this description of civil unrest presents it as an insurrection sanctioned by God. We might draw connections here with some of the other elegies examined in the chapter. For instance, Lorde's elegy reimagines the flooding of Jackson in 1979 as a form of divine punishment visited upon Mississippi for the state's failure to convict Milam and Bryant for Till's murder. Similarly, the final lines of Giovanni's elegy for King imply that the post-assassination riots in 1968 are a punitive force representing the wrath of God.

However, we must also acknowledge that Smith's couplet comprises two separate sentences. Thus, while the 'sweet smoke' of the couplet's final line almost certainly gestures towards the Ferguson protests, it is also possible to read 'what the lord has made' in the preceding line as referring to something else – something separate – which Smith places in contiguity with the protests for emphasis (2014: n.p). For instance, it may be a reference to Psalm 118: 24: 'This is the day which the Lord hath made; we will rejoice and be glad in it' (KJV 2001: 420). If so, we might read the poem's penultimate line as a departure from the abject fatigue and sorrow of the poem's opening, towards a more joyful and celebratory gesture, embodied by the 'sweet smoke' of the final line (Smith 2014: n.p). Or, we might read a wry irony in the penultimate line; a gesture towards the complex world of both beauty and horror that 'the lord has made' (2014: n.p).

Ultimately, like the final lines of the preceding stanza, which exist in various iterations across different poems, this final couplet refuses to resolve into an easy and clearly defined meaning. The lines contain an instability that reflects the unsettled nature of the poem more broadly. This sense of unsettledness that the poem embodies is yet another gesture of resistance; formal resolution in the poem, though consolatory, might potentially operate as an acceptance of Brown's murder. Smith's poem permits no such consolation. Instead, it echoes the popular protest chant, 'no justice, no peace,' which the civil rights activist Al Sharpton describes as a vocalization encapsulating the notion that 'until we see fairness and accountability, we will not remain silent' (2014: para 5). Embodying the sentiment of this activist slogan, Smith's poem refuses to remain static or serene in the face of brutality. It is, in its very unsettledness, a rallying cry for justice and equality.

There are many other poems that might have been included here in a discussion of elegies that respond to racial injustice. Some of these have been mentioned earlier in the chapter. In terms of contemporary work, the online *Black Lives Matter Poetry Reader* (2016) provides a useful starting point for further reading, including work by Fatimah Asghar, Kwame Dawes, Jericho Brown, Kyle Dargan, Rita Dove and Claudia Rankine.[17] The purpose of choosing these particular poems has been to provide an overview; a broad strokes survey of elegies written in response to racial injustice across various particular historical moments, rather than a conclusive and exhaustive study. The aim has been to demonstrate the complexity, nuance and diversity of responses – in form, in content, in affect and in intent – to loss on a scale that includes, but also extends beyond, the personal. The losses elegized within these poems are shared, communal and public, rather than individualized and private. Despite similarities, they cannot be reduced to one particular poetic – or elegiac – approach. While connections and correlations may be drawn between them, they are each unique and distinctive. While the previous chapter examined how Black elegies, particularly those by women writers, have historically been received in particular ways – as 'eulogistic,' as 'vengeful' or 'bitter,' as 'militant,' as 'safe,' as 'non-revolutionary,' as demonstrating a 'useless pain' or 'slavish false consciousness' – this chapter has sought to destabilize and disrupt these categorizations through its close readings, in order to foreground the intricacies, ambivalences, variances and conflicting emotions that each of the poems embody (Hussen 2013: 306; 213).

But, equally, the purpose of this chapter has been to demonstrate that the notion that elegies by Black writers might represent an exceptional or anomalous achievement within a tradition that supposedly belongs to white European writers is, and always has been, untenable. The genealogical model of elegy as a fixed Eurocentric genre or form which writers who are not white men have occasionally sought to adopt is an inaccurate one; a colonial hang-up that needs to be reconfigured and reimagined. What is required is a seismic shift in the way that the so-called tradition of elegy is conceptualized; a total reconstruction in which, to paraphrase bell hooks, white patriarchal culture is no longer understood as 'the' location where elegy exists (1990: 109–10). The next chapter will explore further possibilities for this reconceptualization, examining what elegy scholarship might learn from trans*feminist theories and queer politics.

Notes

1. See Hudson-Weems (1988: 24); S.M. Smith (2015: 179); Wagner (2010: 190, 195); Bush (2013: 10); and McMurtry-Chubb (2017: 622).
2. For a thorough account of this rhetoric, see Houck (2005).
3. This line also gestures towards the much-photographed post-trial kiss between Carolyn and Roy Bryant, which Houck describes as a 'pornographic osculation,' and a 'public display of intraracial sexual desire,' which 'finally redeemed the Northern Threat to the Southern Way' (2005: 254).
4. See Jackson Ford for more on Brooks's move away from the ballad form in her later work (2010: 371); and see Vrana for more on Brooks's rejection of a balladic form that enable the types of delusion Carolyn Bryant harbours in 'A Bronzeville Mother' (2018: 18).
5. 'Grey, adj. 4d' *Oxford English Dictionary Online*. Available online: https://www.oed.com/view/Entry/81341?rskey=POkkum&result=1&isAdvanced=false#eid (accessed 6 May 2021).
6. See Collins and Margo (2007) for more on this.
7. See, for instance, KJV (2001) 1 Peter 3: 9 'Not rendering evil for evil…' (785); Deuteronomy 32: 35 'To me belongeth vengeance and recompence…' (155); Hebrews 10: 30 'For we know him that hath said, Vengeance belongeth to me, I will recompense, saith the Lord…' (778); Leviticus 19: 18 'Thou shalt not avenge, nor bear any grudge against the children of thy people, but thou shalt love thy neighbour as thyself…' (88); Proverbs 20: 22 'Say not thou, I will recompense evil, but wait on the Lord…' (440); Romans 12: 19 'Dearly beloved, avenge not yourselves […] Vengeance is mine; I will repay, saith the Lord' (735).
8. It is important to note here that, according to Mary Jane Lupton, the 1972 version of the poem in *Good News about the Earth* capitalizes the word 'Black,' while the 1989 version in *Good Woman* does not (2006: 46). This is an interesting point, given that Clifton's selective capitalization is often remarked upon in descriptions of her work. Holladay describes how, in her poems, 'few words merit capitalization,' while Lupton describes a lack of capitalization as 'typical of Clifton's style' (Holladay 2004: 19; Lupton 2006: 46). It is worth considering whether the decision to

de-capitalize the word may have been that of the later collection's editor, A. Poulin Jr, rather than Clifton's.

9   Okigbo's poetic influences for these poems are manifold, and include Stephane Mallarmé, Raja Ratnam, Malcolm Cowley and Rabindranath Tagore (outlined in a preface to the *Transition* versions); Gerard Manley Hopkins (See Romanus N. Egudu 2003); Herman Melville and Kwabena Nketia (see Obumselu 2010).
10 For more on Okigbo as 'self-sacrificing soldier,' see Abba (2017: 261).
11 See Echeruo (2004: 20–5) for all three versions.
12 The phrase 'No in thunder,' Egudu states, originates from a correspondence between Herman Melville and Nathaniel Hawthorne; while his 'silent sisters' echo Gerard Manley Hopkins's Franciscan nuns from 'The Wreck of the Deutschland' (2003: 33).
13 See Diala (2015: 88–93) for more on Igbo drum elegies.
14 I examine the *Split this Rock* version here unless otherwise stated (2014: n.p).
15 While this chapter focuses on the context of police violence towards Black men and women in the United States, it should be noted that the United Kingdom also has significant issues of institutional racism within the police. See, for instance, Nazir Afzal 'Black people dying in police custody should surprise no one,' *The Guardian* (2020).
16 There is a good deal more to be unpacked on the complexities of these two positions – violence and non-violence – though unfortunately, it is beyond the scope of this book to do so here. For more on the these positions in relation to grievability, see Butler's *The Force of Non-Violence* (2020), particularly Chapter 1 (27–65).
17 See H.K. Hummel's *Black Lives Matter Reader* (2016).

3

Abstracted grief, precarious grief: Rethinking elegy via transfeminism and queer necropolitics

In the Introduction to this book, we encountered some of the ways in which a heteropatriarchal gendered binary underpins genealogical approaches to elegy. This binary frequently associates a supposedly feminine (or feminized) aesthetic with excess – of emotion and/or of language – as well as with inauthenticity, irrationality, indecorousness and a lack of control while associating a masculine (or masculinized) aesthetic with proportion, minimalism, moderation and reason. To challenge this gendered binary and its usage in genealogical formations, this chapter examines elegies by trans* writers who disrupt and trouble its paradigms.[1]

Trans* voices have been largely – if not entirely – absented from elegy scholarship to date and this chapter seeks to address that lack of representation, while also examining the possibilities that trans*feminist and queer theories offer for reconceptualizing elegy beyond genealogical models and gendered binaries. Situating itself not only within the context of a Mbembeian necropolitics but also – following Haritaworn, Kuntsman and Posocco's edited book of essays (2014) – a queer necropolitics, the chapter examines elegiac poems by Joshua Jennifer Espinoza, Ryka Aoki and Qwo-Li Driskill. Each of these poems addresses themes of queer and trans* loss and death as a result of gendered hate violence and discrimination, as well as the material conditions of precarity that arise from living under constant threat of literal death through violence and/or figurative death through erasure. In doing so, the chapter seeks to identify concrete means for rethinking elegy in ways that are not dependent on gendered binaries and that do not exclude or marginalize trans* voices.

Re-makings, multiplicities, displacements: Beyond binary concepts of gender

In reconceptualizing elegy beyond a heteropatriarchal binary, one potential approach would be to situate work that falls outside of that binary within a conceptual space 'beyond' its parameters. However, attempts to think 'beyond the binary' often serve to exclude certain voices in the process of aiming to include others. Paddy McQueen argues against 'beyond-the-binary' formulations since, though a gendered binary 'can work to exclude some trans identities,' the act of eliminating binary terms altogether can consequently 'remove a central crux through which we construct a relation-to-self' (2016: 682, 678–9). A wholesale rejection of a gendered binary, then, potentially excludes voices of trans* individuals who identify themselves within it.[2]

Moreover, Talia Mae Bettcher warns against conceiving of trans* expressions as conforming to a 'beyond-the-binary model,' or as occupying an 'in between space,' as to do so is 'precisely to assume a dominant interpretation' (2014: 390). In other words, to consider the binary categories 'male' and 'female' as fixed and static – and the trans* body as occupying a space outside of those paradigms – is just another means of sustaining binary formations. Rather than working to disrupt the established binary, it instead situates trans* individuals in a liminal space of othering and non-categorization.

And a gendered binary does not provide an accurate representation of gender expression. Butler argues that variations of gender which do not fit within binary paradigms 'are as much a part of gender as its most normative instance,' and to presume that the term 'gender' refers only to heteronormative expressions of masculinity and femininity is to 'consolidate the power of the norm to constrain the definition of gender' (2004: 42). For Butler then, the concept of gender cannot be represented by a binary model since it already spans beyond the limits of a binary to incorporate a continuum of various and nuanced expressions. How, then, might we rethink approaches to elegy in ways that avoid excluding both those voices which identify within a gendered binary and those that do not?

We might begin by considering the perspective of Antonella Corsani and Timothy S. Murphy. They argue that understanding heterosexuality as 'a political regime' enables us to circumvent the 'dialectic of the sexes,' by allowing the possibility of employing 'political strategies of deterritorializing "man and woman,"' in order to 'politically, philosophically and symbolically' destroy them as categories (2007: 108). Though they emphasize a necessity for moving 'beyond' what they term 'a logic of binary oppositions,' their means of doing so is through a 'displacement of the subject "woman" toward a complex and heterogeneous multiplicity of feminist subjectivities' (2007: 110–11). Building on the writing of Monique Wittig, Adriana Cavarero and Gloria Anzaldúa, they endorse 'approaches that deconstruct the very concept of "woman," in favour of 'the political theory of disordered and undisciplined multiplicity,' and 'the displacement of categories, discourses, forms of politics and borders' (2007: 111–12). Within their queer feminist conception, identities are 'not fixed' or 'congealed,' but rather, 'shifting,' 'fractured,' 'uncongealed' and 'deviant' (2007: 113). Individuals are 'a multiplicity,' who inhabit 'several worlds in contradictory ways,' while 'unity with others' is understood as 'a process of partial (and never totalizing) assemblages' (2007: 113).

To put it more simply, for Corsani and Murphy heterosexuality is not simply a category of sexual orientation, but rather a form of political authority and control. Their use of Deleuze and Guattari's term 'deterritorializing' implies not only a weakening of the boundaries that delineate the categories 'man' and 'woman,' but also a subjectivity in a constant state of flux, fluidity, unrestraint and breakdown. According to their formulation, moving 'beyond' a gendered binary means moving towards a nuanced, various, multifaceted and diverse range of feminist subjectivities. This enables a better understanding of the various overlapping, intersectional oppressions that the binary categories of gender cannot adequately represent. Their political theory is one that works against homogeneity, control and order. Within it, individual identities are unstable, fluctuating, ruptured, irregular and inconsistent. Notions of community, empathy and solidarity – the interrelations and connectivities that a 'unity with others' might signify – are partial; only ever incomplete or fragmentary (Corsani and Murphy 2007: 113). As assemblages, these unities are rhizomatic in nature; they are non-hierarchical and nonlinear, resisting chronological and narrative organizational structures that have a distinct origin or end point.

We might, in addition, consider Butler's concept of gender as that which is open to a 'continual remaking' (2004: 10). In their view, the terms 'masculine' and 'feminine' are 'notoriously changeable' with meanings that alter 'radically depending upon geopolitical boundaries and cultural constraints on who is imagining whom, and for what purpose' (2004: 10). They are 'never settled once and for all but are constantly in the process of being remade' (2004: 10). Thus, for Butler, binary categories of gender are necessarily already in flux at both a personal and a semantic level. A gendered binary is therefore always contingent upon contextual factors. Moreover, this binary operates as a 'restrictive discourse,' which 'performs a regulatory operation of power that naturalizes the hegemonic instance and forecloses the thinkability of its disruption' (2004: 42–3). Like Corsani and Murphy, Butler perceives a gendered binary as a form of hegemonic power and control that shuts out possibilities of thinking beyond its own boundaries. Conversely, as an expression that is open to a 'continual remaking,' their conception of gender is – again, like Corsani and Murphy's – non-totalizing in its scope; it has no fixed beginning or end point, but rather is characterized by constant transformation (Butler 2004: 10). This formulation of gender allows for the circumvention of binary thought-structures in favour of a non-spatial and non-linear continuum in which diverse expressions and articulations are continually passing into one another.

We might also consider Bettcher's analysis, which specifically addresses the lived experiences of trans* individuals. Within trans* communities, gender practices and their meanings are, Bettcher asserts, 'not stable,' but rather 'variable and contested' (2014: 389). Because of this, not only are trans* communities 'in resistant relation to a dominant world,' but they also allow for the recognition of 'a multiplicity of trans worlds in relation to a multiplicity of dominant ones' (2014: 389–90). For Bettcher, a gendered binary might be replaced with the recognition of 'the existence of multiple worlds of sense, worlds in which terms such as "woman" have different, resistant meanings' (2014: 403). Thus, like Butler, Bettcher outlines how gender is not fixed, but rather in a state of continual flux, and contingent upon contextual factors. Much like Corsani and Murphy, Bettcher also endorses a displacement of binary terms towards a more diverse and nuanced multiplicity of subjectivities. To rethink elegy beyond heteropatriarchal binaries, elegy scholarship would need to think outside of its rigid system of gender categorization. What these queer and trans* feminist theories offer for elegy scholarship are various possibilities for moving beyond these categories in ways that open up space for the inclusion of both the voices that identify within them and those that do not.

Necropolitics: Precarity, dehumanization and grievability

To further open out Corsani and Murphy's formulation of heterosexuality as 'a political regime,' Butler's conception of the gendered binary as performing 'a regulatory operation of power' and Bettcher's concept of a 'dominant world,' to which trans* communities are in 'resistant relation,' we might return to Mbembe's term 'necropolitics' (Bettcher 2014: 389–90; Butler 2004: 42–3; Corsani and Murphy 2007: 108; Mbembe 2019). Mbembe highlights 'contemporary forms of subjugating life to the power of death'; in other words, the ways in which expressions of sovereignty and power exercise control over 'who is able to live and who must die' (2019: 92; 66). His terms – 'necropolitics' and 'necropower' – denote certain 'topographies of cruelty' (in particular, 'the plantation and the colony'), wherein these contemporary subjugations are played out (2019: 92).

In a book of essays titled *Queer Necropolitics*, various theorists examine and develop these terms specifically in relation to 'queer subjects' and 'queerly abjected populations,' who are – through a combination of cultural, moral and economic factors – 'marked for death' (Haritaworn, Kuntsman and Posocco 2014: 20). For instance, Sima Shakhsari asserts that bodies which 'fail to materialize,' within the 'heterosexual hegemony,' are abjected, and considered 'not worth protecting, saving, or grieving' (2014: 102). For Shakhsari – just as for Butler, and Corsani and Murphy – heterosexual hegemony is a 'political regime,' or 'regulatory operation of power'; one that operates as a manifestation of necropolitics, delineating whose lives are valuable and whose are not (Butler 2004: 42–3; Corsani and Murphy 2007: 108). Similarly, Aren Z. Aizura outlines how 'gender non-conforming bodies' are subjected to erasures from public discourse that not only 'dehumanize and diminish' them but condemn them 'to disposability' (2014: 130–1). Thus, for Aizura, it is through the systematic structural erasure of non-binary bodies that heterosexual hegemony establishes and sustains a condition of necropolitics.

Further, Elijah Adiv Edelman attributes such 'displacement and erasure' to the fact that non-binary bodies 'operate as a threat' to heterosexual hegemony, since they 'fail to be capitally,' and 'ideologically productive' (2014: 176–7). A gendered binary, then, operates as a means of regulating the value of an individual based on their ideological conformity to heteropatriarchal systems and their ability to engage in a neoliberal economy. In Edelman's view it is 'biopolitical technologies,' as well as 'necrocapitalistic reformation[s] of space,' that enable the 'destruction, erasure and death,' of non-binary bodies that fail to 'become acceptable' within society (2014: 177). Thus, these erasures and displacements are inextricably linked with technologies designed and employed by states and corporations to surveil, identify, discipline and control human bodies and the population; as well as with social restructurings of space such as in urban gentrification.

Queer necropolitics, in other words, signifies the condition in which capitalism and its spatialities demarcate certain queer bodies as disposable. Operating outside of the gendered binary categories of heterosexual hegemony, these bodies are understood as threatening or as valueless because they are considered capitalistically unproductive and, as a result, are dehumanized, excluded and erased. As Butler argues, this level of dehumanization and erasure renders bodies as 'already not quite living,' or 'living in a state of suspension between life and death' (2006: 36). Such lives – not afforded the same protections as other lives – do not 'qualify as "grievable"' within public discourse and hegemonic structures (Butler 2006: 32). In a similar way, Mbembe uses the phrases '*death-worlds*' and 'status of the *living dead*,' to describe, respectively, necropolitical spaces and the necropolitical condition to which certain forms of existence are subjected (2019: 92; emphasis author's). To exist within a necropolitical condition, then, is to occupy a condition of death that may be deferred but is nevertheless considered – by hegemonic structures – as acceptable and inevitable.

Mbembe's description of the necropolitical – and the queer necropolitics outlined in Haritaworn, Kuntsman and Posocco's edited collection of essays – enables us to concretely conceive of heterosexual hegemony as a 'political regime' and as a 'regulatory operation of power' that precludes any possibility of deviation from itself (Butler 2004: 42–3; Corsani and Murphy 2007: 108). Both concepts provide us with an important and specific cultural context for examining elegiac poems by trans* writers. However, it is nonetheless crucial to emphasize that to read trans* elegies in relation to necropolitics is not the only way in which they can be read. To imply that trans* elegiac work can *only* be read as engaging with a necropolitical condition would not only flatten out the many varied ways in which these elegists engage with the mode, but also potentially draw dubious, well-worn associations between trans* or queer subjectivity and death. Rather, this chapter aims to examine the various issues each poem raises for rethinking questions of gender, elegy and mourning through a Mbembian and queer necropolitical lens. In doing so, it examines the ways in which they draw our attention to the sociopolitical conditions in which certain queer bodies are dehumanized and/or 'marked for death' (Haritaworn, Kuntsman and Posocco 2014: 20).

Abstract bodies and the complicit reader: Joshua Jennifer Espinoza's 'Poem (Let us Live)'

In 2016, the Gay & Lesbian Alliance Against Defamation (GLAAD) published that twenty-seven transgender people were killed in the United States that year, nearly all of them trans women of colour (Schmider 2016: para 2). Further, they assert that this number 'does not include transgender people whose deaths were not reported due to misgendering in police reports, news stories, and sometimes by the victim's family' (Schmider 2016: para 2). Similarly, the National Coalition of Anti-Violence Programs' 2016 Report states that – excluding those killed during the 2016 Pulse Nightclub shooting in Orlando (whose number included trans* individuals) – 68 per cent of anti-LGBTQ homicides targeted transgender and gender-non-conforming people (Waters 2017: 9). Of the 1,036 incidents of hate-violence reported across the United States, 21 per cent were towards transgender women (Waters 2017: 9). More recently, according to the National Center for Transgender Equality, the murder of trans* people in 2020 surpassed 2019 figures 'in just seven months' (National Center for Transgender Equality 2020: para 1). These statistics illustrate a context in which trans* individuals – and trans women in particular – are at serious risk of hate-motivated violence and murder.

Rather than focusing on the death of a single individual, Espinoza's 'Poem (Let us Live)' – from her second book *There Should Be Flowers* (2016) – attends to multiple losses of trans women's lives within this context of violence, as well as the anticipation of further losses of life should these circumstances go unaddressed. The 'us' of the poem's subtitle – ('Let *Us* Live') – emphasizes that Espinoza is speaking for a community of trans women whose lives are at risk from transmisogynistic violence. The apostrophized 'you' within the poem is not only a direct address to the reader but, more specifically, an address to those outside of this community; in other words, to a reader assumed to be cisgender (a person whose gender identity corresponds to that assigned at birth). In this way, the poem's address positions the reader from the outset as a representative of cis-heteropatriarchal hegemony and – with its plea towards the reader to 'Let Us Live' – as both complicit and responsible within that cultural structure.

We might draw a parallel between the opening of Espinoza's poem and that of Smith's in the previous chapter. Both poems begin by articulating a deep weariness at having to address the subject of systemic violence and death. While Smith's poem expresses fatigue in response to the task of addressing the police killing of a young Black man, Espinoza's poem opens by articulating exhaustion in response to the various ways in which transfeminine bodies are abstracted within public discourse. By denoting the action of separating oneself – or turning one's mind away from – a situation, the word 'abstraction' implies that there exists within society a hegemonic refusal to adequately acknowledge the reality of transmisogyny and hate-violence. By stating that 'people die from' this abstraction, Espinoza maps a direct correlation between cis-heteropatriarchal society's tendency to actively turn their minds away from instances of transmisogynistic violence; and the frequency with which such violence occurs (2016: 75). In *Queer Necropolitics*, Aizura writes that it is a lack of 'discursive recognition,' that erases the humanity of gender-non-conforming bodies, thus rendering them disposable (2014: 130–1). Denoting a lack of awareness about what is taking place in one's surroundings, the word 'abstraction' gestures towards the lack of 'discursive recognition,' that erases '(certain) queer bodies from public discourse' (Aizura 2014: 130–1). In this way, Espinoza's lines emphasize how this lack – in other words, the erasure of trans women's lives from public social consciousness – sustains the very circumstances in which transmisogynistic violence takes place (Aizuara 2014: 130–1).

But the word 'abstraction' also refers to the action of perceiving something in the abstract; as detached from its particular and singular characteristics. This meaning gestures towards the way in which public discourse – for example, the police reports and news stories that misreport or misgender victims of violence – abstracts individual trans women's deaths from their specific contextual details. Indeed, in her article on trans* commemorative events (specifically Transgender Day of Remembrance) Sarah Lamble describes the way in which 'each case is *abstracted* from its history and context: [e]ach murder is decontextualized and reabsorbed within a unified narrative and a universalized body of the dead trans subject' (2008: 28; emphasis mine). Espinoza's opening lines emphasize the way in which public discourse abstracts individual trans women's deaths from their specific contextual details, subsuming them into narratives that serve particular agendas.

Moreover, the word 'abstraction' signifies the action of articulating in abstract terms; of expressing something as an idea rather than as a concrete reality. In this way, Espinoza's opening lines highlight that, dissociated from lived experiences of hate-violence, cis-heteropatriarchy is only able to conceive of trans women's death in the abstract, rather than in material terms. From its opening lines, then, Espinoza's poem is situated within a necropolitical discourse that addresses the social condition in which trans women's bodies are dehumanized and marked as disposable through the rhetorical process of abstraction.

In the poem, Espinoza characterizes the reader's engagement with transmisogynistic violence as brief, superficial and cursory, taking place in the arena of social media via the decision of whether to share stories about dead trans women online. This portrayal positions the reader in the role of an arbiter deciding whose death is worthy of note and whose is not. As with the obituary which, Butler argues, 'functions as the instrument by which grievability is publicly distributed,' the act of sharing stories of trans women's deaths is 'a means by which a life becomes, or fails to become, a publicly grievable life, [...] the means by which a life becomes noteworthy' (2006: 34). Conversely, the decision not to share a story is to decide that a life is not worthy of grieving. In this sense, social media platforms like Facebook constitute a form of biopolitical technology that 'serves to demarcate that which is valuable from that which is not,' while within the poem, the reader is designated as actively mediating the potential erasures and displacements that such biopolitical technology enables (Edelman 2014: 177).

What this rhetorical position of mediation – in which the poem positions the reader – circumvents is a possibility for understanding the act of sharing stories of trans women's deaths on social media as an act of cis-allyship, solidarity, empathy or sadness, or of educating others. As Lamble suggests, '[b]y recognizing the pain of others, we tell ourselves, we engage in a shared sense of humanity' (2008: 35). But, as Lamble's assertion makes clear, this is a narrative that is self-produced; it is something that a sharer tells themselves. As Lamble further notes, such acts enable an indication of political and social awareness 'without moving outside the comfort zone of moral authority and self-knowing' (2008: 35). For the assumed cis reader of the poem, the act of sharing stories about trans women's deaths on Facebook is one that takes place from a position of both safety and privilege. By addressing the poem to a cis-heteropatriarchal readership, Espinoza permits the reader no circumvention of complicity within a matrix of transmisogynistic erasure and displacement: in not sharing these stories, they are participating in that erasure; and in sharing them, they are afforded a sense of allyship, empathy or solidarity which poses no actual risk to themselves. Forced to acknowledge a position of privilege abstracted from the concrete reality of the death itself, Espinoza thus turns the abstraction experienced by trans women in public discourse back upon the reader.

The poem emphasizes the alienation, estrangement and lack of intimacy that social media platforms like Facebook embody – as what Mbembe terms a 'plastic and simulated form of living' – in which a network of 'friends' is often made up of people one has never met or that one knows only vaguely (2019: 14). The poem indicates that the reader understands dead trans women – whose stories they are deciding whether or not to share – as 'flowers' (Espinoza 2016: 75). This attributed understanding implies dehumanization, aestheticization and romanticization. Flowers are objectified living beings that are grown, cut and gifted because of their visual beauty. As poetic metaphor, they are employed to evoke femininity, fragility and the ephemerality of life. To metaphorize dead trans women as 'flowers' is to consider them as visually pleasing commodities that possess an inherent quality of fragility and ephemerality (2016: 75).

The essential characteristic of fragility that the metaphor implies overlooks the systemic conditions that facilitate and sustain transmisogynistic violence. By portraying them as adopting and maintaining this metaphor, Espinoza characterizes the reader as a curatorial figure; a collector of aestheticized trans women's bodies for the purpose of sharing them with social media acquaintances. This act of sharing is likened to a 'whisper,' a barely audible or secretive utterance with hostile or conspiratorial associations (2016: 75). In this way, the act of sharing the stories of trans women's deaths on Facebook is depicted as a nominal gesture which fails to fully constitute a form of public discourse. In sum, these lines emphasize the violence inherent within a cis-heteropatriarchal act of 'speaking' dead trans women's bodies; an act of figuratively taking possession and aesthetically commodifying, which fails to address the social circumstances which cause and contribute to their deaths.

An index of accountabilities

The poem's central impetus is to emphasize that the deaths of trans women do not occur ex nihilo. To do so the poem incorporates a list of elements that participate in and contribute to them. This list begins with 'words,' highlighting the role of language in the construction and affirmation of heteropatriarchal structures and in the dynamic of transmisogynistic violence (Espinoza 2016: 75). As Dean Pierce asserts, language operates as an instrument 'of psychological harm' that is, in turn, 'used to rationalize or justify acts of physical violence and social discrimination' (2001: 48). Moreover, while language used in dominant social discourse 'reflects the worth and meaning a culture assigns to it,' trans* voices are largely excluded or absented from that discourse (Pierce 2001: 48). This absence has, he argues, intensified to a point where those who fall outside of heterosexual hegemonic binaries are subjected to 'public condemnation' by right-wing conservatives who 'use erroneous information and traditional language,' as a means of circulating and perpetuating ideological myths which are used to 'create fear [...] and work to maintain the cultural silence about and mistrust of queer people' (Pierce 2001: 58). This echoes Aizura's description of 'structural exclusions' that 'dehumanize and diminish gender non-conforming bodies,' whereby the absences and erasures of voices and bodies from dominant social discourse operate as a means of rendering those bodies disposable (2014: 130–1).

Similarly, AnnJanette Rosga argues that 'there can be no cordoning off of language from violence,' since violent hate-crimes '"borrow" or enact elements of state power,' that – rather than representing impartiality – require '[c]ontinuous rhetorical labor' in order to maintain their 'historically gendered and racialized character' (2001: 249–51). In other words, constant linguistic efforts are required to maintain cis-heteropatriarchal systems, while violent hate-crimes in turn adopt and perform the hierarchies inscribed within these systems. Acts of violent hate-crime re-inscribe these hierarchies in a sequence of reciprocal cause and effect. Language is therefore inextricable from the violence that hate-crimes enact; it is an instrument of violence within a vicious cycle that reinforces ideologies which render trans women's bodies dehumanized, excluded and erased.

Following on from 'words,' Espinoza's list continues by registering corporeal elements that participate and contribute to trans women's deaths, beginning with 'hands' (Espinoza 2016: 75). This emphasizes that transmisogynistic violence is, inherently, a physical act. It forces the reader to acknowledge the actuality of transmisogynistic violence as a corporeal action inflicted by an individual or individuals upon another. In other words, it refuses the reader the opportunity to consider the deaths only in abstract terms. Next on the list is 'guns,' which is considered alongside corporeal elements like 'flesh,' and 'teeth' (2016: 75). Charles Fruehling Springwood asserts that the relationship between a gun-owner and their gun is a 'mode of affective embodiment, or embodied habit, in which the gun so easily merges with its owner, forming and conforming to the body, dissolving into one's person unconsciously' (2014: 453–4). Springwood outlines the way in which owner and gun 'form an assemblage in which both are actants, allowing the characteristics of each to interpenetrate [...] both materially and semiotically' (2014: 456). Within this assemblage – or, in Springwood's terms, 'co-constructed coupling' – guns 'insinuate themselves into the desiring and gendered body of the would-be shooter, and a new machine emerges' (2014: 459). Thus, for Springwood a gun functions as a part or an extension of the body. Springwood conceives of the act of carrying a gun as both a practice in biopower and a 'corporeal politics,' that 'frame[s] the affective space in which discourses of danger, fear, security, and violence are performed' (2014: 461). Thus, the corporeal assemblage of body-and-gun is a means of participating in cultural systems that enable instances of hate-violence to take place. Moreover, he outlines the gun as a 'highly charged object of sexual force,' a phallocentric entity metaphorically understood as symbolic of masculine desire, which enables the body to be understood as a weapon (2014: 464–5).

As in Springwood's understanding, Espinoza's poem designates the gun as a part of the body by situating it alongside other corporeal elements. This not only designates guns as a form of biopolitical technology enforcing the necropolitical – in which the 'destruction, erasure and death' of trans women is made 'acceptable' – but also gestures towards the matrix of heteropatriarchal desire within which the gun, as both biopolitical object and as hate-crime weapon, is situated (Edelman 2014: 177). The additional corporeal elements on Espinoza's list return the reader to the concrete somatic reality of transmisogynistic violence as a physical action performed by one body, or bodies, upon another. But, more than this, they operate as a means of breaking down the body – specifically the body of the perpetrator/s – into discrete corporeal parts. In this way, they enact a mirroring, in which violence against the transfeminine body is reflected back upon the person or persons responsible. Through metonymy, these corporeal elements represent the abstraction of the perpetrating body into figurative corporeal units.

While the list's inclusion of both 'men' and 'women' serves to extend responsibility for trans women's deaths beyond the actions of a singular individual, it also reinforces the accountability of cis-heteropatriarchal systems (Espinoza 2016: 75). In other words, it is the rigid classification of persons according to this gendered binary – and those that identify themselves and others in this way – that contributes to and participates in trans women's deaths. Rhetorically addressed as a representative of cis-heteropatriarchy, the reader is refused any space to circumvent their own accountability. To uphold and sustain a gendered binary is to tacitly contribute to the circumstances in which transmisogynistic violence takes place. Situating these binary terms alongside 'laws,' 'policies' and 'police,' further highlights their role through parallel structure (Espinoza 2016: 75). In other words, situating them contiguously with these terms designates the binary categories 'man' and 'woman' as disciplinary mechanisms of legislative regulation and enforcement.

The roles of 'laws,' 'policies,' and 'police' operate in various ways (2016: 75). Che Gossett outlines how trans women disproportionately face 'malign neglect and social abandonment,' that includes criminalization; 'police brutalization'; violence and murder within police custody; and 'penal technologies of torture and execution' (2014: 41). Thus, the disciplinary mechanisms listed in the poem are materially responsible for trans women's deaths. Additionally, if we follow Butler's assertion that 'laws, rules, and policies' operate as a form of regulation – as the 'legal instruments through which persons are made regular' – we might also read them as ideologically disciplinary mechanisms that constitute a means of keeping in line those who transgress boundaries of gender (2004: 40). Bettcher refers to this kind of regulation as 'reality enforcement,' which includes gender segregation in 'public restrooms and changing rooms, domestic violence shelters, homeless shelters, shared hospital rooms, and jails and prisons,' as well as 'same-sex searches by police officers and other security officials,' all of which subject trans women to 'violations of privacy and offenses of indecency' (2014: 396-7). We might add to these disciplinary mechanisms the 'high rates of poverty, unemployment, and homelessness' that Schmider outlines in a GLAAD article on transmisogynistic violence (2016: para 4). Espinoza's inclusion of these legal and political mechanisms signposts the explicit as well as the incremental state and social violences that contribute to trans women's deaths. In doing so, the poem maps an implicit connection between transmisogynistic violence and the social contexts of vulnerability, precarity, ill health, insufficient support and lack of social care within which trans women are frequently forced to exist.

The final element listed in the poem's index of accountabilities is 'witnesses' (Espinoza 2016: 75). As Lamble argues, '[w]hen responsibility belongs to a single perpetrator, the rest of us are positioned as innocent bystanders' (2008: 34). The act of sharing stories of trans women's deaths on social media operates as a means of situating oneself in a – supposedly innocent – position of witness. In Lamble's view, a position of innocence is 'secured through outpourings of public sympathy,' and this is particularly the case 'when we are called to remember those who we did not know personally' (2008: 34-5). Narratives apportioning blame to a singular individual for an act of transmisogynistic violence enable heteropatriarchal and transmisogynistic hierarchies to be 'left fully and forcefully intact' (Lamble 2008: 34). Thus, for Lamble, a position of witness is not only one of sympathy but also one of complicity (2008: 38).

Espinoza's inclusion of this term refuses the reader a position of 'witness' by invalidating its supposed innocence. The poem rejects a narrative that apportions blame to a single perpetrator, instead attributing responsibility to a nexus of elements: the cis-heteropatriarchal binary; legislative and disciplinary mechanisms; social conditions of vulnerability and precarity; and everyone, including (or especially) the reader of the poem who – as a supposed bystander, spectator or witness – enables these circumstances, systems and mechanisms to remain in place. Within this index of accountabilities, it is ultimately the reader who is invested with the agency to address these circumstances and enact change. In the final lines, Espinoza denies the status of the poem *as poem*, instead presenting it as a plea, appeal or entreaty for the lives of trans women. By investing the reader with such agency over trans women's lives, Espinoza designates and positions them as an embodiment of the sovereignty and power that, in Mbembe's formulation of necropolitics, exercises control over 'who is able to live and who must die' (2019: 66). In other words, Espinoza characterizes the reader not only as complicit within – but also as an enforcer of – necropolitical conditions.

Irregularity and memorial: Ryka Aoki's 'The Woman of Water Dreams'

Ryka Aoki's 'The Woman of Water Dreams' – from her book *Why Dust Shall Never Settle Upon This Soul* (2015) – is a rich and complex poem exploring issues relating to gender regulation, trans* commemorative practices, and the cis-heteronormative gaze. The poem addresses trans* deaths commemorated by Transgender Day of Remembrance – as well as an unnamed queer death by suicide – and explores conditions produced by living under constant threat of transmisogynistic violence. The poem is a long sequence comprising six sections, each with a different focus.

The first of these sections addresses themes of indeterminacy and non-rationality. The opening lines ask the reader to reflect upon irrational numbers: those that cannot be expressed as an integer, whole number, or fraction and which, if written as a decimal, would go on forever. Thus, the poem opens with a focus on elements that fall outside of easy categorization and are infinite in their non-rationality. Oblique references to irregular celestial orbits and quantum chaos build upon these notions of indeterminacy, irregularity and disruption. The chaotic movements of the sun and moon, the splitting of a nucleus, and the image of a donut operate as representations of irregularity and a lack – or destruction – of centrality (Aoki 2015: 5). We might interpret these images of irregularity in various ways. For instance, Eva Hayward argues that '[t]he body (trans or not) is not a pure, coherent, and positive integrity,' but rather 'a question of experiencing multiple and continually varying interactions between what can be defined indifferently as coherent transformation, decentered certainty, or limited possibility' (2008: 72–3). Aoki's irregular images similarly reject systems that privilege rationality and that conceive of bodies as consistent, unified wholes.

We might also read them in relation to Mbembe's assertion that 'late-modern political criticism has […] made the concept of reason into one of the most important elements in both the project of modernity and the topos of sovereignty' and as a result, 'the ultimate expression of sovereignty is the production of general norms by a body (the demos) comprising free and equal individuals' (2019: 67). In other words, logic, reason and rationality are privileged over emotion and non-rationality in the establishment and preservation of autonomy and power, each of which is produced through a policing of hegemonic standards in dominant discourse. This policing allows for bodies that transgress these boundaries to be understood as irrational, irregular, chaotic, or indeterminate. Aoki's celebration of irregularity, then, actively works against hegemonic standards by undermining a rationality that conceives of the paradigmatic body as an integral unit.

The inclusion of a cat which is 'dead or frightened,' presents a more ambivalent figure (Aoki 2015: 5). Like the subject of Schrödinger's paradoxical thought-experiment – or at least its common interpretations – it signifies a state of being both alive and dead at the same time. As 'dead or frightened,' it occupies a space of continual deferral, suspended in a liminal space between fear and death (2015: 5). Mbembe asserts that contemporary necropolitics is responsible for 'new and unique forms of social existence in which vast populations are subjected to living conditions that confer upon them the status of the *living dead*' (2019: 92; emphasis his). In its occupation of a liminal space between fear and death, the cat in the poem gestures towards conditions of precarity experienced by non-gender-conforming individuals who live under these kinds of conditions.

Situating the value relations of rationality and non-rationality within a context of death, Aoki emphasizes how rationality only 'makes sense' in the face of chaos. Within the context of transphobic and transmisogynistic violence, she juxtaposes this act of 'making sense' with terror (2015: 5). We might associate the practice of 'making sense' with Butler's term 'regulation': an 'institutionalization of the process by which persons are made regular' (2004: 40). Aoki's 'rational value,' that 'makes sense' only in relation to that which is irrational, operates as an allegory for the policing of gender expression whereby normative definitions are solidified by pathologizing expressions that transgress their parameters (Aoki 2015: 5). In a discussion of 'identity enforcement,' Bettcher argues that 'it is precisely the fact that transpeople do not have their self-identifications taken seriously that is so deeply bound up with transphobic hostility and violence' (2007: 51, 54). This explicitly sketches a relation between identity enforcement – i.e. the act of 'making sense' of a person's gender according to normative definitions – and transphobic hate-violence.

Lamble outlines a similar correlation between 'dominant power relations of sex and gender norms,' and the erasure of trans* individuals within public discourse that consequently 'makes it difficult [...] to secure such basic rights and services as health care and housing' (2008: 28). For Lamble, the act of 'making sense' of a person's gender according to normative definitions relates to an elision of trans* bodies that directly contributes to conditions of precarious living. By gesturing towards the violence inherent in the privileging of so-called rationality over identities that cannot easily be categorized within its taxonomies, Aoki signposts the spaces of precarity that trans* bodies are forced to occupy, specifically as a result of this practice of 'making sense,' which deems such bodies irregular, irrational and chaotic. Ultimately, then, these reflections upon irregularity within the poem's opening section are ambivalent. On the one hand, the orbit of the sun and moon, the splitting of a composite subatomic particle, and a fondness for decentered confectionery represent a celebration of uncategorizability within systems of rationality. On the other hand, the cat – which occupies a contingent space of death and fear – and the association between the practice of 'making sense' and terror, both serve to highlight that hegemonic systems of rationality create conditions of precarity for trans* bodies.

Commemorative violences

The second section of 'The Woman of Water Dreams' focuses on Transgender Day of Remembrance (TDOR), an event that occurs annually in November with the specific purpose of remembering those killed by transphobic hate-violence. Aoki critically examines its commemorative practices, emphasizing the potential erasures that it can perform. Rather than presenting TDOR as an honoring of the dead, the poem offers a depiction of a commemorative practice in which the names of the deceased are appropriated and erased. Aoki does this firstly through employment of the pastoral convention of pathetic fallacy, likening the commemorated trans* dead to the falling of autumn foliage from deciduous trees (2015: 8). This not only highlights TDOR's placement in the calendar year, but also exploits metaphoric connections between autumn and death.

However, their changing colour also signposts the whitewashing that critics argue can take place at trans* commemorative events, both in the sense of eliding racial backgrounds of the dead; and in the glossing over of less socially acceptable elements of their lives. In her critique of the TDOR archive, Lamble argues that it 'includes no information on age, race, class, ability, or particular circumstances of each individual who was murdered,' which amounts to a 'narrative decoding of racial violence' where 'difference is subsumed within sameness' (2008: 28). This erasure of personal details renders the deceased, in

Lamble's terms, 'decontextualized and reabsorbed within a unified narrative and a universalized body of the dead trans subject' (2008: 28). Aoki's depiction of victims' names as 'sainted' echoes Lamble's suggestion that 'undesirable facts or complex dimensions of identity are often omitted from the story so as to produce a good-victim narrative' (Aoki 2015: 8; Lamble 2008: 27; emphasis author's). Thus, the autumn leaves metaphor symbolizes both the event's potential erasures of race and ethnicity; and the way in which public discourse frames the dead in terms that elide complexities of their identity.

Secondly, as 'mispronounced,' their names are subjected to a spoken violence (Aoki 2015: 8). In the context of education, Carmen Fariña argues that '[m]ispronouncing a student's name essentially renders that student invisible' (2016: para 13). Likewise, in a study of microaggressions in the classroom, Rita Kohli and Daniel Solórzano found that the mispronunciation of a name can impact upon an individual's 'sense of self and worldview' (2012: 19). Aoki's depiction of victims' names as 'mispronounced,' signposts the way in which TDOR unintentionally sustains certain marginalizations and erasures of trans* identities within its commemorative practices (2015: 8). In addition, Aoki emphasizes a tendency for public discourses to subsume trans* deaths under a broader anti-violence banner that fails to recognize the specific brutalities which transphobic hate-violence enacts. The poem criticizes platitudes that condemn 'all hatred' and that serve to draw attention away from the specific issue that an original declaration or gesture is intended to evoke: in this case, that transphobic and transmisogynistic hate-violence is a form of systemic violence targeted at a specific group of people because of who they are (2015: 8). In sum, then, Aoki's poem performs a complex critique of TDOR's commemorative practices, outlining the various erasures, violences and misdirections that are potentially enacted within them.

Further contradictions within these practices are highlighted by juxtaposing images of the 'acceptable' (living) queer body alongside concrete imagery of transphobic violence and death. The poem presents various stereotypes of queer identity as flamboyant and carnivalesque, alongside the figure of an 'almost-tenure-track' professor, whose presence in the poem implies that when certain kinds of queer activism are put in service of cultural capital – such as the advancement of an academic career – their integrity is potentially compromised (Aoki 2015: 10). The figures of 'prophets,' and 'mermaids' gesture towards a concept of queer identity as theorized through a cis-heteropatriarchal academic lens: the former as individuals whose marginalization affords them a unique perspective on the human condition, and the latter as individuals whose uncategorizability is viewed as mirroring mermaid narratives (Aoki 2015: 10).[3] Though these figures have frequently been adopted as positive archetypes by queer and trans* communities, their contiguity with the 'almost-tenure-track' professor gestures towards an appropriation of these figures by liberal and cis-heteropatriarchal channels – i.e., the media and academia – as a means of representing the 'acceptable' queer body to liberal, cis-heteronormative audiences (2015: 10). These figures represent bodies from which, in Lamble's terms, 'undesirable facts or complex dimensions of identity' have been elided (2008: 27).

These complexities are replaced by larger-than-life, festive and caricatural qualities that, in turn, operate in contradistinction to the violent details of broken teeth and jawbones that follow in the poem, which foreground transmisogynistic violence in its concrete reality. Focusing specifically on parts of the mouth, these violent details signpost the way in which transphobic violence operates explicitly as a means of silencing trans* voices. Moreover, as visceral details severed from any individual, history or context within the poem, they echo Lamble's assertion that, through the privileging of 'gruesome details of violence,' TDOR commemorative practices can potentially define trans* bodies only 'by the details of brutality,' which ultimately render the institutional and systemic foundations of that violence invisible (2008: 28).

Depicting the event as '[f]alse lashes and fables,' Aoki gestures towards dynamics of artifice and construction involved in these commemorative practices (2015: 10). Iconographic of exaggerated expressions of femininity, '[f]alse lashes' symbolize embellishment and beautification, while 'fables' indicate the narrativizing of a story that makes a moral point about human nature (Aoki 2015: 10). These symbols imply a constructed image of the deceased in which virtues are enhanced or exaggerated, and in which less socially acceptable qualities are elided. Moreover, as 'fables' rather than facts, it is implied that these deaths are utilized in the service of a larger social narrative (2015: 10). As we have seen in Espinoza's critique of sharing stories of trans women's deaths online, the narrativization of transmisogynistic violence as the act of an individual – rather than as a product of social systems – enables mourners to overlook their own complicity within these systems. And, as in Espinoza's poetic critique, Aoki depicts commemorative practices as a means by which mourners can circumvent their own participation in – or upholding of – conditions that allow transmisogynistic and transphobic violence to take place.

The third section of the poem reflects further upon queer death. It opens with a shift in focus towards the death by suicide of an unnamed individual, referred to in the poem only as 'she' (Aoki 2015: 11). In its simplicity and tragedy, the first line operates as a jolt for the reader, shifting the narrative direction from the commemoration of multiple deaths to the recounting of one that is singular and specific. While the person is described with reference to their unique and particular literary interests – which conflate the magical and otherworldly with the real – repetition of the phrase, 'the way queer folks do,' within the stanza undermines the impact of this shift by depicting the death by suicide in a casual tone as something matter-of-fact, typical, characteristic, or even predictable (2015: 11). The repetition of this phrase serves to render it slogan-like: a repeated motto used by dominant discourses to dismiss behaviours deemed supposedly 'irregular'. In this way, Aoki illustrates for the reader a tendency for queer deaths by suicide to be normalized. Rather than acknowledging the institutional structures of power and violence that contribute to their frequency, this kind of linguistic phrasing serves instead to dismiss death by suicide as somehow characteristic of queerness. Aoki's ironic repetition of the phrase within the poem acts as a means of highlighting how its homogenizing language serves to reaffirm social structures that impose categories of regularity upon individuals and, moreover, sustain conditions that enable homophobic and transphobic violence to take place. By depicting queer death by suicide as something 'normal' or 'regular,' the ironic phrase 'the way queer folks do' reinforces the idea that queer bodies are disposable, and that it is the bodies themselves that are responsible for that disposability (2015: 11).

It is within this section of the poem that we encounter the lines from which the poem's title derives (Aoki 2015: 11). These lines indicate the act of desiring something of which one is deprived, or to which one has no access. Moreover, the lines that follow reflect on various cultural rituals of observation, commemoration and identity: Obon (the Japanese Buddhist custom honoring the spirits of one's ancestors), vigils (the act of Christian devotional watching) and Chanukah (the Jewish day of commemoration) (2015: 12). Within Buddhist funerary practices, water has substantial meaning as the most powerful element, representing longevity as well as the power to give and take life.[4] In Christianity, water represents life and living; while in Judaism the narrative of the desert journey in which water is lacking has led to interpretations of water and its deprivation as an appreciation for the life that God provides. Thus, 'water dreams' might be understood as a specific desire for longevity of life; for being allowed to live and appreciate being alive; and for agency over one's own life and death (Aoki 2015: 11). As we have seen, Mbembe describes necropolitics as a condition in which the state has the 'power and capacity to dictate who is able to live and who must die' (2019: 66). Aoki's 'woman of water dreams' works against this necropolitical condition as a symbol of the desire for autonomy and sovereignty over one's life in the face of systemic erasure and death (2015: 11).

Ohana: familial relations and their failures

Describing the world in corporeal terms – as a body ejaculating, vomiting and imprisoning those who 'live without apology' – Aoki depicts society as a matrix of desire, disgust and fear of lives that transgress normative binaries (2015: 13). The world operates as a space of abjection for trans* individuals, in which their bodies are rejected by 'ohana' with whom they were never acquainted (2015: 13). The Hawaiian word *ohana* – which means 'family', but in a much broader sense than in Western conceptions – is a term that is bound up with Hawaiian Indigenous relationships to environment. As Kekuhi Kealiikanakaoleohaililani and Christian P. Giardina argue, it denotes the 'ability to identify the water source to whom one is related, to embrace as family the natural phenomenon that are part of the organic lived world' (2016: 63–4). Thus, the term *ohana*, understood as 'family', includes not only biological relatives (both alive and deceased), but also – in a non-hierarchical way – certain plants, guardian animals, weather phenomena and geological formations (Kealiikanakaoleohaililani and Giardina 2016: 63). These relationships go beyond Western conceptions of family relations, operating as 'part of natural consciousness' like a kind of 'second sense' (Puku'i and Handy cited in Kealiikanakaoleohaililani and Giardina 2016: 63).

It is also a term bound up with the cycle of life and death, in which 'there is no absolute beginning or finality of ending; there is only the beginning and ending of cycles,' and in which 'there is no forgetting exactly who [one is] biologically, physically, psychologically, and genealogically because [one is] alertly aware of the dynamic continuity of our relationships and these cycles' (Kealiikanakaoleohaililani and Giardina 2016: 63–4). In this way, Aoki's depiction of being rejected by unfamiliar *ohana* signifies not only an exile from familial relationships but a severance from any fixed grounding within the world, as well as a detachment from natural consciousness, from a connection to identity and community, and from a coherent sense of participation in the cycle of life and death. Thus, the 'woman of water dreams' also represents a desire to re-establish these connections; to figuratively re-identify with the metaphorical 'water source to whom one is related' (Kealiikanakaoleohaililani and Giardina 2016: 63). Working against the alienation of necropolitical conditions, it signifies a desire for holistic forms of belonging based on connections with nature, environment, non-human animals, heritage and a less totalizing concept of death than that for which Western discourses allow.

In the fourth section of the poem, themes of family and familial relation are further opened out, beginning with a domestic interaction between the poem's speaker and their mother. The mother's misgendered laments about her 'son' and 'his' wasted life, lack of marriage and ownership of property represent cis-heteronormative ideas of relationships and identities (Aoki 2015: 15). Perceived through this regulating lens, the speaker's life is understood not simply as irregular, but as unproductive and indeterminate: it is 'wasted' because it does not include a career plan, a marriage or the ownership of a home; and it is 'wasted' because it is considered misused in the service of something unknown (i.e. 'Lord-knows-what') (2015: 15). These views reflect Edelman's assertion that displacement and erasure are inevitable for bodies 'that fail to be capitally productive (e.g. engaging in the formal economy) along with failing to be ideologically productive' (2014: 176–7).

In Edelman's view, within a condition of necropolitics, human bodies are 'manipulated and regulated by sovereign powers' in the pursuit of this 'ideological and capital productivity,' and 'bodies that stand in the way of capital productivity' are rendered 'pathological' (2014: 176–7). The speaker's mother represents a necropolitical policing and regulation of the queer body enacted in the space of the family home. Her extreme right-wing conservative views on queerness and trans* identity portray some of the ways in which the erasure and displacement of ideologically and/or capitalistically 'non-productive' bodies play out at the level of the personal (Aoki 2015: 15). For instance, her use of the third-person singular neuter pronoun 'it' to designate gay people not only reflects a refusal of homosexuality and trans* identities but operates as a dehumanizing gesture. As Kate Scott argues, referring to another person using the pronoun 'it' operates as a homophobic slur that associates the subject with 'inanimate objects or animals, rather than with human beings' (2016: 79).

Similarly, the mother's engagement with rumours about 'immigrants and AIDS' signifies a concern for moral panic issues (Aoki 2015: 15). Chas Critcher suggests that moral panics gain frequency 'in times of rapid or unsettling social change' in order to reaffirm 'the basic moral values of society' (2008: 1136). Jeffrey Weeks argues that moral anxieties about AIDS reflect 'deeply rooted fears about the unprecedented rate of change in sexual behaviour and social mores,' while Kenneth Thompson – citing Simon Watney – asserts that they reflect an 'ideological policing of sexuality, especially in the matters of representations'

(Weeks 2010: 83; Thompson 2005: 76). Similarly, Jamie G. Longazel argues that moral panics about immigration are constructions that rely upon 'entrenched racial anxieties and symbolic war-on-crime linkages between racial minorities and criminality' (2012: 97). Such linkages, he suggests – citing Ian Haney López – are 'concerned with protecting the wealth, power, and prestige' of those who possess them (2012: 98). Thus, in the poem the speaker's mother represents the transmission of an anxiety rhetoric that, at its core, seeks to uphold established cis-heteropatriarchal values and police bodies which do not adhere to their parameters. The purpose of this rhetoric – played out at a personal level – is not only to uphold an ideological status quo, but also to sustain the economic power structures that exist within it.

Irregular bodies, irregular selves

Aoki depicts a series of moments that represent temporalities occurring just before an instance of violence takes place: either a rhetorical violence on social media or a physical violence in the street. An instant of anticipatory imminence existing before harm is inflicted, this temporality is characterized by precarity and vulnerability, in which violence is always about to happen. Like that occupied by the cat in the opening of the poem, these temporalities are liminal moments situated between fear and death. By repeatedly occupying these temporalities within the poem, Aoki highlights the constant threat to which trans* bodies are subjected. The poem emphasizes how these violences play out not only within public and virtual spaces, but also within the private and the familial. The theme of precarity that these temporalities embody is taken up and extended later in lines which make reference to Pyotr Ilyich Tchaikovsky, Stirling Dickinson and Henry David Thoreau (Aoki 2015: 18). Historical figures whose sexuality has been the source of speculation in public discourse, and who represent fragility, vulnerability, pathology and erasure, these three men operate as icons of indeterminate or unregulatable identity.

Tchaikovsky's death from cholera was rumoured to have been self-inflicted from knowingly drinking unboiled water, and he has been the subject of much retroactive psychological profiling. As Judith Peraino argues, he has been attributed with 'every kind of psychological malady, including neurosis, hallucinations, depression, mania, psychopathy, split personality, temporary insanity, hysteria, hysteron-epilepsy, and phobia' (2005: 82–3). An example of this unsubstantiated pathology can be found on Wikipedia: one page suggests that Tchaikovsky suffered from a neurosis called the Glass Delusion, in which subjects believe themselves to be breakable like glass (there is no citation to substantiate this and it appears to be based entirely on myth).[5] Moreover, Natalia Minibayeva asserts that Tchaikovsky's music was 'for a long time linked inseparably to a distorted image of his personality,' due to a number of factors including censorship of his biographical materials and inaccessibility to his archive (2014: 164). As a result, 'speculations emerged, ranging from undocumented assertions of insanity to descriptions of an egoism exacerbated by homosexuality' (Minibayeva 2014: 164). In this way, the figure of Tchaikovsky exemplifies a tendency within public discourse to pathologize indeterminate or uncategorizable sexuality.

In the poem – in which he 'litters the asylums' – he is associated with both pathology and chaos; both the words 'litter' and 'asylums' signify disorder, one suggesting a lack of orderliness and the other signifying a site for treating mental distress (Aoki 2015: 18). Tchaikovsky represents the pathologized and ideologically unproductive non-binary body understood *as* litter: as waste requiring disposal. Having failed to be ideologically productive according to hegemonic systems of 'regularity,' he is displaced into the abject space of the asylum in which pathologized individuals – those who disrupt hegemonic conceptions of rationality and reason – are contained.

Alluded to as someone who tears the 'wings' from 'Lady's slipper' orchids, Stirling Dickinson – an artist after whom the Dickinson's lady's slipper orchid (*Cypripedium dicinsonianum*) is named – represents an ambivalent figure in the poem (Aoki 2015: 18). His biographer John Virtue, 'described him as asexual,' despite widespread rumours that he engaged in same-sex partnerships (Pinley Covert 2017: 129–30). In this sense, he represents the retrospective erasure of homosexuality. Further, in the late 1950s, major US newspapers ran stories 'alleging that Dickinson was a threat to national security (a veiled reference to suspected homosexuality at the time)' (Pinley Covert 2017: 130). Thus, Dickinson also represents the queer body conceived of as a threat to the state, or, in Edelman's terms, a body 'marked as ideologically suspect through biopolitical evaluation' (2014: 177). However, in the poem Dickinson is engaged in the violent destruction of a flower known for being difficult to cultivate; he is ripping its petals off as a child might rip the wings off an insect (Aoki 2015: 18). This implies that there is more complexity to his presence than simply representing the erased or displaced queer body.

Pinley Covert asserts that Dickinson was able to dispel the aforementioned newspaper accusations because of his prominence as 'a central figure in San Miguel's international tourism industry,' having the full support of 'political and business leaders from across the state of Guanajuato' (2017: 130–1). As a crucial influence in the promotion of San Miguel as a tourism destination, Dickinson was instrumental in establishing 'an industry that catered to foreign rather than Mexican tastes' (2017: 37). Pinley Covert argues that by privileging 'certain histories, sites, and traditions over others,' this promotion enabled local power to shift 'to those who crafted the narrative,' i.e. to people like Dickinson, who was the director for the *Escuela Universitaria de Bellas Artes*, and to 'those with capital to invest in hotels, restaurants, and shops' (2017: 37–8). Thus, in addition to representing the queer body as erased, or marked as ideologically uncertain, Dickinson also represents colonial occupation – specifically of central Mexico by the United States – particularly if we follow Mbembe's definition of colonial occupation as the 'writing' of 'a new set of social and spatial relations on the ground,' including, but not limited to 'the subversion of existing property arrangements' (2019: 79). Dickinson's violence in the poem – towards a flower named after him – might therefore be read as a gesture towards his complicity in the gentrification of San Miguel de Allende, a spatial restructuring that led to the erasure and displacement of local histories and traditions. In this way, he operates as an ambivalent figure of both queer erasure and ideological suspicion; but also of white colonial power exerted over the Global South.

Finally, Thoreau operates in the poem as a figure of the abjected queer body (Aoki 2015: 18). Henry Abelove outlines how some critics perceived his book, *Walden* as 'disastrous,' because it explicitly rejected normative social values, promoting an eschewal of matrimony and the 'casting off [of] all ties of family,' both of which, at the time, were perceived to be inviolable (1993: 17–18). Moreover, Ralph Waldo Emerson's eulogy to Thoreau sought to repudiate such conceptions of him as a critic of normative values, but in doing so 'assimilated Thoreau to the grand narrative of connubiality [...] which [he] had previously been thought of as disrupting' (Abelove 1993: 19). His question voiced in the poem – 'Where am I' – if read in relation to Emerson's eulogy, emphasizes the displacement performed by subsuming his identity into a narrative of heteronormativity (Aoki 2015: 18). As a means of transforming the identity of an 'irregular' social outsider into one that was more socially acceptable, Emerson's eulogy operates as a form of identity regulation; an act of 'making regular' according to hegemonic value structures. That Thoreau is, in the poem, 'claw[ing]' his articulation in flat lungs alludes to his death from pulmonary tuberculosis or, as it was commonly known at the time, consumption (2015: 18). As a word that suggests an action of fighting-against, to 'claw' implies a struggle with impending death. However, if read as a response to Emerson's eulogy, this clawing action functions as a gesture of fighting against the consumption of his identity within grand narratives of heteronormative matrimony and heterosexual desire; in other words, a gesture of fighting-against the erasure and displacement of his so-called 'irregularity'.

Mbembe argues that '[t]he romance of sovereignty,' upon which necropolitics hinges, 'rests on the belief that the subject is both master and controlling author of [their] own meaning' (2019: 67–8). In the final section of the poem, Aoki highlights how supposedly 'irregular' bodies are not permitted this sovereignty but are instead situated within a paradoxical semantic space constructed by a cis-heteronormative lens (2015: 20). Within this space, the trans* body is inscribed with an excess of meaning that renders it disposable; and, simultaneously, it is subjected to an erasure of meaning that renders that same body invisible. Like the temporalities of 'just before' – where the threat of bodily harm is continuously imminent yet deferred – the poem's final section emphasizes the liminal spaces of precarity which 'irregular' bodies are forced to inhabit. Here, the act of being oneself – i.e. unapologetically expressing one's irregularity – requires a giving up of power to forces of disorder (represented here by an image of quantum chaos). The word 'cede' echoes lines in the second section in which the names of trans* people are 'ceded to anonymous candles' in the commemorative practices of TDOR (Aoki 2015: 18; 8). Thus, expressing the 'irregular' self necessitates a surrender to the possibility of death, and through that death, anonymity.

Conceived in this way, the act of being oneself unapologetically within cis-heteropatriarchal hegemony is, in one sense, to be already dead. Thus, Aoki's temporalities of 'just before' are analogous to Mbembe's *'death-worlds,'* in which certain marginalized populations occupy a 'status of the *living dead*' (2019: 92; emphasis author's). However, as Edelman argues, '[e]ven within [...] barren death worlds [...] fissures can be wrenched open through which vitality, and life, emerge' (2014: 187). Aoki's poem also operates as this kind of fissure, wrenching open necropolitical spaces of precarity to allow life to emerge. The cat's survival and the giving over of one's power to 'butterflies' and 'baryons' are images of vitality and life, resistant to the erasures and displacements of so-called 'irregularity' which processes of identity regulation enact (Aoki 2015: 20). Like the irrational numbers in its opening and closing sections, 'The Woman of Water Dreams' explicitly refuses to 'resolve' into a singular monolithic narrative (2015: 20). Rather, the poem works against the structures of so-called rationality it critiques, resisting the violence that systems of 'making sense' perform (2015: 20).

Body as site of colonial struggle: Qwo-Li Driskill's 'Pedagogy'

Cherokee Two-Spirit poet, activist and scholar Qwo-Li Driskill's poem 'Pedagogy' – anthologized in *Sovereign Erotics: A Collection of Two-Spirit Literature* – has two epigraphs: the first from 'Highway 126' by Deborah Miranda (an Ohlone-Costanoan Esselen Nation of California, Chumash and Jewish poet and scholar); and the second from 'Crazy Grandpa Whispers' by Chrystos (a Menominee lesbian and Two-Spirit poet and lecturer) (Driskill et al. 2011: 182–4).

Miranda's poem, dedicated to her partner Margo Solod, is from the collection *The Zen of La Llorona*. It explores the practice of healing using natural herbs and medicines. Driskill's epigraphic inclusion of Miranda's lines thus situates 'Pedagogy' within a thematic sphere of healing and recovery. Chrystos's poem, from their collection *Not Vanishing*, enacts a dialogue between an ancestral Indigenous American voice calling for active resistance to settler colonialism and the voice of the poem's speaker, who responds by arguing that such resistance leads either to institutionalization or incarceration (Chrystos 1988: 1). In this way, Driskill's epigraphical inclusion of Chrystos's lines situates 'Pedagogy' within a discussion of how to effectively resist – and survive – white imperialist and colonial violence, within a context that forecloses the possibility of such resistance. From the outset, then, Driskill's poem uses queer and Two-Spirit voices to position hir poem within a context of healing from – and resistance against – white colonial violence.[6]

The poem begins with a catalogue of bodily damages. The speaker's journey to work is characterized by worry, specifically about family illnesses and precarities: cancer, gallstones, hepatitis C, depression, HIV, carbon monoxide poisoning, toxic air pollution, and the possibility that loved ones will be killed or injured by, among other people, the police (Driskill et al. 2011: 183). It is an overwhelming itemization of the material conditions of precarity to which Indigenous American bodies – and more specifically, Two-Spirit bodies – are subjected. The list implicitly gestures towards lack of access to adequate physical and mental healthcare; to below-standard living conditions; to environmental pollution; to physical and verbal abuse; and to a lack of protection provided by – and an antagonistic threat from – aggressive law enforcement. The preface to Chrystos's *Not Vanishing* lists similar material conditions to which Indigenous American communities are subjected.

Butler defines precarity as a 'politically induced condition in which certain populations suffer from failing social and economic networks of support and become differentially exposed to injury, violence, and death' (2009: ii). Moreover, '[s]tructural forms of violence take their toll on the body, wearing the body down, de-constituting its corporeal existence' (Butler 2020; 138). Both Driskill's and Chrystos's lists emphasize forms of precarity that correspond with Butler's definitions and descriptions. The worries that build in Driskill's poem catalogue the somatic and psychological effects of enduring both economic and physical precarity, sketching a nexus of precarities within which the Indigenous American body is situated. Butler further emphasizes that the construction of social institutions takes place in part as a means of lessening conditions of precarity to ensure that 'populations have the means available by which life can be secured' (2009: ii). Driskill's catalogue of bodily damages embodies Butler's assertion that when 'certain populations suffer from failing social and economic networks of support,' they are 'at heightened risk of disease, poverty, starvation, displacement, and of exposure to violence without protection' (2009: ii).

It is, according to Butler, those who 'live their genders' in ways that are not 'intelligible' according to normative standards who are at 'heightened risk' of precarity through violence and harassment (2009: ii-iii). In 'Stolen From Our Bodies,' Driskill writes of 'people like me [who] are routinely killed,' citing the violent hate-motivated murders of Two-Spirit individuals F.C. Martinez Jr. and Amy Soos, twenty-five-year-old Hopi trans woman Alejandro Ray Lucero and twenty-one-year-old trans man Brandon Teena (2004: 56). Denoting an expression of gender, the term *Two-Spirit* cannot be understood in terms of cis-heteropatriarchal binary categories or aligned with identities represented by terms such as 'LGBTQ' and 'queer'. The term, Driskill asserts, designates not just one category of gender, but several tribal categories that exist outside of European concepts of gender (2010: 72). As an 'intentionally complex' term, it is intended to be 'inclusive, ambiguous, and fluid,' deliberately challenging the 'labels and taxonomies' of the 'white-dominated GLBTQ community' (2010: 72-3). Unlike European constructions of identity, it is a term that is 'intimately connected to land, community, and history,' and further it is bound up with an understanding of 'the ways colonial projects continually police sexual and gender lines' (2010: 72-3).

The material precarities and violences visited upon Indigenous American bodies in Driskill's poem cannot be understood as separate from the violent erasures and displacements enacted upon Indigenous American expressions of gender by European systems of categorization. These erasures and displacements are rooted in British and US colonial history, as Driskill outlines in *Asegi Stories*.

As part of a plan whose purpose was to take over jurisdiction of Indigenous lands and create communities that could be assimilated under British political control, Indigenous systems of gender were characterized by these colonial powers as 'deficient,' 'savage,' 'backward' and 'perverse' (Driskill 2016: 76–7; 82–3). The displacement of individuals from their communities to a British-controlled plantation culture operated as a means of interrupting Indigenous systems of gender in order to 'recenter a heteropatriarchal family structure, and transform Native people into British subjects' (Driskill 2016: 82–3). Disregarding Indigenous identities, British colonialists mapped their own accounts of gender and sexuality onto Indigenous bodies (Driskill 2016: 75–6). This mapping operated as a biopolitical means of realizing the colonization of Indigenous land (Driskill 2016: 89, 124–5). Thus, Driskill's catalogue of contemporary Indigenous American somatic and psychological precarities in the poem must be understood in the context of these colonial and biopolitical erasures and displacements.

The historical erasure of Indigenous gender identities – in which Two-Spirit identities were *'rendered invisible'* through the mapping and rewriting of Indigenous bodies by colonial heteropatriarchy – operates as the foundation upon which contemporary conditions of precarity are built (Driskill 2016: 89; emphasis author's). By describing 'marks' and 'scars' obtained in conflicts fought 'on and over' Indigenous American bodies, Driskill highlights not only these historical struggles for colonial power, but also the way in which these struggles are inscribed upon the body (Driskill et al. 2011: 183). We can read these lines in relation to Mbembe's description of the colony as 'a site in which [...] "peace" is more likely to assume the face of "endless war"' and in which 'the political [...] under the guise of war' inscribes certain human bodies within the order of power (2019: 76; 66). The 'marks' and 'scars' in the poem represent both a literal inscription of war upon the body and a figurative representation of the psychological effects of deracination and erasure. In 'Stolen From Our Bodies,' Driskill describes how the ideological enforcement of a 'colonized sexuality' renders Indigenous American non-binary genders 'degraded, ignored, condemned and destroyed' (2004: 54). Hir assertion that Indigenous American sexualities 'harbor bruises left by a white supremacist culture,' emphasizes an understanding of sexuality both as part of the body and as having sustained a bodily injury (2004: 54). Colonial heteropatriarchy's ideological erasure of Indigenous genders is a violence that 'marks' and 'scars' bodies in the same way as do the toxic effects of economic precarity and the brutalities of hate-motivated violence.

Material precarity in the classroom

The poem's title refers to the practice of teaching as well as to the theory and principles of education. The speaker of the poem is an educator and the poem in large part addresses a student, or a constituency of students, who experience a similar level of economic and physical precarity. In the same way that the speaker catalogues various worries about familial illness and economic hardship, the addressed student is also concerned about their mother's cancer treatment and the metastasis of cancer cells in her lungs (Driskill et al. 2011: 183). The similarities between their concerns establish between them a level of familiarity, intimacy and solidarity that goes beyond standard student–teacher relationships. They are connected through shared worries about the material realities that their precarious living conditions produce: how to afford food and what to do about family illnesses. In this way, Driskill's address goes beyond that of the didact or the Socratic, offering pastoral care that extends beyond the classroom.

In the poem, these material realities are situated in contradistinction to the abstract discussions that take place within that classroom. By contrasting these different forms of engagement with precarity – lived experience vs. abstract discussion – Driskill highlights the disparity between them; they are discrete, disconnected and do not permeate one another. In the poem, the classroom is characterized as focusing on Aristotelian modes of persuasion – *ethos*, *pathos* and *logos* – rhetorical devices used to construct arguments. *Ethos* draws upon an audience's shared moral values and attitudes; *pathos* draws upon an audience's emotions, particularly sadness and empathy; while *logos* draws upon data and statistics to persuade – or mislead – an audience (Driskill et al. 2011: 183). The fear articulated in the poem's opening – of harm and verbal abuse that may be suffered by the speaker's loved ones – clearly emphasizes how moral values are not shared within society, and gestures towards the way in which both emotions and statistics can be manipulated to produce hate and violence.

The classroom is also characterized by the student's need to use words like 'power,' 'privilege,' 'oppression' and 'binary': crucial terms for understanding discourses of Feminism, Queer Theory, Gender and Critical Race Studies (Driskill et al. 2011: 183). Like Aristotelian modes of persuasion, these words represent means by which conditions of precarity are understood in theoretical rather than material terms. Specifically, they represent the linguistic means by which the material lived experiences of precarity are abstracted for the purposes of academic discussion. Like Espinoza's critique of sharing stories of trans women's deaths online, and Aoki's depiction of the professor 'in the new Queer Studies Department,' Driskill's listing of these theoretical terms gestures towards a tendency – particularly within academic spaces – to understand precarity only in abstract terms (Aoki 2015: 10).

Driskill emphasizes this disparity – between material conditions of precarity and the academic spaces in which they are discussed – in questions that ask what the classroom has to do with anyone experiencing these conditions (2011: 183). In hir article 'Doubleweaving Two-Spirit Critiques,' Driskill highlights the way in which Indigenous American voices – and the ongoing conditions of colonial heteropatriarchy – are systematically unseen in 'scholarly and political consciousness and imagination,' including within queer critiques that seek to be inclusive in their scope (2010: 78). Indigenous peoples are 'constantly disappeared through the stories that non-Native people tell, or don't tell' (Driskill 2010: 79). Thus, as a site of learning and knowledge, the classroom is not an impartial and objective pedagogical space, but a locus in which erasures of Indigenous histories and subjectivities – and the histories of colonial violence – continue to take place. Indeed, in the context of Indigenous American history, the classroom is an explicitly colonial space. The House Concurrent Resolution 108 implemented in 1953 was a policy that forced Indigenous students to attend boarding schools run by the Bureau of Indian Affairs, as a means of 'rapidly assimilat[ing] them into mainstream society' (Tighe 2014: 8). These means of enforced assimilation included not only the prohibition of Indigenous American languages in favour of English, but also numerous abuses including the forced cutting of hair, an important part of Indigenous identity. The classroom, then, is not an apolitical space but rather a site in which colonial struggles continue to play out. It is a space that privileges Eurocentric learning while erasing Indigenous American histories.

Driskill's poem emphasizes that, for Indigenous Americans, inhabiting the classroom has less to do with knowledge and more to do with survival. The poem's speaker explains that their own presence in the classroom stems from an economic need, specifically one driven by food poverty (Driskill et al. 2011: 184). The student, on the other hand, is in the classroom because it offers a means of survival against a nation 'whose tongue yearns' for their 'blood' (Driskill et al. 2011: 184). Driskill's metaphor depicts the United States as a predatory and vampiric figure. It resembles Mark Neocleous's reading of vampire metaphors in the writing of Karl Marx, which represent state authority and its capitalist economic and political systems living vampire-like on living labour and 'capitalized blood' (Marx cited in Neocleous 2003: 669–70). Moreover, it resembles what Mbembe describes as 'the power of capital' as a 'bloody process of devouring' (2019: 14). Specifically, Driskill's metaphor depicts the United States as thirsting for, and feeding from, the blood of Indigenous Americans. As in Edelman's formulation of necrocapitalism – in which bodies that are considered ideologically unproductive are rendered pathological – Driskill's metaphor gestures towards the way in which Indigenous American bodies are understood by necrocapitalistic ideologies as unproductive and are therefore rendered pathological through socially and structurally enforced material conditions of precarity (Edelman 2014: 177).

Driskill's nation-as-vampire metaphor also flips common interpretations of the vampire figure on its head. Neocleous – citing Donna Haraway – outlines how vampire metaphors are often used to designate otherness, ambiguity, shifting identity, a crisis of categorization, a disruption of 'the usual rules of interaction' and the 'politics of identity' (2003: 673). He describes how in cultural studies, the figure of the vampire is interpreted as representing 'oppressed and marginalized groups,' including 'transgressive sexuality' (2003: 673). In Driskill's metaphor, however, it is the colonizer nation who is 'other'. Through violent so-called 'civilization' projects, deracination, the stealing of land, policing of bodies and the prohibition of languages and traditions, it is the nation-state that represents disruption to the 'usual rules of interaction' (Neocleous 2003: 673).

Nation as carceral space; nation as predator

In Driskill's poem, the nation is not only a vampire-like predator but also a prison. The speaker prays that the student will be able to smuggle out from the classroom words as if they are concealed weapons; just as a makeshift shank or shiv functions as a means of escape from a hostile prison environment. And the speaker hopes that they might learn how to 'saw' their way through the 'iron bars' of the country (Driskill et al. 2011: 184). In this second metaphor, Driskill portrays the country as a prison-industrial-complex writ large; a carceral space on a national scale.

Despite being 'subject to more violent crime than any other US ethnic group,' Indigenous Americans have the highest incarceration rate (Tighe 2014: 2; 12). Indigenous American activist Stormy Ogden describes this disproportionately high rate as 'genocidal' (2014: 64). Economic inequality – in 2014, 27 per cent of Indigenous Americans lived below the poverty line compared with 11.6 per cent of white Americans – and its attendant effects, such as 'lack of educational opportunities, high unemployment, permanent residency issues, homelessness, mental illness, substance abuse, and geographic isolation' are key contributory factors here; as are 'racist practices in arrest, conviction, and sentencing patterns' (Davis 1998: para 6; Tighe 2014: 2). Two-Spirit individuals also face a high risk of incarceration because of their non-binary gender identities. As Rosenberg and Oswin have asserted, trans* individuals are 'incarcerated at a disproportionately high rate' (2015: 1269–70). Thus, Driskill's depiction of the United States as a prison not only situates itself within a nexus of intersecting oppressions, but gestures towards the fact that incarceration is a very real risk for those who occupy this nexus. As weapons with which they might cut through the 'iron bars' of the nation, language in Driskill's poem operates as a means of escaping that potential reality (Driskill et al. 2011: 184).

Moreover, Rosenberg and Oswin's sketch of carceral spaces – in which 'gender regulation is a standard element of social control,' and in which non-binary individuals are subjected to 'severe harassment, medical neglect, and violence' – echoes the physical and mental family illnesses, concerns about police violence and verbal harassment earlier in the poem (Rosenberg and Oswin 2015: 1277; Dean Spade cited in Rosenberg and Oswin 2015: 1273). In this way, Driskill's metaphor of the United States as a prison casts the nation as a macrocosm of the penal institution. Regardless of whether literally incarcerated within the US prison system, Indigenous American bodies – and, in particular, Two-Spirit bodies – are already figuratively incarcerated by colonial and heteropatriarchal hierarchies that operate within society.

It is also worth noting that the US prison-industrial complex is dependent on the dispossession of Indigenous land for its existence. Stephanie Lumsden argues that – along with the settler fiction of *Terra Nullius*, which understood colonized Indigenous American land as 'unowned' – it was in large part the 'capitalist treatment of land as a natural resource for economic development,' which led to the systematic erasure of Indigenous communities and their land (2017: para 3). When that land later lost value due to shifts in global markets, it became 'a convenient place for the state to invest in prison building' (Lumsden 2017: para 3). Thus, in Lumsden's view, it is only because of the appropriation of Indigenous American land that a prison-industrial complex is able to exist. In this sense, Driskill's metaphor highlights how, through its capitalist colonial history, the United States is wholly defined by its carceral qualities which are written into the very land upon which it exists.

Moreover, Davis argues that the prison-industrial complex offers a means by which the 'social problems that burden people who are ensconced in poverty' may be concealed from public view (1998: para 1). Issues such as '[h]omelessness, unemployment, drug addiction, mental illness, and illiteracy' within marginalized communities are 'solved' by incarcerating large numbers of these populations within penal infrastructures (Davis 1998: para 1). Thus, Driskill's characterization of the United States as a prison gestures towards the necropolitical condition in which Indigenous Americans are subjected to systematic structural erasures from public discourse that condemn them 'to disposability' (Aizura 2014: 130-1).

In the final lines of the poem, Driskill returns to a metaphor of the nation as a vampire-like predator; a country lying in wait for Indigenous American bodies with 'teeth' recently 'sharpened' (Driskill et al. 2011: 184). As Theodor Adorno writes of predators in *Negative Dialectics*, hunger is not enough of a motivating factor for attacking prey; predators require 'additional impulses,' which 'fuse into rage at the victim, a rage whose expression in turn serves the end of frightening and paralyzing the victim' (2004: 22). This predatory rage – Adorno argues – is 'rationalized by projection'; as he later outlines, 'the animal to be devoured must be evil,' or rather, rationalized as evil to justify the devouring (2004: 22). Driskill's metaphor depicts white imperialist America as embodying this fusion of desire to consume and its synthesis with rationalization; a rage based on colonial idealism (2011: 184).

In another sense, the metaphor depicts the nation as what KC Councilor calls an 'eating body politic,' in which Indigenous American bodies are consumed and digested by the national body, which is itself a representation of the 'ideal (white) citizen body' (2017: 140, 142). As Councilor argues, metaphors of digestion within a context of national rhetoric emphasize assimilation; the process of 'making one element like another' (2017: 141). Thus, Driskill's metaphor gestures not only towards the figurative consumption of Indigenous American bodies through violence, but also towards the ways in which Indigenous cultures are erased in order that Indigenous American bodies might be assimilated into a US body politic, synecdochally represented by the white American body (Councilor 2017: 146).

Contained within Driskill's compounding of predator and prison metaphors is the implication that the apostrophized Indigenous American student has the potential to refuse the role of prey within this Adornoian predator–prey dynamic, or the role of food within Councilor's 'eating body politic' (2017: 140). The word 'sharpened' in Driskill's depiction of the United States as a nation with 'teeth' echoes the figuration of language as 'sharpened spoons,' with which they might escape literal or figurative carceral spaces (Driskill et al. 2011: 184). Language, then, may afford a potential means of protection against the nation's predatory attacks. We might understand the poem's title – 'Pedagogy' – as designating that the poem itself performs an act of teaching. But Driskill refuses to present the academic classroom as a simple and straightforward means of escape from the material conditions of precarity; it is unable to 'save' either the addressed student/s or the Indigenous American communities that Driskill's use of the pronoun 'us' implies (Driskill et al. 2011: 184).

The poem designates the classroom not as a politically neutral level playing field, but as a space of colonial struggle that can offer only conditional protections through the implementation of language as a weapon. Unlike Miranda's epigraph, Driskill's own poem is less about the possibility of healing and more concerned with educating readers about the material conditions of illness and precarity that Indigenous Americans are subjected to because of white colonial heteropatriarchal structures. Like Chrystos's poem, it addresses the possibility of survival within a context that forecloses possibilities of resistance. The economic and physical precarities – and the allusions to incarceration within the poem – highlight the ways in which Indigenous American bodies are condemned 'to disposability' (Aizura 2014: 130–1). In this way, 'Pedagogy' articulates what it is like to embody a necropolitical condition; to be 'marked for death' within a system that does not adequately offer protection from harm and sufficient means for survival (Haritaworn, Kuntsman and Posocco 2014: 20).

Towards some conclusions

Each of these three poems addresses issues of precarity. Espinoza's poem is concerned with the physical and ontological precarities that trans women face living under threat of hate-motivated violence and murder. Aoki's poem repeatedly occupies temporalities of precarity. And Driskill's poem addresses economic and material precarities to which Indigenous Americans are subjected. Similarly, each of the poems confronts issues of erasure. Espinoza's poem highlights the erasive dynamics of aestheticization, romanticization and dehumanization that exist in the act of sharing stories of trans women's deaths online. Aoki's poem critiques erasures that take place in trans* commemorative practices like TDOR; forms of language used to erase the particularities of queer individuals who die by suicide; and the incremental everyday erasures that trans* people experience in public and private spaces. Driskill's poem highlights the structural erasure of Indigenous American bodies through incarceration within the US penal system; and the erasure of Indigenous American history in academic spaces.

Moreover, each of the poems addresses issues of abstraction. Espinoza's poem is concerned with the abstraction of trans women's bodies; and the poem turns that abstractive dynamic back towards a reader implicated as complicit with heteropatriarchal structures. Aoki's poem examines the abstractions within public trans* commemorative mourning practices; as well as the abstraction of queer identities in carnivalesque and flamboyant representations of queerness. Driskill's poem critiques the ways in which material conditions of precarity are abstracted in the classroom through rhetorical language. Finally, each of these poems draws attention to the necropolitical conditions in which queer and trans* bodies are 'marked for death'; considered 'not worth protecting, saving or grieving'; or dehumanized and rendered disposable because they are not considered capitally or ideologically productive according to necrocapitalistic ideas (Aizura 2014: 130–1; Edelman 2014: 176–7; Haritaworn, Kuntsman and Posocco 2014: 20). In other words, they each gesture towards 'contemporary forms of subjugating life to the power of death' (Mbembe 2019: 92).

Despite these shared threads, these connections should not be read as delineating a monolithic trans* narrative or depicting a unitary trans* experience of grief, loss, mourning or death. As Eli R. Green states, to assume there is 'only one "trans-politic"' fails to acknowledge 'the diversity of trans culture and politics' (2006: 240). And, as McQueen argues, it is critical that important differences between trans* identities are not denied or erased (2016: 672–3). Instead, these commonalities of theme and concordant structures of thought operate as potential strands of dialogue between three very different poetic articulations, each of which affords an understanding of the various intersectional oppressions to which trans* individuals are subjected. Following Bettcher, we might understand them as representing 'multiple worlds of sense,' in which terms like 'precarity,' 'abstraction' and 'erasure' have different and nuanced meanings (2014: 403).

What these poems signpost for elegy scholarship is the exclusion and marginalization of trans* voices within genealogical constructions; and the inadequacy of a gendered binary as a means of categorizing and understanding elegies. As Driskill emphasizes, academic analyses that adhere to binaries of sexuality and gender 'risk colluding with master narratives' (2010: 75). As we have seen in the previous chapter, marginalized voices cannot simply be assimilated into genealogical constructions that understand a tradition of elegy as Eurocentric, heteropatriarchal, linear and chronological. This misleading representation of elegy operates, to borrow again from Driskill, as a 'colonial project' whose purpose is to sustain the marginalization of certain voices (2010: 84).

Rethinking elegy beyond genealogical constructions, we might call upon the theoretical approaches outlined in this chapter as a means of circumventing the totalizing gestures and taxonomic categorizations upon which genealogical formations rely. For instance, applying Corsani and Murphy's perspectives on gender binaries allows us to reimagine genealogical constructions themselves – and their reliance on principles of whiteness, patriarchy and heteronormativity – as 'political regimes': means of asserting political authority and control governing whose elegies are read, studied and critically examined; and how they are interpreted (2007: 108). To move beyond a 'logic of binary oppositions' in understanding elegy would enable the inclusion of a 'heterogenous multiplicity' of subjectivities, reflecting 'several worlds in contradictory ways,' and thereby allowing for a fuller representation of the intersecting oppressions at work within the context of individual elegies (2007: 110, 113). Such an approach would need to be rhizomatic in nature; which is to say, non-hierarchical, nonlinear and resistant to chronological and narrative organizational structures. Unlike genealogies, which map out a tradition as an arborescent sequence of literary inheritances, this would require the rejection of such narrative configurations.

We might also envision elegy as subject to 'continual remakings' – as in Butler's conception of gender – in which conventions are unstable and changeable; and in which 'permutations,' and transgressions are part of a continually shifting mode (2004: 42). Or equally, as in Bettcher's analysis, we might recognize 'multiple worlds of sense' within elegy, in which different terms – including gendered terms, but also, for instance, diverse and nuanced expressions of loss and mourning – have different and resistant meanings (2014: 403). These perspectives offer elegy scholarship the possibility of opening up spaces that do not exclude and marginalize voices designated as 'other' by and within genealogical constructions. They facilitate the possibility of a nuanced, rhizomatic approach to elegy, in which connections are nonlinear and non-hierarchical; in which voices are multiplicitous and heterogenous; in which terms (gendered or otherwise) are fluid and unstable; and which establish no definitive chronological origin or end point.

Notes

1. The umbrella term trans* (with an asterisk) refers here to individuals or groups who are not cisgender, and includes, among others, non-binary, genderqueer, agender, third gender, bi-gender, gender-non-conforming and Two-Spirit identities.
2. As in, for instance, trans women, transfeminine or bi-gender individuals.
3. See, for instance, Hurley (2014); Spencer (2014); and Hayward (2017).
4. See Margaret Gouin (2012: 49; 106) for more on this.
5. Available online: https://en.wikipedia.org/wiki/Glass_delusion (accessed 6 May 2021). Though Wikipedia is by its own admission not a reliable source for academic research, the page has nonetheless been accessed by over 130,000 people over the last four years (Data based on Wikipedia's own pageview analysis as of 18 January 2021). For more on the Glass Delusion, see Gill Speak (1990).
6. Hir is Driskill's preferred pronoun.

4

Anti-museum, anti-archive and personal elegy: Writing the human back into being

As we have seen in the previous chapters, the understanding of elegy as a genealogy which is both Eurocentric and arborescent – that is, predicated on principles of literary descent and inheritance – enables the erasure of important socio-historical and contextual factors. If we destabilize this genealogical model, and the white, patriarchal and heteronormative thought structures upon which it relies, the question remains: what other, alternative potential approaches might elegy scholarship adopt?

In the previous chapter, we explored how drawing on trans*feminist and queer theories enables a reconsideration of elegy as a mode that is fluid, non-hierarchical, nonlinear and rhizomatic. In resistance to chronological, narrative and binary organizational structures that have a specific origin and end point, we might consider elegy – borrowing from Corsani and Murphy's approach to gender and identity – as an assemblage or a collection of assemblages. Following Butler, we might consider these assemblages as characterized by constant transformation and remaking. This reconsideration of elegy requires a rejection of what Mbembe terms 'abstract universalism'; the rhetorical assumption that white, cis-masculine and heterosexual subjectivities reflect universal experience and/or that these subjectivities constitute a standard against which all other experiences might be measured (2019: 9). As a mode, then, elegy might be understood, not as a fixed and static form or genre, but a continually evolving poetic mood adopted in a wide variety of contexts by a range of poets of various identities.

Undoubtedly, this approach will appear to some, in comparison with the genealogical model, somewhat nebulous and inexplicit; in short, intellectually fuzzy. But it is worth emphasizing that the supposedly straightforward and clear-cut delineations of the genealogical model are not factual but constructed. And it is those constructions which have facilitated and enabled the exclusion and marginalization of work by writers of colour, women writers and trans* writers from the so-called 'tradition'. In order to rethink scholarly approaches to elegy, perhaps a little healthy ambiguity and nuance is useful, even necessary.

Mbembe's concept of the anti-museum provides a helpful model for thinking through alternative approaches to elegy beyond the genealogical. He argues that the museum is a 'powerful device of separation,' which has 'not always been an unconditional place of reception for the multiple faces of humanity taken in its unity' (2019: 171). Within its parameters, 'subjugated or humiliated humanities' have been 'assigned different and unequal symbolic statuses' (2019: 171). They are, he argues, spaces of 'neutralization and domestication of forces' (2019: 172). He further asserts that the inclusion of the figure of the slave within museum spaces reinforces and sanctifies separations and inequalities upon which they are ideologically founded (2019: 171). We might draw a comparison here between this critique of the museum space and Morrison's critique of a white literary establishment's inclusion of Black writing as a 'gathering of a culture's difference into the skirts of the Queen,' effecting a 'neutralization' whose purpose is to sustain racial hierarchies (1988: 134). What both perspectives critique are the ways in which hegemonic institutional structures are unable, in their existing form, to hold space for 'subjugated or humiliated humanities' in any meaningful way, precisely because that current form is based on 'difference, hierarchy, and inequality' (Mbembe 2019: 171). This is, in essence, a similar point to that which this book has sought to make about genealogical formations of elegy: that they are unable, in their current structure, to make meaningful space for elegies written by writers of colour, women writers and trans* writers because of principles of whiteness, patriarchy and heteronormativity upon which they are based.

In resistance to the museum, Mbembe envisages the *anti-museum*, which he describes as 'the figure of another place, one of radical hospitality' (2019: 172). It is a space whose purpose is explicitly to sustain and safeguard the 'slave's spectral dimension,' providing the means for 'its apparitions' to exist by 'breaking and entering,' and through haunting and absence (2019: 172). For Mbembe, this is the anti-museum's key purpose – a means of holding and preserving conceptual space for the figure of the slave – and for this reason, it cannot be adopted wholesale as a model for rethinking approaches to elegy. But Mbembe's resistant anti-museum space nonetheless provides a helpful paradigm; a conceptual framework for considering what an anti-genealogical approach might look like. The anti-museum is, at one and the same time, both an institutional and non-institutional space; or, rather, it is an institutional space that does not, by inclusion, make its exhibits 'of the institution'. In a similar way, anti-genealogical approaches to elegy might hold space for elegiac work without drawing it into a genealogical whole; without incorporating it into a so-called 'tradition'; without calcifying it into an established arborescent order or taxonomy. The anti-museum not only centres 'subjugated and humiliated humanities,' but also the 'history that the concept of archive struggles to contain' (2019: 171–2). For Mbembe, archives produce 'a specular device'; they reflect gendered and racialized 'fantasies' that, in turn, produce concrete realities (2019: 173). Anti-genealogical approaches might equally centre excluded and marginalized voices; and challenge realities produced by the white imaginary, the patriarchal imaginary and the heteronormative imaginary.

Finally, the anti-museum is a space of 'radical hospitality' (Mbembe 2019: 9). As such, it is underpinned by a progressive re-understanding of the relationship between museum and exhibitor/exhibit, as analogous to that between a guest and a host. While there are obvious problems with reading Mbembe's concept through the lens of a European thinker (particularly given his critique of understanding the archive as belonging to Europe), it is nonetheless useful to consider 'radical hospitality' in relation to Jacques Derrida's writing on the meaning of hospitality, to understand how it might be interpreted and implemented.

Derrida highlights the 'aporia,' or 'limitation' that exists within the 'self-contradictory concept' of hospitality, namely that it is predicated upon a condition that the host 'remains the *patron*, the master of the household, on the condition that he maintains his own authority' (2000: 4–5; emphasis his). Hospitality, he argues, enacts a 'folding [of] the foreign other into the internal law of the host,' which is – in the 'Indo-European history of hospitality' – the 'law of the household, domestic lineage, family' (2000: 7; 13). Dependent upon an understanding of the 'other as stranger,' it is predicated upon 'circles of conditionality that are family, nation, state, and citizenship' (2000: 8). While we cannot know, according to Derrida, what hospitality truly is, its meaning is underpinned by an unequal relationship of host and guest, which bears similarities both to the relationship Mbembe critiques between museum and exhibitor/exhibit, and to the relationship between the canon of traditional elegy (as white, patriarchal, Eurocentric/Anglo-American and centred upon the 'English elegy') and elegies by writers not included within that 'tradition'. This unequal relationship is conditioned by the understanding that one party (the host) has ownership over the space into which the other (the guest) is welcomed or invited, and that party, therefore by extension, has authority over the rules that determine that space. From the outset, Derrida argues, hospitality 'governs the threshold – and hence it forbids in some way even what it seems to allow to […] pass across it' (2000: 14). Thus, hospitality, as Derrida describes it, also defines the relational dynamics of the museum and the elegy, if we understand those curating the museum or the elegiac tradition as occupying the position of the 'host'; and the exhibitor/exhibit or elegist of colour, trans* elegist or woman elegist as occupying the position of the 'guest'.

How, then, might we understand *radical* hospitality? Firstly, we must differentiate between radical hospitality and what Ilsup Ahn describes as 'soft hospitality': namely kindness, tolerance, generosity or acceptance (2010: 258). It is also, in the context discussed here, distinct from the Christian theological meaning Ahn proposes, as modelled on the concepts of forgiveness and 'invisible debt' (2010: 258). *Radical* hospitality, as described here, is not simply about literally or figuratively 'welcoming strangers'. It is, rather, a troubling – or, indeed, a reinvention – of the unequal relation between guest and host (and, by extension, museum and exhibitor/exhibit; and elegiac 'tradition' and elegy/elegist). It is a disturbance of the concept of host as owner, master or sovereign of space; a disruption to the laws of 'household' and 'domestic lineage'; and to the 'circles of conditionality' that define hospitality (Derrida 2000: 13; 8). In other words, it is an upturning of the guest–host relation whereby the guest (or, exhibitor/exhibit; elegy/elegist) does not require an invitation into the space; can enact a transformation upon the space; and has a stake in the ownership of it. Much like Derrida's description of the visitation, '[a]nyone can come at any time and can come in without needing a key to the door. There are no customs checks with a visitation' (2000: 14). It is, in other words, characterized by an elimination of the threshold and the internal laws of ownership and lineage that define traditional hospitality. We might also say that it is a space in which the so-called 'foreign other' is neither 'foreign,' nor 'other,' because the space itself is defined by a constellation of multiple othernesses and commonalities (Derrida 2000: 7).

These proposals towards rethinking approaches to elegy beyond genealogical models are, by necessity, tentative, exploratory and speculative. The focus of this book has been to interrogate and destabilize the genealogical model and the principles that underpin it; in short, to highlight why ways of rethinking elegy are necessary. Having critiqued singular, clear-cut and definitive constructions as a part of its project, it would be disingenuous to consequently offer a singular, clear-cut and definitive solution. This book is a small part of a much broader conversation that includes a huge number of initiatives, projects and social actions that are challenging and disrupting white supremacist, patriarchal and heteronormative systems, including struggles to decolonize curricula and syllabi, heritage, museum spaces, libraries, archives and literary canons.

Rather than ending this book with the kind of totalizing gesture it has so far critiqued, these tentative, exploratory and speculative ideas are put into practice in the examination of three elegies presented under the rubric of personal elegy. These elegies were chosen for their resistance to necropoetical themes as outlined in the introduction: the principles, precepts and techniques which serve to determine whose lives are publicly grievable, namely whiteness, patriarchal forms of masculinity and heteronormative binaries (including the trope of emotional restraint). These elegies are brought into contiguity here through analysis in order to constitute an assemblage of grieving subjectivities. There is no attempt, in other words, to unify them according to an organizing principle other than that they each deal with personal losses of one kind or another. They represent voices that, in genealogical constructions of elegy, have historically been underrepresented, marginalized or excluded: Solmaz Sharif is an Iranian-American poet, Kay Ulanday Barrett is a transgender queer and disabled Pilipinx-amerikan poet, and Meg Day is a queer, trans and deaf poet.[1] And each poem is approached with a spirit of 'radical hospitality'; that is, as a part of a constellation of multiple othernesses and commonalities.

Mourning through the cracks: Fragile intimacy in Solmaz Sharif's 'Personal Effects'

Solmaz Sharif is an Iranian-American poet, born in Turkey to Iranian parents. Her poem, 'Personal Effects' – from her debut collection *Look* (2016) – is an elegy for her uncle Amoo, a soldier killed in the Iran–Iraq war (1980–1988) when Sharif was a child. The title of the poem operates on a number of levels: while it is a legal phrase often used in wills to describe items of possession left to a successor, it also has significance in the language of the US military, where the 'safeguarding' of a deceased soldier's personal effects is part of the 'sacred duty' of the Mortuary affairs specialist (Bourlier 2016: 18). Throughout *Look*, Sharif employs a range of linguistic terms and phrases from the *Department of Defense Dictionary of Military and Associated Terms* (2007) to perform what R. Shareah Taleghani calls a 'subversive […] act of translation,' in which she 'rewrites, rewords and recontextualizes' the 'seemingly neutral' and 'mundane' US military language (2020: 51). The poem's title embodies an example of this subversive translation and recontextualization since, in addition to denoting items belonging to a deceased person, it also gestures towards the consequences, forces and impacts (i.e. the effects) of her uncle's death, which the poem's speaker experiences on a personal level.

One of the poem's central gestures is the study of, and reflection upon, photographs of the poet's uncle who, it is implied, she has never met (or has not met since childhood). The poem opens with an epigraph from Sontag's *On Photography* which likens cameras – as 'fantasy-machines' – to guns and cars. By including this epigraph, Sharif reminds us that, as Sontag asserts, 'there is something predatory in the act of taking a picture,' and that to take a person's picture is a form of violation or a 'soft murder,' in that it 'turns people into objects that can be symbolically possessed' (2005: 10). Sontag's description might also be applied to the poetic mode of elegy as a whole, whose purpose is to 'capture' in language a person 'as they never see themselves,' just as a photograph 'captures' a person in an image (2005: 10). From the outset, then, the poem is wary of its own medium, drawing attention to the impossibility of knowing a person through a photograph – or, indeed, through poetry – alone. Amoo, in other words, is more than the poem and more than the pictures described within it; his knowability exceeds the poem and eludes both the poem's speaker and reader. This sense of an impossibility of knowing operates as a subtle undermining of the poem's title, as understood in the military sense. It works against the implication that personal effects might be imbued with a symbolic or sanctified significance and that, in the absence of the deceased, such objects might stand in for them. This is, in essence, what the poem documents: the failure of personal effects – photographs in an album, the contents of a person's pockets, the small daily things a person loves – to allow us to fully know a person; and attempts to construct a sense of intimacy with Amoo despite that failure.

By recontextualizing US military language, Sharif highlights the dynamic of capitalist exchange which underlies it. From the perspective of this language, the poem tells us, Amoo is a 'LOW DOLLAR VALUE' item accounted for in numerical terms (Sharif 2016: 64). This capitalized phrase, according to a 1969 Logistics Management document, is an inventory management cost category term whose aim is 'to focus management resources at those points in the supply system where the greatest benefits will be gained' (1969: 9–8). The document gives the example of an engine part to illustrate such an item, which – as opposed to the high-dollar-value item – is not considered to have 'the highest potential return on the dollar spent' (1969: 9–8). A 1961 Dictionary of US Army terms describes it as '[a]n end item or repair part' whose dollar value 'does not exceed $1,000 annually'; while a 1953 Military Supply document describes it as a 'so-called useless item' (1961: 318; 155). Finally, the 1994 *Department of Defense Dictionary* describes it as an 'item which normally requires considerably less management effort than those in the other management intensity groupings' (1994: 222). A 'LOW DOLLAR VALUE' item, then, is a part of a capitalist military-industrial supply chain whose purpose is to maximize profit and resources for the benefit of the state (Sharif 2016: 64). To describe a person as a 'LOW DOLLAR VALUE' item is to performatively render them an expendable commodity within this supply chain, no different from a piece of obsolete or broken machinery; an object, therefore, unworthy of significant organizational effort (Sharif 2016: 64). Its lexical purpose, as applied to a person, is to dehumanize; to judge a human life as cheap and disposable.

As reduced to a 'budgeted […] X number,' the poem implies that this human loss is strategically planned for with precision; the cost of the telephone call to the family dispatching the news of the soldier's death is offset against the amount that will consequently be saved in 'rations' and 'cigarettes' as a result (Sharif 2016: 64). In other words, what Sharif highlights is that this military language is one of accounting rather than accountability; that it reflects the assessment of human life according to principles of asset and expenditure. Its function, in short, is to translate a person into profit and loss. Within this lexical framework, death is understood simply as a shift on a balance sheet. As Butler argues, '[t]o be subject to a calculation is already to have entered the gray zone of the ungrievable' (2020: 107).

Throughout the poem, we are continually reminded of the human impact – the personal effects – of this lexical framing: Amoo's father quietly sobbing in private; his mother's inconsolable grief and guilt. Through these reminders, Sharif restores to these cold, euphemistic phrases the human dimension they are designed to obscure. These kind of military phrases or names, to borrow from Mbembe, 'refer little to things but instead pass above or alongside them,' in order to enact 'disfiguration and distortion' (2019: 7). By placing them firmly in the centre of these moments of human emotion, the poem refuses them their neutrality and distance. At the same time, it reveals their mechanisms as linguistic agents of capitalist dehumanization, designed to obfuscate their own purpose. Thus, Sharif's poem fulfils a function that Mbembe describes as 'return[ing] to life what had been abandoned to the powers of death' (2019: 8).

We might contrast the poem's recontextualization of this military-industrial language with its critique of the ideological construction of the martyr. Sharif's description of a museum 'for the martyrs' might be read within the context of what Younes Saramifar calls 'a master narrative of martyrdom and legacy of the war' (Sharif 2016: 63; Saramifar 2019a: 135). This narrative, Saramifar argues, is an 'ideology advocated by the Islamic Republic of Iran' since the Iran–Iraq war; an ideology rooted in the Shi'i religious account of the martyrdom of the Prophet Muhammad's grandson, Husayn ibn Ali, in the Battle of Karbala in the year 680 (2019a: 135). Ali-Asghar Seyed-Gohrab calls this ideology a 'vogue' or 'cult of martyrdom' which is often 'idealized and even glamorized' (2016: 89). This 'vogue', he argues, has altered 'the public sphere' of Iran into a 'museum of martyrdom' (2016: 89–90). Within this ideological framework, families were 'congratulated' for their loss rather than consoled and, according to Seyed-Gohrab, were expected to express happiness about their loss, while '[l]amentation for the dead was considered shameful' (2016: 90). Similarly, Saramifar explores how state-sanctioned war memorial sites are 'designed to speak of martyrdom and not pain,' while 'constant surveillance and suppression of unsanctioned memories' prevent the articulation of counter-narratives that explore loss and mourning (2019b: 127; 140).

Sharif's descriptions of a museum of martyrs as 'some metal shelf' and a 'white archival box' operate as a critique of this ideology (2016: 63). Both images imply a library system of bureaucratic filing rather than a holy site or shrine. The word 'shelf,' suggests the act of putting something aside or filing it away out of sight, while the 'white archival box,' draws a connection between the burying of a coffin (a white box) and the filing away of documents (Sharif 2016: 63). According to Mbembe, the archive is 'a breaching, an opening, and a separation, a fissure and a breaking, a crazing and a disjunction, a crevasse and a rift, or indeed a tear' (2019: 172). It is 'made of cuts,' and 'cracks,' and to explore it is to 'revisit traces' (Mbembe 2019: 172–3). It 'does not necessarily produce visibility,' but rather a 'reality-generating hallucination' (Mbembe 2019: 173). These Mbembian images of archive and shelf seem to reflect what Saramifar – reading Iranian memorial sites through Cathy Caruth – describes as gestures that are 'connected to forgetting rather than remembering' (2019b: 130). In the examination of memorial sites, Saramifar draws attention to individuals who 'resist' the 'state-sanctioned narrative' by mourning 'through its cracks,' finding space to enable 'organic histories to live through them vicariously' (2019b: 131–2). The poem's refusal of this narrative in favour of the speaker's own 'myth-making' represents a similar kind of resistance; a mourning through the cracks of state-institutionalized commemorative practices (Sharif 2016: 63).

Moreover, the poem's 'myth-making' is also a resistance to – and a mourning through the cracks of – the militarized language of the *Department of Defense Dictionary* which, in the poem, represents a Western superpower whose involvement in the Iran–Iraq war included supplying intelligence, finance and chemical weapons materials to Iraq (Ayatollahi Tabaar 2019: 495–6). This language, Sharif reminds us, is designed to 'NEUTRALIZE,' by assuming a position of objectivity; or by removing from the language any accountability for the violence of war. Further, the poem highlights that its purpose is to determine which subjects may be understood as persons worthy of mourning and which are 'COLLATERAL DAMAGE' (2016: 64; 68). Unlike the cold US military euphemisms, the Iranian ideology of martyrdom mirrors language often used to describe American soldiers killed in action: phrases like 'fallen comrades' and 'fallen heroes' (Bourlier 2016: 18). Both these latter types of language involve a reverential mythification of the deceased; a gesture of apotheosis which resembles tropes often employed by traditional elegies as a way of providing consolation and resolution to mourning and loss. In resistance to these two contrasting ideological responses to the losses of the war dead – the neutralized distance of the US military and the Iranian state-sanctioned responses that frame the dead as martyrs – the poem explores alternative approaches to mourning.

We can see these alternative approaches throughout the poem, in which the speaker documents their attempts to construct forms of physical and psychical intimacy with Amoo. Various sections describe endeavours to build connections through an engagement with photographic images. As Sontag points out, photographs offer an opportunity for a family to 'bear[…] witness to its connectedness,' and to symbolically repeat the 'imperiled continuity' of family life (2005: 5–6). As a presence accessible through photographic images, Amoo exists in the poem largely as 'ghostly traces,' mediated by the speaker's gaze (Sontag 2005: 5–6). He is, in each instance, suspended in time, in the act of undertaking a simple act or gesture: smoking a cigarette, holding a weapon, posing, standing by a pond or peeling a piece of fruit. These photographic gestures are often imbued with a deep sense of vulnerability; one which might be read in relation to Sontag's description of a life 'heading towards [its] own destruction' (2005: 55). His image, in other words, is only visible through – and defined by – the lens of his death. In this way, we might understand these photographs – these personal effects – as what Sara Ahmed calls 'sticky objects': objects which have 'become sticky, or saturated with affect, as sites of personal and social tension' (2014b: 11). As with any set of personal effects, whose meaning is imbued with the absent presence of their deceased owner, the photographs function as a 'sign that gets repeated and accumulates affective value,' just as a 'sticky finger' might attract dust (2014b: 90). They are characterized by a sense of 'withness,' whereby they are bound relationally to the absent person, as well as ideologically to the way in which they died and the circumstances in which they are mourned (2014b: 91).

Amoo is, for most of the poem, a static figure permanently caught in a temporal moment; stopped in the midst of an interpretable action or gesture. It is a suspension, Sharif reminds us, 'by STANDING ORDER'; in other words, one precipitated by a long-standing military operating procedure command (2016: 57). But the phrase 'STANDING ORDER' also operates as part of the military-industrial lexical framework which understands people as profit, since a standing order also refers to an instruction of regular payment (Sharif 2016: 57). Within this state of suspension, Amoo operates as what Sontag calls a 'death mask' or 'trace' of the real; a preserved impression of lost time figuratively imprinted by a military-industrial tread (2005: 120). This sense of impression repeats as a motif throughout the poem: in references to the 'weight' of Amoo's feet as he marches; in the act of rolling and pressing pasta into shapes; and in the action of pressing a 'dog tag' into the temple (Sharif 2016: 60; 61; 67). Repeatedly, we are reminded of marks on a surface left behind by force. It is through impressions 'made by bodily others,' Ahmed argues, that a sense of the collective – of 'feelings-in-common' takes shape (2004: 27). These marks, 'left by the press of one surface upon another,' like the photographs – and, indeed, personal effects more broadly – become 'a sign of absence, or a sign of presence that "is no longer"' (2004: 30).

Sharif's poem seeks to construct links of fragile intimacy through the photographs by finding sites of commonality – sites of 'feelings-in-common,' in Ahmed's terms – between the speaker and Amoo (2004: 27). The sensory experience of smoking a cigarette acts as a corporeal link between them; an adolescent love for the kind of military clothing he wore operates as a shared fashion aesthetic (Sharif 2016: 56; 71). She imagines for him a list of, largely sensory, things he might have been 'moved' by: certain foods, smells, sensations and acts of kindness (2016: 70). In intuiting for him a rich, complex sensory and emotional life, Sharif restores a sense of humanity of which he has been stripped, both by his death in war and by the military-industrial language used by the global powers that supported the opposing side.

As Ahmed argues, it is 'what moves us, or what affects us such that we are no longer in the same place,' that connects us to others (2004: 27). Sharif's imagined list of things Amoo might have been 'moved' by includes sensory experiences involving the 'proximity of others': the washed hair of a woman, the arms and mouth of a loved one, kindness to others, a game of chess (Ahmed 2004: 27). Through these imagined interactions of affective 'movement,' Sharif builds a network of human connections for Amoo. These moments of connection contrast with, and run counter to, his movement 'across a minefield' towards his death (Sharif 2016: 70). That this latter movement is precipitated by the force of what Sharif calls an invisible hand, one that is 'all our hands combined,' also establishes a sense of accountability for his death; an accountability that is denied him by both the US Department of Defense language and the Iranian government's ideology of martyrdom (2016: 70). That accountability is one which is shared collectively, not only on a macro-scale by the nations which participated in the war, but also on a micro-scale by both the poem's speaker and the reader. In other words, the impressions 'made by bodily others,' leave marks upon all of us; and to be moved by another is to be connected to them regardless of intention (2004: 27).

A further sense of connection can be seen in two sections of the poem that mirror one another. Both sections create a sense of emphasis through anaphora: one using the word 'but,' and the other, the word 'and' (Sharif 2016: 61; 83). Both conjunctions – 'but' and 'and' – are linguistic connectives used as a means of joining clauses or sentences together. That the first of these sections repeatedly begins lines with the word 'but' highlights the separation between Amoo and the military duties required of him, as well as the temporal and geographical separation between Amoo and the poem's speaker (Sharif 2016: 61). The word 'but,' implies a voltaic shift in thought; its anaphoric repetition creates a constant sense of shifting direction, which is mirrored in Amoo's movements both as a soldier sneaking into town to phone home and as a figure in the speaker's thoughts (2016: 61).

The second section's anaphoric repetition of 'and' creates a sense of accrual, reflecting its focus on imagined personal effects; namely things that Amoo might have had in his pockets (2016: 83). Both poetic sections involve a blurring of distinction between the viewpoints of the speaker and of Amoo. In the first, the poem shifts from his point of view – as a reluctant soldier missing his family – to hers as she imagines this perspective from a point of spatial and temporal removal. In the second, this blurring of viewpoints intensifies to a point where their perspectives merge in a 'rearview' mirror; a blurring which creates a sense of empathic connection (2016: 83).

This empathic connection is echoed at two points in the poem, in which a blurring of distinctions between the speaker's body and Amoo's is repeated. The speaker twice describes writing about having burned her finger on an oven and, consequently, smelling the 'trenches,' where her uncle lost control of his bladder (Sharif 2016: 80; 86). These written lines, the poem tells us, provoke a response of disapproval or disbelief in others, which they justify by suggesting that the speaker 'doesn't know' (Sharif 2016: 80; 86). Exactly what is not known is not made clear; whether it is simply an implication that, if one knew better, they would not write such a thing, or whether what is not known is the lived experience of war. In any case, these lines represent a blurring of bodily boundaries between the speaker and Amoo, organized around a burn or a bodily wound.

As Ahmed suggests, a wound 'functions as a trace of where the surface of another entity (however imaginary) has impressed upon the body' (2004: 27). It is, she argues, through an experience of such a wound that 'we come to have a sense of our skin as bodily surface, as something that keeps us apart from others' (2004: 29). But, she goes on, it is 'through such painful encounters between this body and other objects [...] that "surfaces" are felt as "being there" in the first place' (2004: 29). It is through this wound, then – this burning of the hand – that the speaker acknowledges both a sense of separation from Amoo and a sense of connection. In not having known him, she cannot – at least from a normative understanding of social connection – create a site of 'feelings-in-common' with him (2004: 27). However, through a feeling of pain and bodily vulnerability that is felt to be shared, the speaker creates a space of intimate connection, in which Amoo's experience is impressed upon her own body.

In the final sections, the speaker imagines meeting with Amoo in the terminal of an airport. In these sections, Sharif performs an emphatic and deliberate refusal of unknowability, firstly by responding 'Yes,' to the imagined question of whether she knows who he is, and secondly by responding, 'How could I not?' (2016: 85; 86). This affirmation is, she acknowledges, a 'half-lie'; Sharif reflects throughout the poem on the fragility and instability of the intimate connections she constructs (2016: 86). As acts of poetic 'myth-making,' they are not normative systems of knowing (2016: 63). But what if, the poem implicitly asks, these normative systems of knowing are inadequate? What if they perform dehumanizing gestures, or enforce ways of knowing that do not reflect a person's emotional experience? Sharif constructs forms of intimacy that create meaning through the cracks of these normative systems. Like the individuals Saramifar describes – who resist 'state-sanctioned' narratives in their mourning practices at memorial sites – Sharif's poem operates as a 'time portal that changes chronology and calendric arrangements of temporality' to demonstrate ways in which the 'past and the present are entangled' (2019b: 132). Personal effects may not provide us with the means to know a person through their absence, but – the poem suggests – there are fragile forms of knowability and empathic connection to be found in engaging with them. This knowability – these connections –

will always inevitably be imperfect, partial, fragile and grounded largely in the imagination. But their purpose is to restore a sense of humanity that has been lost within normative systems of knowing.

Inherited grief: Kay Ulanday Barrett's 'While looking at photo albums'

Kay Ulanday Barrett is a transgender queer and disabled Pilipinx-amerikan poet. Their poem, 'While looking at photo albums' appears in their collection *More Than Organs* (2020). In addition to documenting grief at the loss of a parent, the poem explores the ways in which loss and grief are transmitted through family generations. In particular, the poem addresses diasporic loss experienced within a family who fled the Philippines prior to, or during, the dictatorship of President Ferdinand Marcos between 1972 and 1981.

Ulanday Barrett's poem comprises a block of text made up of fragments punctuated by en-dashes. In one sense, these dashes operate as interrupters, parenthetically separating each broken phrase. In this way, they enable the poem to reflect, formally and aesthetically, the disintegration of the self, following the loss of a parent. In another sense, a dash signifies a connection between words or phrases. So, they also operate as a kind of connective tissue within the poem, holding and binding the separated fragments and maintaining cohesion within them. We might also note that a dash resembles a mathematical minus sign, a symbol representing subtraction or, to put it differently, representing loss. Considered in this way, the dashes suffuse the poem's monolithic shape with marks that function as a continual reminder of the absence or lack that loss enacts upon the bereaved.

The poem's central motif is water; its images are frequently pluvial, fluvial or oceanic in nature. These images are anchored, in the third and fourth line, by the statement that the poet's mother's maiden name, Ulanday, means 'of the rain' (2020: 50). If we read this image of rain as a gesture towards pathetic fallacy – whereby it functions as a metaphor for the sorrow of loss – the poem implies that this sorrow is a form of inheritance; something that is shared from one family generation to another, or it is encoded within the identity of the family unit. Indeed, the lines that follow, which point out how biology textbooks describe the patterns of pouring, appear to support this idea. Moreover, the opening lines specify that this interpretation – that Ulanday means 'of the rain' – is the 'first definition' they learned (2020: 50). This suggests that it operates as a key part of the family's personal mythos; a kind of nominative determinism, in which sorrow or sadness is a fate into which one is born.

Described as a 'pouring,' the name represents an abundant outflowing, a continuous stream, or an unrestrained release of emotion (Ulanday Barrett 2020: 50). However, described as having a 'pattern,' and as a 'definition,' this outflowing also has a shape or design; it offers a model to be imitated (2020: 50). In other words, if we read the image of the rain in the poet's name as representing inherited sorrow and loss, it is – paradoxically – a sorrow that is both uncontrollable and unrestricted, but also controlled and co-ordinated according to a prefigured plan. Indeed, it is – as the poem tells us – biology textbooks that put forward the idea that 'pouring' follows a 'pattern' (2020: 50). However, this troubles the idea of inherited loss as something that is prefigured within family identity by suggesting it is one that is institutionally taught and perhaps uncritically received. In the notes for *Living a Feminist Life*, writing in response to trans exclusionary radical feminist arguments about sex differences, Ahmed writes, 'Biology 101? Well, patriarchy wrote that textbook' (2017: 269). Ahmed's point is that widely accepted, so-called 'common sense' knowledge distributed in institutional contexts often exhibits unexamined biases. Ulanday Barrett's inclusion of the biology book's reminder that 'pouring' – and, by extension, sorrow – has a purpose, potentially emphasizes a similar idea: that the conception of loss as something predetermined and encoded, or as something that follows a pre-prescribed and easily intelligible pattern, is one that might be questioned (2020: 50). After all, according to the biology books, the poet's inherited name (as Ulanday Barrett reminds us) means 'release' – an outpouring of emotion or a liberation from emotional tension (2020: 50). But for the poetic speaker's mother it has a different meaning altogether: to 'flee' and to 'leave' (2020: 50). Thus, the poem implies, what the textbooks tell us might not always reflect subjective meanings.

The term 'flee' denotes the action of making an escape; of disappearing or evading (2020: 50). 'Leave,' however, is a contronym; it gestures both towards departure and towards that which remains as leavings; that which is, in other words, left behind (2020: 50). In the poem, this contronymic understanding of the name's meaning marks the construction of a complex, multidimensional image of the poet's mother working to support her family; and as a Catholic revolutionary forced to migrate to the United States, a migration which is evenly weighted as both an escape (a 'fleeing') and the action of leaving something important behind. She is represented as an exhausted and partial self, broken down and eroded by extraneous forces. These forces are fluvial in nature, suggesting they are linked to the 'rain' and 'pouring' – or, in another sense, the sorrow – of the family namesake (Ulanday Barrett 2020: 50). The family is described in terms that imply a shoring up against these fluvial forces – ones that erode the speaker's mother to a 'drained sediment' (2020: 50). This shoring up occurs within a lonely space of night-time work in which rosaries provide a means of fixity and stability. Here, as in Catholicism more broadly, rosaries represent a means of devotion whose purpose is to aid in the endurance of hardship; a rosary is a string of beads used as a physical means of counting and reciting devotional prayers, often having a total of fifty-nine beads. We may draw similarities here between the rosaries in the poem, and the poem's structure itself. As a sequence of textual fragments connected by dashes – sixty-one in total – the poem resembles a string of rosary beads in its form.

The poem's reference to 'nuns in barricade' evokes the People Power Revolution – or EDSA Revolution, named after Epifano de los Santos Avenue in Manila, where it took place – a civil resistance movement that led to the end of Marcos's presidency (Roces 2006: 144; Ulanday Barrett 2020: 50). Marcos became president of the Philippines in 1965, and in September 1972 he declared martial law towards the end of what was constitutionally meant to be his final term of office (Wurfel 1977: 5). The legal justification he gave for instituting a suspension of ordinary government was 'the existence of an armed rebellion led by the Maoist New People's Army,' and many civilians were detained and tortured on suspicion of affiliation with, or support for, this rebellion (Wurfel 1977: 6). A catalyst for the EDSA Revolution was the assassination of Senator Benigno Aquino, who in 1983 was shot by military officers after returning to Manila from the United States, following a heart bypass operation. Aquino's shooting, and his wife's insistence on an open casket funeral, intensified pre-existing protests to new levels. Under pressure from the United States, Marcos announced a snap election, in which Aquino's widow ran as a popular opponent (Rodell 2002: 21–4).

However, when the elections took place, Marcos was declared the winner despite widespread accusations of tampering and military intimidation. In response, a small group of officials planned a coup to overthrow Marcos, but when Marcos learned of their plot and ordered their arrest, they assembled – along with other rebel forces – at the military quarters of Camp Auginaldo situated on Epifano de los Santos Avenue. Civilians began to turn out in support of the rebels, and by the following day they numbered in the hundreds of thousands. As George N. Katsiaficas asserts, 'people cut down trees and lampposts. City buses were commandeered to form barricades [...]. So many people jammed the highways and streets around the rebel camps that military units loyal to Marcos could not advance' (2013: 50).

Ulanday Barrett's poem refers specifically to the role of 'nuns in barricade' in the civil uprising (2020: 50). During the EDSA Revolution, nuns played a key role in activism against the Marcos regime. According to Roces, nuns would stand 'in front of military barricades to protect demonstrators from potential violence,' by 'using their bodies as buffer to shield and protect the workers' (2006: 137; 142–3). They would link arms 'at the forefront of [...] picket lines to protect striking workers,' who were at risk of 'military arrest and detention' during illegal strikes (Roces 2006: 142–3). During the EDSA Revolution in particular, '[n]uns armed with rosaries knelt down before armoured personnel carriers and pleaded with the military' (Roces 2006: 144). By likening their family – and, more specifically, their mother – to 'nuns in barricade' the poem's speaker draws an explicit connection between their mother and images of protection against violence; of women's political activism, social justice and strength in the face of violent forces; and what Roces refers to as 'moral guardians' who are 'independent of men' and operating outside a traditional 'familial context' (Roces 2006: 137; 140; Ulanday Barrett 2020: 50). Like the 'nuns in barricade,' the speaker's mother is, in other words, active, progressive, brave and operating at the front line where a violence is taking place (Ulanday Barrett 2020: 50).

This image is complicated further by the description of women in the speaker's family as 'like checkpoints' (Ulanday Barrett 2020: 50). While the speaker's mother is associated with the courageous and progressive activism of the EDSA Revolution's nuns, there is also a parallel drawn with the manned roadblocks of martial law. As Eloisa D. Palazo writes, military checkpoints were used extensively during the Marcos regime, 'as a measure against the mounting insurgency problems of the country' (1989: 211). Their principal purposes, she argues, were to 'establish an effective territorial defense,' to 'maintain peace and order,' and to 'provide an atmosphere conducive to the social, economic and political development' of the region (Palazo 1989: 211). Justin Schon, however, describes how checkpoints are, 'one of the most terrifying locations for civilians' during a conflict, describing them as both 'physical impediments to travel' and as 'spaces of "anticipated violence"' (2016: 281; 282). He argues that this uncertainty about the potential for violence and 'tense interactions' magnifies this fear, 'regardless of whether they are managed by governments, rebel groups, civilians looking to make some extra money, or militias' (2016: 282; 286–7).

While it stands to reason that checkpoints would be, as the speaker of the poem says, what the women in their family know, it is more complex to unpack what might be meant by the statement that these women 'hone' in the speaker's heart 'like checkpoints' (Ulanday Barrett 2020: 50). The word 'hone' carries connotations of pining or craving, moaning or wailing, sharpening (as of a blade), refining or perfecting, providing strength or firmness, or the motion of heading directly for (as in 'to hone in on') (2020: 50). Perhaps Ulanday Barrett is signposting how the memories of these women sharpen over time into something like an obstructive or protective barrier. Perhaps there is a suggestion that they provide strength to the speaker's spirit like the protective barricades of the nuns. In fragmented phrases whose meanings accrete as the poem progresses – in the same way that silt accumulates in a riverbed – Ulanday Barrett juxtaposes these two forms of blockade: the protective barrier of the activist and the obstructive barrier of the regime's roadblock. In this way, the reader's attention is drawn to the way in which barriers and borders operate as both a form of defence and a form of constraint.

In the latter part of the poem, the lines call back to the water images in the poem's opening, returning to the idea that 'pouring' (as a figurative action that represents the outpouring of emotion – i.e. crying) is a quality embedded within the speaker's name and therefore might be understood as a defining characteristic with which they are born (Ulanday Barrett 2020: 50). However, while the poem explores and questions nominative determinism as family mythos, it in no way straightforwardly accepts or refutes it, refusing to settle on an explicit position. While the poem instructs a transformation of the body into both 'harbor' and 'oars,' it also retains a liquid quality as something that can be poured (2020: 50). In this way, the poem ends with the speaker's body representing both a 'pouring' (as liquid) and a 'purpose' (as an object with a clear design) (2020: 50). In other words, on the question of whether one is born to suffer because one's name implies suffering, the poem ends ambivalently. Suffering, it seems to imply, is both inherent and of the world; it is something that is part of being human, but also something that is made outside of us by external forces. The liquidness of the body (the 'pouring') is an involuntary response to loss, while the act of making part of oneself into 'oars' is an act of agency, a moving forward or a movement against it (2020: 50). For Ulanday Barrett, then, inheritances are complicated; we carry the legacies of our parents with us and spread them on the things we touch. Our bodies and our lives are transformed by the griefs we experience, and those that our families have experienced before us. But we are agents within those griefs; we can resist the ways in which they act like forces upon us.

The transformation of a body into a 'harbor,' echoes the nun's barricade as a form of protective shelter and containment (2020: 50). In its continual returning to different forms of both pouring and containment (in the nuns' barricade, the checkpoint and the 'harbor'), the poem occupies a space of ambivalence on the ideas of both holding in and being held (2020: 50). Both offer potential dangers and benefits. Pouring has the potential for release but may also erode, carrying parts of the self away with it. It is an inevitability of grief; a sense of emptying out that liquefies, but it also allows for the development of strength and agency, enabling the fashioning of 'oars' that will assist forward progression. Containment may signify protection (as in the 'harbor,' or the nun's barricade) but it may also signify constraint and impediment (2020: 50). While the poem ultimately refuses to reconcile these ambivalences, the final line suggests a transformation of 'pouring,' into 'purpose' with the instruction to use the 'oars,' as a means of travel to seek out the speaker's mother, for whose death they were unable to be present (2020: 50). This, the poem ultimately implies, may be the function of grief: it enables us to embark upon the discovery of what we have lost.

Deafness and 'cure': Meg Day's 'Elegy in Translation'

Meg Day's 'Elegy in Translation' was originally published in the online poetry magazine *TYPO* and re-published on *Poem-a-Day,* the daily poetry series on *The Academy of American Poets* website, on 18 March 2018. Day is a queer, trans and deaf poet whose elegy appears, at first glance, to lament the end of an intimate relationship. But the poem troubles the trope of lost love by utilizing the space of elegy to criticize ableist notions about 'curing' deafness. In this way, the poem operates as a lament in response to the multiple violences and marginalizations that D/deaf people experience.

The poem begins with an epigraph from a song by Canadian folk music group The Be Good Tanyas from their album *Blue Horse* (Ford, F., S. Parton and others 2000). The song is about loss and describes dreaming of a person who is no longer around. This implies the poem's register is one of lament for someone loved and lost. The poem opens with a request for forgiveness, appearing to establish for the poem a tone of apology or prayer. However, it is densely packed with an irony that builds as the poem progresses. While it appears that forgiveness is being asked for the 'deafness' of the poem's speaker, we gradually learn that the word 'deafness' carries, in this context, a more figurative and specific meaning (Day 2018: n.p). It is not, in this instance, a general condition of hearing loss, but rather, the inability to hear the spoken name of the person to whom the poem is addressed, i.e. an ex-lover.

This name is described in the poem through articulatory phonetics; the various ways in which speech sounds are formed in and by the mouths of others. From Day's description of these phonetics, we might infer that the name begins with a bilabial consonant (involving a coming together of the lips) followed by a rounded vowel (involving a rounding of the lips) and an interdental consonant (involving the tongue between the teeth coupled with an exhalation, as in *th*). Day's descriptions are oceanic in nature; the articulation in its totality is likened to a 'wave,' and the tongue to a 'fluke,' the tail of a whale as it might appear in the ocean (2018: n.p). These images lend power and force to the name; they carry connotations of chaos, vastness and might. At the same time, they imply violence: a 'fluke' also means the barb at the end of a spear, while the description of the spoken name as a 'blow' suggests an unanticipated attack (Day 2018: n.p). Thus, through these images Day establishes a correlation between the addressee of the poem and the potentially overwhelming force of the ocean. As the poem progresses, a further connection is drawn between the ex-lover's name and an 'oblivious' instruction to hold a 'conch' to one's ear, in which the speaker might hear 'loud & clear,' the sounds of a 'highway' (Day 2018: n.p). As 'oblivious,' both are presented as something unconscious, unmindful, forgetful or lacking in awareness (Day 2018: n.p). And both are described as similar in their 'blueness,' suggesting that they are suffused with sorrow, dejection or misery (Day 2018: n.p).

The reference to holding a conch to one's ear invokes seashell resonance, the folk myth whereby, when a shell is held to the ear, noise from the surrounding environment and sounds from the human body (blood flowing and muscles acting) resonate within the shell to create a sound like that made by the sea. Stefan Helmreich describes the shell in this common folk myth as a 'mouth, [a] damp and resonant grotto, and doppelgänger ear – an eerie object becoming (never entirely) a disenchanted scientific thing' (2012–2013: 26). As a 'mouth,' he argues, it is a channel 'for voices from a communal past,' while as 'doppelgänger ear,' it is a 'resonant' chamber 'of individual, located experience' (2012–2013: 26). For a D/deaf person, however, it is neither of these things; instructing a D/deaf person to hold a conch to their ear is an ableist request. It gestures not only towards obliviousness – as highlighted in the 'oblivious blue' of the poem – but also towards 'rudimentary devices such as shells, animal horns and simple tubes' used '[t]hroughout history […] to provide air amplification of sound for deaf people' (Ross et al. 2014: 534). In this way, the ex-lover's spoken name, the instruction to hold a 'conch' to one's ear, and the sound of the highway – are linked as signifiers that operate, for the poem's speaker, as ableist in nature (Day 2018: n.p).

Seashells operate as a metonym for the process of hearing. Studies in the history of otology suggest that Empedocles, the Greek philosopher who first described the cochlea – the spiral-shaped space in the inner ear which incorporates the sensory organ of hearing – named it as κοχλος, after a 'seashell found in the Mediterranean region' (Flávio Nogueira Júnior et al. 2007: 694). Like Helmreich's 'doppelgänger ear,' a seashell might be understood as a figurative stand-in for the anatomy of the hearing body (2012–2013: 26). Or, if we understand the instruction to hold a 'conch' to the ear as semantically disconnected from its material association with hearing and non-hearing bodies, we might consider it as a figurative command to intuitively 'listen' (again, an ableist metaphor) to one's internal resonances; as Helmreich puts it, the '"resonant chamber" of individual, located experience' (2012–2013: 26). So, we might also read the sound of the highway, heard 'loud & clear,' as figurative; as a symbol for realizing, definitively and conclusively that it is time to leave a relationship (or, 'hit the road,' so to speak) (Day 2018: n.p).

In the seventh line, there is a shift in focus towards a different kind of loss; one that puts the 'conch' into a different context. With use of the word 'kin,' Day creates a familial connection with other D/deaf persons; not just in the present, but also in the past. The speaker's hands – their means of communication – are 'bloated' or swollen with the 'name signs' of other D/deaf people, for whom the folk myth of seashell resonance represents a notion of potential 'cure' (2018: n.p). By depicting these figurative kin as waiting for the sound of water 'heard' within the seashell, the line resituates the 'conch' as an allegory for the different 'rudimentary devices' that Ross et al. describe as being used '[t]hroughout history [...] to provide air amplification of sound for deaf people' (Ross et al. 2014: 534).

Further, this recasts Helmreich's notion of the shell as 'doppelgänger ear' in a different light (2012–2013: 26). Day's line subtly foregrounds hands as means of speech for D/deaf people, explicitly referring to their 'name signs' (2018: n.p). In this way, the notion of shell as 'doppelgänger ear' is an ableist construction; a means of culture and medicine enforcing the idea that deafness is a deficit – particularly in relation to interpersonal communication – that requires 'correcting' or normalizing through prosthesis (Helmreich 2012–2013: 26). We might, for instance, draw connections between the image of the 'conch' in the poem and the controversial medical practice of cochlear implant surgery (Day 2018: n.p). In an article on the sensationalizing of cochlear implant activation, Amelia Cooper highlights the 'erroneous message' that 'cochlear implants fully transform deaf individuals into hearing ones'; the 'fallacy that cochlear implants are a one-size-fits-all solution'; and the problems that arise from these ideas such as, 'linguistic deprivation if sign language is excluded,' and the 'inherently negative implication,' that 'deafness is a medical disability that should be cured rather than a cultural identity that should be celebrated and respected' (2019: 469–71).

The ableist notion that deafness is a physical or communicatory deficit in need of 'fixing' is one that is further critiqued in the poem's subsequent lines. The poem catalogues items that have, at one time or another, been understood as a 'cure' for deafness or hearing problems, including 'oil'; animal 'grease' and 'fat'; fruit stones; sticks and rocks (Day 2018: n.p). These so-called 'cures' are widely documented folk myths. Andreas Markides outlines how the Roman patrician Celsus recommended 'emollient oil,' as a cure for 'ear-wax,' while the website My Hearing Centers lists 'bear fat,' and David Owen mentions 'peach kernels fried in hog lard,' in his book *Volume Control* (Markides 1982: 481; My Hearing Centers 2020: para 2; Owen 2019: 117). Further, Ross and colleagues describe 'placement of a stiff rod on the skull or teeth of the deaf person' (Ross et al. 2014: 533).

By designating each of these 'cures' as old wives' tales, Day establishes them as folkloric superstitions built around the ableist understanding of deafness as a medical impairment or physical deficit rather than a cultural identity. The poem gestures towards the pathologizing of deafness and the drive to normalize an understanding of it as a disability rather than a way of being. As Cooper outlines, the word '"Deaf" with an uppercase "D" refers to a cultural identity,' and many who identify as Deaf 'do not need nor want to be "fixed"' (Cooper 2019: 469–71). Esme Cleall, who examines perceptions of deafness in the nineteenth century, highlights how a desire for 'educating the deaf into "normality" implied that deafness, and ultimately the deaf, were best erased,' and reflects upon a common tendency in the 'late nineteenth century Anglophone world,' whereby hearing persons 'actively sought to forget deafness' (2015: 3). Day's poem highlights that these ideas are still prevalent within society and continue to inflect interpersonal relationships between D/deaf and hearing persons.

The speaker of Day's poem registers their own complicity with these ableist interactions and structures. The statement that they had mistaken their deafness for a 'wound' that could be healed resituates the poem from a vehicle of interpersonal relationship loss to a critique of the pervasive nature of ableist conceptions of deafness (Day 2018: n.p). The social prevalence of pathologizing deafness, and the reinforcement of that idea within the failed relationship had – the poem suggests – caused the speaker to perceive their own deafness in this way. The poem redresses this not only by critiquing the spurious 'cures' that have been practised medically throughout history and by challenging the pathologizing notions that underlie these practices, but also by presenting orally spoken language as an inadequate means of communication in comparison with sign language.

We have encountered this earlier, when the speaker refers to 'name signs' of their 'kin' accumulating in their hands, as if there are too many to articulate (Day 2018: n.p). Later in the poem, Day once again gives primacy to the hands as a means of communicating, this time as a means of listening rather than speaking. As 'wasted,' the ex-lover's orally spoken words are without use, starved or squandered (2018: n.p). Further, these words facilitated the visiting of figurative places to which the speaker feels it would have been better not to go. Day highlights the gravity of this failure of communication by counterpointing different forms of misunderstanding. These misunderstood phrases are, for the most part, presented playfully or humorously as an inconsequential misapprehension of popular song lyrics. In contrast, however, one instance has a more sinister undertone; one that signposts the threat that a failure of communication can potentially present. In other words, while some forms of misunderstanding are harmless, others carry the possibility of damage, in this case to the image of the self. This example brings to light the deeply problematic nature of a relationship whose end has been, up to this point, seemingly elegized in the poem. Having categorized the speaker as without worth, the ex-lover is aligned with the old wives who falsely believed that deafness is a deficit in need of a 'cure'. In other words, in a reversal of the poem's ostensible elegiac focus, the ex-lover represents and embodies ableist notions against which the poem is arguing, and the poem laments the pathologizing violences experienced by D/deaf persons on both a sociocultural and an interpersonal level.

This reversal is reinforced at the end of the poem which, like the opening, focuses on the mouth. Bringing to a climactic point the motif of misunderstanding and miscommunication between ableist ex-lover and D/deaf speaker, the poem draws a visual connection between three oral gestures performed by the ex-lover: how their mouth, when not speaking, looks the same when they are thinking and when they are exhaling smoke. The connection between these oral states, the poem's speaker tells us, is that they each have the same 'sound,' and the poem ends with a colon after which nothing follows (Day 2018: n.p). In other words, the colon implies that what follows is silence. This poetic gesture troubles the primacy that hearing persons give to oral speech as a mode of communication. Two of the ex-lover's gestures imply a mouth without movement, while the third – 'blowing smoke' – is a colloquial phrase that suggests the intention of deliberately confusing or misleading someone (Day 2018: n.p). Thus, whether speaking or not, the ex-lover conveys nothing; they are effectively silent and silenced.

This silence is also significant in relation to the poem's challenging of ableist perceptions of D/deafness as a medical condition that requires 'curing'. As Cleall highlights, 'the trope of silence is almost "iconic" in hearing representations of deafness, used "extensively" by hearing people to evoke the lives of deaf people' (2015: 13). She argues that this trope operates as a form of active silencing, in which D/deaf persons are imagined as 'unable to "speak up," "naturally" silent, and easily forgotten' (Cleall 2015: 13). The ending of Day's poem subverts this trope, turning silence back towards the hearing body of the ex-lover.

Throughout, we have seen how the primacy of oral speech in this interpersonal relationship has led to negative outcomes: unable to hear the ex-lover through sign language, the poem's speaker registers repeated failures in communication and unpleasant experiences. By turning the ableist trope of silence back upon the hearing body of the ex-lover, the poem highlights how it is the primacy given to oral speech by hearing persons that creates and perpetuates notions of silence. A key part of this primacy is the expectation that D/deaf persons should participate in communication with hearing persons through oral speech, lip reading, or by 'fixing' their D/deafness via surgical means, rather than hearing persons communicating through sign language. Thus, Day's poem draws attention to the trope of silence as a construction of the ableist imagination, while any responsibility for silence and failure in communication sits squarely with the hearing person.

It is interesting to note that Day's commentary about the poem on the *Poem-A-Day* website outlines how the version on the site is an 'incomplete rendering', drawing our attention to a missing component: a 'contrapuntal poem [...] in American sign language' (Day 2018: n.p). This is an interesting omission, and one that reinforces the arguments Day makes within the text of the poem. Does this omission reflect the same kind of erasure and marginalization to which the poem is drawing our attention? This question remains unanswered, as the absence of the contrapuntal poem is not explained. For whatever reason, we are only able to engage with the poem on a textual level. While the reasons for its absence may be logistical rather than ideological, it is interesting to consider that it nonetheless reflects a primacy often given to certain forms of communication over others.

Postscript

As outlined in the introduction to this chapter, the critical approach to these poems is intended to be tentative, exploratory and speculative. The poems discussed represent an assemblage of grieving subjectivities, each vastly different in their poetic tones, contexts and aesthetics. In approaching them with a spirit of Mbembian 'radical hospitality' understood through Derrida's critique of the guest–host dynamic, the intention has been to perform a troubling of the unequal relation between critic and critical subject. To put it differently, in order to disturb the laws and conditions that define the relationship between critic and critiqued, the chapter has attempted to allow the three poems – as a constellation of othernesses and commonalities – to enact a transformation over the space of the book by upturning the usual sovereignty of the critic-writer.

Obviously, this attempt could only ever be partial, just as – according to Corsani and Murphy – notions of community, empathy and solidarity can only ever be partial, incomplete or fragmentary (2007: 113). But, in eschewing the scholarly tendency to draw the threads of these poems neatly together, this chapter has sought to present them as an assemblage that is rhizomatic in nature, resisting the chronological and narrative organizational structures that the genealogical model represents. No doubt this will seem, for some, an unsatisfactory end to this book. But to finish with a distinct end point would simply reinforce a genealogical structure, while a neat drawing together of threads would enact the same kind of 'neutralization and domestication of forces' that Mbembe critiques in the museum space (2019: 172). Since the museum space – and by extension – genealogical models of elegy cannot in their existing forms hold space for 'subjugated or humiliated humanities' in any meaningful way, I would prefer to end on a note of unsettledness, of opening up and opening out, and of potential transformation (Mbembe 2019: 171).

Note

1   Pilipinx is the gender-neutral alternative to Pilipino/Pilipina, indicating an individual of Philippine or Philippine-American identity; the 'P' replaces the 'F' of 'Filipinx' as a means of decolonizing language usage. The term 'amerikan' is an alternative spelling of 'American' which seeks to foreground the country's oppressive imperialist social, cultural and political dynamics.

References

Abba, A. A. (2017), 'Christopher Okigbo's Poetics and the Politics of Canonization', *MATATU*, 49: 260–79.

Abelove, H. (1993), 'From Thoreau to Queer Politics', *The Yale Journal of Criticism*, 6 (2): 17–27.

Adamson, B. (2016), '"Thugs," "Crooks," and "Rebellious Negroes": Racist and Racialized Media Coverage of Michael Brown and the Ferguson Demonstrations', *Harvard Journal on Racial and Ethnic Justice*, 32: 189–278.

Adorno, T. W. (2004), *Negative Dialectics*, trans. E. B. Ashton, London & New York: Routledge.

Afzal, N (2020), 'Black People Dying in Police Custody Should Surprise No One', *The Guardian*, Thursday 11 June. Available online: https://www.theguardian.com/uk-news/2020/jun/11/black-deaths-in-police-custody-the-tip-of-an-iceberg-of-racist-treatment (accessed 6 May 2021).

Ahmed, S. (2004), 'Collective Feelings or, the Impressions Left by Others', *Theory, Culture and Society*, 21 (2): 25–42.

Ahmed, S. (2014a), 'Selfcare as Warfare', *feministkilljoys*, 25 August. Available online: https://feministkilljoys.com/2014/08/25/selfcare-as-warfare/(accessed 6 May 2021).

Ahmed, S. (2014b), *The Cultural Politics of Emotion*, 2nd edn, Edinburgh: Edinburgh University Press.

Ahmed, S. (2017), *Living a Feminist Life*, Durham and London: Duke University Press.

Ahn, I. (2010), 'Economy of "Invisible Debt" and Ethics of Radical Hospitality: Toward a Paradigm Change of Hospitality from "Gift" to "Forgiveness"', *Journal of Religious Ethics*, 38 (2): 243–67.

Aizura, A. Z. (2014), 'Trans Feminine Value, Racialized Others and the Limits of Necropolitics', in J. Haritaworn, A. Kuntsman and S. Posocco (eds), *Queer Necropolitics*, 129–48, Abingdon: Routledge.

Anderson, D. S. (2018), 'What Happened to the Key Figures in the Emmett Till Case?', *Mississippi Clarion Ledger*, 13 September. Available online: https://eu.clarionledger.com/story/news/2018/09/13/what-happened-key-figures-emmett-till-case/1275626002/ (accessed 6 May 2021).

Aoki, R. (2015), *Why Dust Shall Never Settle upon This Soul*, Toronto: Biyuti Publishing.

Awkward, M. (1995), *Negotiating Difference: Race, Gender, and the Politics of Positionality*, Chicago: University of Chicago Press.

Ayatollahi Tabaar, M. (2019), 'Factional Politics in the Iran-Iraq War', *Journal of Strategic Studies*, 42 (3–4): 480–506.

Becker, U. (2000), *The Continuum Encyclopedia of Symbols*, London: A&C Black.

Bergan, D. E. (2009), 'The Draft Lottery and Attitudes towards the Vietnam War', *Public Opinion Quarterly*, 73 (2): 379–84.

Berlant, L. (1988), 'The Female Complaint', *Social Text*, 19/20: 237–59.

Bettcher, T. M. (2007), 'Evil Deceivers and Make-Believers: On Transphobic Violence and the Politics of Illusion', *Hypatia*, 22 (3): 43–65.

Bettcher, T. M. (2014), 'Trapped in the Wrong Theory: Rethinking Trans Oppression and Resistance', *Signs: Journal of Women in Culture and Society*, 39 (2): 383–406.

Biggs, D. (2018), 'Clearing, "Wasting," and Regreening: An Environmental History of Bare Hills in Central Vietnam', *The Journal of Asian Studies*, 77 (4): 1037–58.

Bigham, D. E. (2005), *On Jordan's Banks: Emancipation and Its Aftermath in the Ohio River Valley*, Lexington: University Press of Kentucky.

Bilbro, J. (2012), 'Who Are Lost and How They're Found: Redemption and Theodicy in Wheatley, Newton, and Cowper', *Early American Literature*, 47 (3): 561–89.

Bly, A. T. (1999), 'Wheatley's On the Death of a Young Lady of Five Years of Age', *The Explicator*, 58 (1): 10–13.

Bourlier, T. (2016), 'Ode to the Mortuary Affairs Specialist', *Double Eagle*, 5 (5): 18–19.

Brady, A. (2006), *English Funerary Elegy in the Seventeenth Century: Laws in Mourning*, Basingstoke, England and New York: Palgrave Macmillan.

Brady, C. (1986), 'Spenser's Irish Crisis: Humanism and Experience in the 1590s', *Past Present*, 111 (1): 17–49.

Broadhurst, C. J. (2010), '"We Didn't Fire a Shot, We Didn't Burn a Building": The Student Reaction at North Carolina State University to the Kent State Shootings, May 1970', *North Carolina Historical Review*, 87 (3): 283–309.

Brooks, G. (2006), *Selected Poems*, New York: Harper Perennial.

Burke, H. M. (1991), 'The Rhetoric and Politics of Marginality: The Subject of Phillis Wheatley', *Tulsa Studies in Women's Literature*, 10 (1): 31–45.

Bush, H. K. (2013), 'Continuing Bonds and Emmett Till's Mother', *Southern Quarterly: A Journal of the Arts in the South*, 50 (3): 9–27.

Butler, J. (2004), *Undoing Gender*, London: Routledge.

Butler, J. (2006), *Precarious Life: The Powers of Mourning and Violence*, London and New York: Verso.

Butler, J. (2009), 'Performativity, Precarity and Sexual Politics', *AIBR: Revista de Antropología Iberoamericana*, 4 (3): i–xiii.

Butler, J. (2016), *Frames of War*, London and New York: Verso.

Butler, J. (2020), *The Force of Non-Violence*, London and New York: Verso.

Card, D. and T. Lemieux (2001), 'Going to College to Avoid the Draft: The Unintended Legacy of the Vietnam War', *The American Economic Review*, 91 (2): 97–102.

Carmichael, S. (1966), *Black Power*, Berkeley: University of California, 29 October. Available online: http://americanradioworks.publicradio.org/features/sayitplain/scarmichael.html (accessed 6 May 2021).

Carney Smith, J., ed. (2006), *Notable Black American Women*, Book 2, Detroit: Gale.

Carretta, V. (2001), 'Introduction', in *Phillis Wheatley: Complete Writings*, xiii–xxxvii, London: Penguin.

Casalicchio, E. (2021), 'Britain's Culture War Extends beyond Brexit', *Politico*, 8 January. Available online: https://www.politico.eu/article/uk-tories-plan-assault-woke-culture-war/ (accessed 6 May 2021).

Caulfield, J. W. (2016), *Overcoming Matthew Arnold: Ethics in Culture and Criticism*, Abingdon: Routledge.

Cavitch, M. (2010), 'American Constitutional Elegy', in K. Weisman (ed), *The Oxford Handbook of the Elegy*, 224–37, Oxford: Oxford University Press.

Chari, V. K. (1976), 'Poetic Emotions and Poetic Semantics', *The Journal of Aesthetics and Art Criticism*, 34 (3): 287–99.

Chrystos (1988), *Not Vanishing*, Vancouver: Press Gang.

Cleall, E. (2015), 'Silencing Deafness: Displacing Disability in the Nineteenth Century', *PORTAL Journal of Multidisciplinary International Studies*, 12 (1): 1–16.

Clifton, L. (2012), *The Collected Poems of Lucille Clifton 1965–2010*, ed. K. Young and M. S. Glaser, Rochester, New York: BOA Editions.

Cohen, Li (2020), 'Police in the U.S. Killed 164 Black People in the First 8 Months of 2020. These Are Their Names', *CBS News Online*, Part I: January–April, 10 September. Available online: https://www.cbsnews.com/pictures/black-people-killed-by-police-in-the-u-s-in-2020/ (accessed 6 May 21).

Collins, W. J. and R. A. Margo (2007), 'The Economic Aftermath of the 1960s Riots in American Cities: Evidence from Property Values', *The Journal of Economic History*, 67 (4): 849–83.

Cooper, A. (2019), 'Hear Me Out–Hearing Each Other for the First Time: The Implications of Cochlear Implant Activation', *Missouri Medicine*, 116 (6): 469–71.

Cooper, B. (1998), '"The White-Black Fault Line": Relevancy of Race and Racism in Spectators' Experiences of Spike Lee's Do the Right Thing', *Howard Journal of Communication*, 9 (3): 205–28.

Corsani, A. and T. S. Murphy (2007), 'Beyond the Myth of Woman: The Becoming-Transfeminist of (Post-)Marxism', *SubStance* 112, 36 (1): 106–38.

Costello, B. (2010), 'Fresh Woods: Elegy and Ecology among the Ruins', in K. Weisman (ed), *The Oxford Handbook of the Elegy*, 324–42, Oxford: Oxford University Press.

Councilor, K. C. (2017), 'Feeding the Body Politic: Metaphors of Digestion in Progressive Era US Immigration Discourse', *Communication and Critical/Cultural Studies*, 14 (2): 139–57.

Cowling, K. (1995), 'Monopoly Capitalism and Stagnation', *Review of Political Economy*, 7 (4): 430–46.

Crenshaw, K. (1989), 'Demarginalizing the Intersection of Race and Sex: A Black Feminist Critique of Antidiscrimination Doctrine, Feminist Theory and Antiracist Politics', *University of Chicago Legal Forum*, 1989 (8): 139–67.

Crewe, J. (2010), 'Elegy in English Drama, 1590–1640', in K. Weisman (ed), *The Oxford Handbook of the Elegy*, 518–32, Oxford: Oxford University Press.

Critcher, C. (2008), 'Moral Panic Analysis: Past, Present and Future', *Sociology Compass*, 2 (4): 1127–44.

Cummings, A. (2005), 'Public Subjects: Race and the Critical Reception of Gwendolyn Brooks, Erica Hunt, and Harryette Mullen', *Frontiers: A Journal of Women Studies*, 26 (2): 3–36

Curran, S. (2010), 'Romantic Elegiac Hybridity', in K. Weisman (ed), *The Oxford Handbook of the Elegy*, 238–50, Oxford: Oxford University Press.

Daddis, G. A. (2013), '"A Better War?": The View from the Nixon Whitehouse', *Journal of Strategic Studies*, 36 (3): 357–84.

Davis, A. (1998), 'Masked Racism: Reflections on the Prison Industrial Complex', *Color Lines*, 10 September. Available online: https://www.colorlines.com/articles/masked-racism-reflections-prison-industrial-complex (accessed 6 May 2021).

Davis, A. (2016), 'The Prosecutor's Ethical Duty to End Mass Incarceration', *Hofstra Law Review*, 45: 1063–85.

Davis, E., L. Clifton and S. Sanchez (2002), 'Lucille Clifton and Sonia Sanchez: A Conversation', *Callaloo*, 25 (4): 1038–74.

Day, M. (2018), 'Elegy in Translation', *poets.org*, Academy of American Poets, 18 March. Available online: https://poets.org/poem/elegy-translation (accessed 6 May 2021).

Debo, A. (2005), 'Reflecting Violence in the Warpland: Gwendolyn Brooks's "Riot"', *African American Review*, 39 (1/2): 143–52.

Derrida, J. (2000), 'Hostipitality', *Angelaki: Journal of Theoretical Humanities*, 5 (3): 3–18.

Diala, I. (2015), 'Okigbo's Drum Elegies', *Research in African Literature*, 46 (3): 85–111.

Do the Right Thing (1989), [Film] Dir. Spike Lee, USA: Universal Pictures.

Doka, K. J. and T. L. Martin (2000), *Men Don't Cry… Women Do: Transcending Gender Stereotypes of Grief*, Philadelphia: Taylor & Francis.

Driskill, Q. (2004), 'Stolen from Our Bodies: First Nations Two Spirits/Queers and the Journey to a Sovereign Erotic', *Studies in American Indian Literature*, Series 2, 16 (2): 50–64.

Driskill, Q. (2010), 'Doubleweaving Two-Spirit Critiques: Building Alliances between Native and Queer Studies', *GLQ: A Journal of Lesbian and Gay Studies*, 16 (1/2): 69–92.

Driskill, Q. (2016), *Asegi Stories: Cherokee Queer and Two-Spirit Memory*, Tucson: University of Arizona Press.

Driskill, Q., D. Heath Justice, D. Miranda and L. Tatonetti, eds (2011), *Sovereign Erotics: A Collection of Two-Spirit Literature*, Tucson: University of Arizona Press.

DuBois, W. E. B. (2007), *The Souls of Black Folk*, ed. B. Hayes Edwards, New York: Oxford University Press.

Eales, Lindsay and Danielle Peers (2020). 'Care Haunts, Hurts, Heals: The Promiscuous Poetics of Queer Crip Mad Care', *Journal of Lesbian Studies*, 25 (3): 163–81.

Earnshaw, O. (2017), 'Mood, Delusions and Poetry: Emotional "Wording of the World" in Psychosis, Philosophy and the Everyday', *Philosophia*, 45: 1697–708.

Echeruo, M. J. C. (2004), 'Christopher Okigbo, *Poetry* Magazine, and the "Lament of the Silent Sisters"', *Research in African Literatures*, 35 (3): 8–25.

Edelman, E. A (2014), '"Walking while Transgender": Necropolitical Regulations of Trans Feminine Bodies of Colour in the Nation's Capital', in J. Haritaworn, A. Kuntsman, and S. Posocco (eds), *Queer Necropolitics*, 172–90, Abingdon: Routledge.

Egudu, R. N. (2003), 'G. M. Hopkins's "The Wreck of the Deutschland" and Christopher Okigbo's "Lament of the Silent Sisters": A Comparative Study', *Comparative Literature Studies*, 40 (1): 26–36.

Elder, A. and N. Giovanni (1982), 'A MELUS Interview: Nikki Giovanni', *MELUS*, 9 (3): 61–75.

English, K. (2017), 'Respect, Dignity and Fairness Conveyed in Capital Letters: Public Editor', *The Star*, 26 May. Available online: https://www.thestar.com/opinion/public_editor/2017/05/26/respect-dignity-and-fairness-conveyed-in-capital-letters-public-editor.html (accessed 6 May 2021).

Espinoza, J. J. (2016), *There Should Be Flowers*, Fairfax, VA: Civil Coping Mechanisms.

Etter, G. W. (2001), 'Totemism and Symbolism in White Supremacist Movements: Images of an Urban Tribal Warrior Culture', *Journal of Gang Research*, 8 (2): 49–75.

Evans, M. (1970), *I Am a Black Woman: Poems*, New York: Morrow.

Fanon, F. (2004), *The Wretched of the Earth*, trans. R. Philcox, New York: Grove Press.

Fariña, C. (2016), 'Chancellor Carmen Fariña's Remarks at the National Association for Bilingual Education Conference', *NYC Department of Education*, 3 March. Available online: https://www.schools.nyc.gov/about-us/news/announcements/contentdetails/2016/03/03/chancellor-carmen-fari%C3%B1a-s-remarks-at-the-national-association-for-bilingual-education-conference (accessed 6 May 21).

Finnegan, R. (2014), *Oral Literature in Africa*, Cambridge: Open Book Publishers.

Flávio Nogueira Jr, J., et al. (2007), 'A Brief History of Otorhinolaryngolgy: Otology, Laryngology and Rhinology', *Brazilian Journal of Otorhinolaryngology*, 73 (5): 693–703.

Ford, F., et al. (2000), *Blue Horse*, Vancouver: Nettwerk (CD).

Foster, L. (2003), 'The Capitalization of Black and White', *Share: Canada's Largest Ethnic Newspaper*, 21 August, 26: 18. Available online: http://www.yorku.ca/lfoster/documents/Foster%20Scanned%20Articles/The%20Capitalization%20of%20Black%20And%20White_Foster_Share_21.08.03.pdf (accessed 6 May 2021).

Fowler, V. C. (1992), *Nikki Giovanni*, New York: Twayne.

Fox, M. V. (2018), 'The Meanings of the Book of Job', *Journal of Biblical Literature*, 137 (1): 7–18.

Franklin, B. A. (1968), 'Army Troops in Capital as Negroes Riot', *New York Times*, 6 April. Available online: http://movies2.nytimes.com/library/national/race/040668race-ra.html (accessed 6 May 2021).

Fruehling Springwood, C. (2014), 'Gun Concealment, Display, and Other Magical Habits of the Body', *Critique of Anthropology*, 34 (4): 450–71.

Fuss, D. (2013), *Dying Modern: A Meditation on Elegy*, Durham and London: Duke University Press.
Gallop, J. (1988), *Thinking through the Body*, New York: Columbia University Press.
Gates, H. L. Jr. (2003), *The Trials of Phillis Wheatley: America's First Black Poet and Her Encounters with the Founding Fathers*, New York: Basic.
Gibson, C. L. (2017), '"Fight the Power": Hip Hop and Civil Unrest in Spike Lee's *Do the Right Thing*', *Black Camera: An International Film Journal*, 8 (2): 183–207.
Gioielli, R. R. (2015), *Environmental Activism and the Urban Crisis: Baltimore, St. Louis, Chicago*, Philadelphia: Temple University Press.
Giovanni, N. (2007), *The Collected Poetry of Nikki Giovanni*, New York: Harper Perennial.
Goldberg, J. (2010), 'Between Men: Literary History and the Work of Mourning', in K. Weisman (ed), *The Oxford Handbook of the Elegy*, 498–517, Oxford: Oxford University Press.
Goldzwig, S. R. (2003), 'LBJ, the Rhetoric of Transcendence, and the Civil Rights Act of 1968', *Rhetoric & Public Affairs*, 6 (1): 25–53.
Gossett, C. (2014), 'We Will Not Rest in Peace: AIDS Activism, Black Radicalism, Queer and/or Trans resistance', in J. Haritaworn, A. Kuntsman and S. Posocco (eds), *Queer Necropolitics*, 31–50, Abingdon: Routledge.
Gouin, M. (2012), *Tibetan Rituals of Death: Buddhist Funerary Practices*, Abingdon: Routledge.
Gray, E. (2010), 'Victoria Dressed in Black: Poetry in an Elegiac Age,' in K. Weisman (ed), *The Oxford Handbook of the Elegy*, 272–88, Oxford: Oxford University Press.
Gray, T. (1981), 'Elegy Written in a Country Churchyard', in *Thomas Gray: Selected Poems*, ed. J. Heath-Stubbs, 21–5, Manchester: Carcanet Press.
Green, E. R. (2006), 'Debating Trans Inclusion in the Feminist Movement', *Journal of Lesbian Studies*, 10 (1–2): 231–48.
Gutzwiller, K. J. (1991), *Theocritus' Pastoral Analogies: The Formation of a Genre*, Madison: University of Wisconsin Press.
Gutzwiller, K. J. (1997), 'Genre Development and Gendered Voices in Erinna and Nossis', in Y. Prins and M. Schrieber (eds), *Dwelling in Possibility: Women Poets and Critics on Poetry*, 202–22, Ithaca: Cornell University Press.
Hamilton, S. (1853), *History of the National Flag of the United States of America*, Philadelphia: Lippincott, Grambo, and Company.
Hammond, J. (2010), 'New World Frontiers: The American Puritan Elegy', in K. Weisman (ed), *The Oxford Handbook of the Elegy*, 206–23, Oxford: Oxford University Press.
Hammond, M. (2010), *Beyond Elegy: Classical Arabic Women's Poetry in Context*, Oxford: Oxford University P/British Academy.
Haritaworn, J., A. Kuntsman, and S. Posocco, eds (2014), *Queer Necropolitics*, Abingdon: Routledge.
Harris, T. (2014), *Martin Luther King Jr., Heroism, and African American Literature*, Tuscaloosa: University of Alabama Press.

Harris, W. (2008), 'Phillis Wheatley, Diaspora Subjectivity, and the African American Canon,' *MELUS*, 33 (3): 27–43.

Hartman, M. (2011), 'An Arab Woman Poet as a Crossover Artist? Reconsidering the Ambivalent Legacy of Al-Khansa', *Tulsa Studies in Women's Literature*, 30 (1): 15–36.

Hatzenbuehler, R. L. (1996), 'Assessing the Meaning of Massacre: Boston (1770) and Kent State (1970)', *Peace & Change*, 21 (2): 208–20.

Hayward, E. (2008), 'More Lessons from a Starfish: Prefixial Flesh and Transspeciated Selves,' *Women's Studies Quarterly*, 36 (3): 64–85.

Hayward, P. (2017), *Making a Splash: Mermaids (and Mer-men) in 20th and 21st Century Audiovisual Media*, Bloomington: Indiana University Press.

Helle, A. (2010), 'Women's Elegies, 1834–Present: Female Authorship and the Affective Politics of Grief', in K. Weisman (ed), *The Oxford Handbook of the Elegy*, 463–80, Oxford: Oxford University Press.

Helmreich, S. (2012–2013), 'Seashell Sound', *Cabinet*, 48: 23–9.

Holladay, H. (2004), *Wild Blessings: The Poetry of Lucille Clifton*, Baton Rouge: LSU Press.

hooks, b. (1990), *Yearning: Race, Gender and Cultural Politics*, Boston: South End Press.

hooks, b. (1992), *Black Looks: Race and Representation*, Boston: South End Press, 1992.

Houck, D. W. (2005), 'Killing Emmett', *Rhetoric & Public Affairs*, 8 (2): 225–62.

Hudson-Weems, C. (1998), 'Resurrecting Emmett Till: the Catalyst of the Modern Civil Rights Movement', *Journal of Black Studies*, 29 (2): 179–88.

Hummel, H. K., ed (2016), *Black Lives Matter Reader*. Available online: https://blacklivesmatterpoetryreader.weebly.com/

Hunter-Young, N. (2018), 'Smoke Screens and Cinematic Representations of The MOVE Bombing', *Public*, 29 (58): 42–9.

Hurley, N. (2014), 'The Little Transgender Mermaid: A Shape-Shifting Tale', in M. Reimer, N. Ali, D. England, and M. Dennis Unra (eds), *Seriality and Texts for Young People: The Compulsion to Repeat*, 258–80, Basingstoke: Palgrave Macmillan.

Hussen, A. (2013), '"Black Rage" and "Useless Pain": Affect, Ambivalence, and Identity after King', *South Atlantic Quarterly*, 112 (2): 303–18.

Izevbaye, D. (2011), 'Living the Myth: Revisiting Okigbo's Art and Commitment', *Tydskrif Vir Letterkunde*, 48 (1): 13–25.

Jablonski, S. (1997), 'Ham's Vicious Race: Slavery and John Milton', *Studies in English Literature 1500–1900*, 37 (1): 173–90.

Jackson Ford, K. (2010), 'The Last Quatrain: Gwendolyn Brooks and the Ends of Ballads', *Twentieth Century Literature*, 56 (3): 371–95.

Jamison, A. (1974), 'Analysis of Selected Poetry of Phillis Wheatley', *The Journal of Negro Education*, 43 (3): 408–16.

Jefferson, T. (1785), *Notes on the State of Virginia*, Philadelphia: Richard and Hall. Available online: http://docsouth.unc.edu/southlit/jefferson/jefferson.html (accessed 6 May 2021).

Jordan, J. (2004), 'The Difficult Miracle of Black Poetry in America or Something Like a Sonnet for Phillis Wheatley', in J. Burrell (ed), *Word: On Being a [Woman] Writer*, 167–79, New York: Feminist Press at CUNY.

Jordan, J. (2007), *Directed by Desire*, ed. J. Heller Levi and S. Miles, Washington: Copper Canyon Press.

Kapai, L. (1995), 'Henrietta Cordelia Ray', in C. Davidson and L. Wagner-Martin (eds), *The Oxford Companion to Women's Writing in the United States*, Oxford: Oxford University Press. Available online: https://www.oxfordreference.com/view/10.1093/acref/9780195066081.001.0001/acref-9780195066081-e-0665?rskey=gRflRD&result=664 (accessed 16 November 2021).

Kaplan, N. (2014), 'The Fire [This] Time': Ferguson, Implicit Bias, and the Michael Brown Grand Jury', *Public Interest Law Reporter*, 20 (1): 52–6.

Katsiaficas, G. N. (2013), *Asia's Unknown Uprisings: People Power in the Philippines, Burma, Tibet, China, Taiwan, Bangladesh, Nepal, Thailand and Indonesia, 1947–2009*, Oakland: PM Press.

Kay, D. (1990), *Melodious Tears: The English Funeral Elegy from Spenser to Milton*, Oxford: Clarendon Press.

Kealiikanakaoleohaililani, K. and C. P. Giardina (2016), 'Embracing the Sacred: An Indigenous Framework for Tomorrow's Sustainability Science', *Sustainability Science*, 11 (1): 57–67.

Kennedy, D. (2007), *Elegy*, Abingdon, Oxon and New York: Routledge.

Kennedy, R. F. (1968), *Remarks to the Cleveland City Club, April 5, 1968*, Cleveland, OH: John F. Kennedy Presidential Library and Museum. Available online: https://www.jfklibrary.org/learn/about-jfk/the-kennedy-family/robert-f-kennedy/robert-f-kennedy-speeches/remarks-to-the-cleveland-city-club-april-5-1968 (accessed 6 May 2021).

Khan, A. (2019), 'Getting Killed by Police Is a Leading Cause of Death for Young Black Men in America', *LA Times*, 16 August. Available online: https://www.latimes.com/science/story/2019-08-15/police-shootings-are-a-leading-cause-of-death-for-black-men (accessed 6 May 2021).

Kiernan, B. (2008), *Blood and Soil: A World History of Genocide and Extermination from Sparta to Darfur*, London: Yale University Press.

King James Holy Bible (KJV) (2001), Nashville: Thomas Nelson.

King Jr., M. (1968a), *I've Been to the Mountaintop*, Mason Temple, Memphis, Tennessee, 3 April. Available online: https://www.americanrhetoric.com/speeches/mlkivebeentothemountaintop.htm (accessed 6 May 2021).

King Jr., M. (1968b), *The Other America*, Grosse Point High School, 14 March. Available online: http://www.gphistorical.org/mlk/mlkspeech/index.htm (accessed 6 May 2021).

Kohli, R. and D. G. Solórzano (2012), 'Teachers, Please Learn Our Names!: Racial Microaggressions and the K-12 Classroom', *Race, Ethnicity and Education*, 15 (4): 1–22.

Krupat, A. (2012), *'That the People Might Live': Loss and Renewal in Native American Elegy*, Ithaca: Cornell University Press.

Kutzinski, V. M. (1992), 'American Literary History as Spatial Practice', *American Literary History*, 4 (3): 550–7.

Lamble, S. (2008), 'Retelling Racialized Violence, Remaking White Innocence: The Politics of Interlocking Oppressions in Transgender Day of Remembrance', *Sexuality Research & Social Policy*, 5 (1): 24–42.

Leslie, Omolara (1973), 'The Poetry of Christopher Okigbo: Its Evolution and Significance', *Ufahamu: A Journal of African Studies*, 4 (1): 47–58.

Levy, P. (2018), *The Great Uprising: Race Riots in Urban America in the 1960s*, New York: Cambridge University Press.

Longazel, J. G. (2012), 'Moral Panic as Racial Degradation Ceremony: Racial Stratification and the Local-Level Backlash against Latino/a Immigrants', *Punishment & Society*, 15 (1): 96–119.

Lorde, A. (2000), *The Collected Poems of Audre Lorde*, New York: W. W. Norton & Company.

Lordi, E. (2018), 'Nikki Giovanni: "Martin Had Faith in the People"', *The Atlantic*, 5 April. Available online: https://www.theatlantic.com/entertainment/archive/2018/04/martin-luther-king-jr-nikki-giovanni-interview/554807/ (accessed 6 May 2021).

Lumsden, S. (2017), 'From Wilderness to Raw Material: How the Dispossession of Native Land Enables the Prison Industrial Complex', *UCLA Center for the Study of Women*, 3 March. Available online: https://csw.ucla.edu/2017/03/03/wilderness-raw-material-dispossession-native-land-enables-prison-industrial-complex/ (accessed 6 May 2021).

Lupton, M. J. (2006), *Lucille Clifton: Her Life and Letters*, Westport, CN: Greenwood Publishing.

Maag, C. (2007), 'Kent State Tape Is Said to Reveal Orders,' *New York Times*, 2 May: A17(L). Available online: https://www.nytimes.com/2007/05/02/us/02kent.html (accessed 6 May 2021).

Malcolm X (1964), *The Ballot or the Bullet*, Cleveland, Ohio, 3 April. Available online: http://www.edchange.org/multicultural/speeches/malcolm_x_ballot.html (accessed 6 May 2021).

Markides, A. (1982), 'Some Unusual Cures of Deafness', *The Journal of Laryngology and Otology*, 96: 479–90.

Marlowe, C. (1993), *Doctor Faustus A- and B- Texts (1604, 1616)*, ed. D. Bevington and E. Rasmussen, Manchester and New York: Manchester University Press.

Marotti, A. F. (1991), 'Patronage, Poetry and Print', *Yearbook of English Studies*, 21: 1–26.

Matson, R. L. (1972), 'Phillis Wheatley – Soul Sister?', *Phylon*, 33 (3): 222–30.

Mbembe, A. (2019), *Necropolitics*, trans. S. Corcoran, Durham and London: Duke University Press.

McMurtry-Chubb, T. (2017), '"Burn This Bitch Down": Mike Brown, Emmett Till, and the Gendered Politics of Black Parenthood', *Nevada Law Journal*, 17 (3): 619–50.

McQueen, P. (2016), 'Feminist and Trans Perspectives on Identity and the UK Gender Recognition Act', *The British Journal of Politics and International Relations*, 18 (3): 671–87.

McSweeney, J. (2014), 'What Is the Necropastoral?', *Poetry Foundation Harriet Blog*, 29 April. Available online: https://www.poetryfoundation.org/harriet/2014/04/what-is-the-necropastoral (accessed 6 May 2021).

Mellor, A. K. (2010), '"Anguish no Cessation Knows": Elegy and the British Woman Poet, 1660–1834', in K. Weisman (ed), *The Oxford Handbook of the Elegy*, 442–62, Oxford: Oxford University Press.

Metress, C. (2003), '"No justice, No Peace": The Figure of Emmett Till in African American Literature', *MELUS*, 28 (1): 87–103.

Mills, C. W. (2013), 'An Illuminating Blackness', *The Black Scholar*, 43 (4): 32–7.

Milton, John (1902), *Lycidas*, ed. H. B. Cotterill, London: Blackie and Son. Available online: http://babel.hathitrust.org/cgi/pt?id=mdp.39015008305289;view=1up;seq=7 (accessed 6 May 2021).

Minchin, T. J. and J. A. Salmond (2011), *After the Dream: Black and White Southerners since 1965*, Lexington: University of Kentucky Press.

Minibayeva, Natalia (2014), '*Per Aspera Ad Astra*: Symphonic Tradition in Tchaikovsky's First Suite for Orchestra', in L. Kearney (ed), *Tchaikovsky and His World*, 163–95, Princeton, NJ: Princeton University Press.

Miranda, D. A. (2005), *The Zen of La Llorona*, Cromer: Salt Publishing.

Moore, G. and U. Beier, eds (1998), *The Penguin Book of Modern African Poetry*, London: Penguin.

Morrison, T. (1988), 'Unspeakable Things Unspoken: The Afro-American Presence in American Literature', in *The Tanner Lectures on Human Values*, 7 October, University of Michigan. Available online: https://tannerlectures.utah.edu/_documents/a-to-z/m/morrison90.pdf (accessed 6 May 2021).

Morton, J. (2013), 'Sacred Shadows: The Significance of Black Madonnas', *The International Journal of Religion and Spirituality in Society*, 2 (2): 103–11.

Murray, J. (2021), 'Politicians Should Not "weaponise" UK History, Says Colonialism Researcher', *The Guardian*, Monday 22 February. Available online: https://www.theguardian.com/culture/2021/feb/22/politicians-should-not-weaponise-uk-history-says-colonialism-researcher (accessed 6 May 2021).

My Hearing Centers (2020), 'Hearing Loss Cures of the Past', 28 March. Available online: https://myhearingcenters.com/blog/hearing-loss-cures-of-the-past/ (accessed 6 May 2021).

National Center for Transgender Equality (2020), 'Murders of Transgender People in 2020 Surpasses Total for Last Year In Just Seven Months', Friday 7 August. Available online: https://transequality.org/blog/murders-of-transgender-people-in-2020-surpasses-total-for-last-year-in-just-seven-months (accessed 6 May 2021).

National Council on Family Relations (1970), 'Statement on the Effects of U.S. Casualties in Viet Nam on American Families', *Journal of Marriage and Family*, 32 (2): 197–9.

Nel, M. (2017), 'Baptised in the Spirit and Fire: Single or Double Baptism', *Neotestamentica*, 50 (1): 165–80.

Neocleous, M. (2003), 'The Political Economy of the Dead: Marx's Vampires', *History of Political Thought*, XXIV (4): 668–84.

Newsweek Archives (2017), 'Take Everything You Need, Baby', 15 April 1968, in 'Photos: The Rampage That Came after Martin Luther King Jr. Was Slayed', 16 January. Available online: https://www.newsweek.com/martin-luther-king-jr-assassination-riots-541664 (accessed 6 May 2021).

Obumselu, B. (2010), 'Cambridge House, Ibadan, 1962–66: Politics and Poetics in Okigbo's Last Years', *Research in African Literatures*, 41 (2): 2–18.

Ogden, S. (2014), 'The Prison-Industrial Complex in Indigenous California', in J. Sudbury (ed), *Global Lockdown: Race, Gender, and the Prison-Industrial Complex*, 57–66, Abingdon: Routledge.

Okigbo, C. (1963), 'Lament of the Silent Sisters', *Transition*, 8: 13–16.

Okigbo, C. (1965), 'Lament of the Drums', *Transition*, 18: 16–17.

O'Neale, S. (1986), 'A Slave's Subtle War: Phillis Wheatley's Use of Biblical Myth and Symbol', *Early American Literature*, 21 (2): 144–65.

Onwuachi-Willig, A. (2016–2017), 'Policing the Boundaries of Whiteness: The Tragedy of Being "Out of Place" from Emmett Till to Trayvon Martin', *Iowa Law Review*, 102 (3): 1113–86.

Onyemaobim, I. O. (2016), 'The Michael Brown Legacy: Police Brutality and Minority Prosecution', *George Mason University Civil Rights Law Journal*, 26 (2): 157–82.

Ostriker, A. (1993), 'Kin and Kin: The Poetry of Lucille Clifton', *The American Poetry Review*, 22 (6): 41–8.

Owen, D. (2019), *Volume Control: Hearing in a Deafening World*, London: Penguin.

Palazo, E. D. (1989), 'Military Checkpoints and the Rule of Law', *Philippine Law Journal*, 64: 211–35.

Peraino, J. (2005), *Listening to the Sirens: Musical Technologies of Queer Identity from Homer to Hedwig*, Berkeley: University of California Press.

Perfetti, S. (2018), 'Biblical Exegesis and Aristotelian Naturalism: Albert the Great, Thomas Aquinas, and the Animals of the Book of Job', *Aisthesis*, 11 (1): 81–96.

Persons, G. A. (1987), 'The Philadelphia Move Incident as an Anomaly in Models of Mayoral Leadership', *Phylon*, 48 (4): 249–60.

Peters, C. (2017), 'Left-wing Academics Are Helping a Minority of Students to Force Their Identity Politics on the Rest of Us", *The Telegraph*, 27 October. Available online: https://www.telegraph.co.uk/news/2017/10/27/left-wing-academics-helping-minority-students-force-identity/ (accessed 6 May 2021).

Pierce, D. (2001), 'Language, Violence, and Queer People', *Journal of Gay & Lesbian Social Services*, 13 (1–2): 47–62.

Pinley Covert, L. (2017), *San Miguel de Allende: Mexicans, Foreigners, and the Making of a World Heritage Site*, Lincoln: University of Nebraska Press.

Poggioli, R. (1975), *The Oaten Flute: Essays on Pastoral Poetry and the Pastoral Ideal*, Cambridge, MA: Harvard University Press.

Potterf, J. E. and J. R. Pohl (2018), 'A Black Teen, a White Cop, and a City in Turmoil: Analyzing Newspaper Reports on Ferguson, Missouri and the Death of Michael Brown', *Journal of Contemporary Criminal Justice*, 34 (4): 421–41.

Priest, M. (2010), '"The Nightmare Is Not Cured": Emmett Till and American Healing', *American Quarterly*, 62 (1): 1–24.

Quinn, J. (1986), 'Move v. The City of Philadelphia', *The Nation*, 29 March, 458–60.

Raboteau, A. J. (1994), 'Fire in the Bones: African-American Christianity and Autobiographical Reflection', *America*, 170 (18): 4–9.

Ramazani, J. (1994), *Poetry of Mourning: The Modern Elegy from Hardy to Heaney*, Chicago: University of Chicago Press.

Rankine, C. (2020), *Just Us*, London: Allen Lane.

Raymond, J. (2004), 'Complications of Interest: Milton, Scotland, Ireland, and National Identity in 1649', *The Review of English Studies (New Series)*, 55 (220): 315–45.

Reese, R. (2011), 'Canada: The Promised Land for U.S. Slaves', *The Western Journal of Black Studies*, 35 (3): 208–17.

Richards, P. M. (1992), 'Phillis Wheatley and Literary Americanization', *American Quarterly*, 44 (2): 163–91.

Rivera Garza, Cristina. (2020), *The Restless Dead: Necrowriting and Disappropriation*, trans. Robin Myers, Nashville, TN: Vanderbilt University Press.

Robinson Marbury, H. (2015), *Pillars of Cloud and Fire: The Politics of Exodus in African American Biblical Interpretation*, New York: New York University Press.

Roces, M. (2006), 'The Militant Nun as Political Activist and Feminist in Martial Law Philippines', in M. Mikula (ed), *Women, Activism and Social Change: Stretching Boundaries*, 136–56, Abingdon: Routledge.

Rodell, P. A. (2002), *Culture and Customs of the Philippines*, Westport, CT: Greenwood Publishing.

Rosenberg, R. and N. Oswin (2015), 'Trans Embodiment in Carceral Space: Hypermasculinity and the US Prison Industrial Complex', *Gender, Place & Culture: A Journal of Feminist Geography*, 22 (9): 1269–86.

Rosga, A. (2001), 'Deadly Words: State Power and the Entanglement of Speech and Violence in Hate Crime', *Law and Critique*, 12 (3): 223–52.

Ross, L., P. Lyon and C. Cathcart (2014), 'Pills, Potions and Devices: Treatments for Hearing Loss Advertised in Mid-Nineteenth Century British Newspapers', *Social History of Medicine*, 27 (3): 530–56.

Sacks, P. M. (1987), *The English Elegy: Studies in the Genre from Spenser to Yeats*, Baltimore and London: The Johns Hopkins University Press.

Sanchez, S. (1987), *Under a Soprano Sky*, Trenton, NJ: Africa World Press.

Sanders, K. and J. L. Jeffries (2013), 'Framing MOVE: A Press' Complicity in the Murder of Women and Children in the City of (Un) Brotherly Love', *Journal of African American Studies*, 17 (4): 566–86.

Saramifar, Y. (2019a), 'Emotions of Felt Memories: Looking for Interplay of Emotions and Histories in Iranian Political Consciousness since Iran-Iraq War (1980–1988)', *Anthropology of Consciousness*, 30 (2): 132–51.

Saramifar, Y. (2019b), 'The South Side of Heaven: A Journey along the Iranian Collective Memory in Iran-Iraq War Memorial Sites', *Anthropology of the Middle East*, 14 (1): 125–41.

Schenck, C. M. (1986), 'Feminism and Deconstruction: Re-Constructing the Elegy', *Tulsa Studies in Women's Literature*, 5 (1): 13–27.

Schiesari, J. (1992), *The Gendering of Melancholia: Feminism, Psychoanalysis, and the Symbolics of Loss in Renaissance Literature*, Ithaca, NY: Cornell University Press.

Schmider, A. (2016), '2016 Was the Deadliest Year on Record for Transgender People', *GLAAD*, 9 November. Available online: https://www.glaad.org/blog/2016-was-deadliest-year-record-transgender-people (accessed 6 May 2021).

Schon, J. (2016), 'The Centrality of Checkpoints for Civilians during Conflict', *Civil Wars*, 18 (3): 281–310.

Scott, K. (2016), 'Pronouns and Procedures: Reference and beyond', *Lingua*, 175: 69–82.

Seyed-Gohrab, A. (2016), '"The Houses of the Tulips": Persian Poetry on the Fallen in the Iran-Iraq War', *International Journal of Persian Literature*, 1 (1): 89–119.

Shakhsari, S. (2014), 'Killing Me Softly with Your Rights: Queer Death and the Politics of Rightful Killing', in J. Haritaworn, A. Kuntsman and S. Posocco (eds), *Queer Necropolitics*, 93–110, Abingdon: Routledge.

Sharif, S. (2016), *Look*, Minneapolis: Graywolf.

Sharpton, A. (2014), 'No Justice, No Peace: Why Mark Duggan's Family Echoed My Rallying Cry', *The Guardian*, 10 January. Available online: https://www.theguardian.com/commentisfree/2014/jan/10/mark-duggan-family-rallying-cry-no-peace-no-justice (accessed 6 May 2021).

Shaw, W. D. (1994), *Elegy and Paradox: Testing the Conventions*, Baltimore and London: The Johns Hopkins University Press.

Shields, J. C. (1994), 'Phillis Wheatley's Subversive Pastoral', *Eighteenth-Century Studies*, 21 (4): 631–47.

Shipley, M. and J. Taylor (2019), 'Life as Eutopia: MOVE's Natural Revolution as a Response to America's Dystopian Reality', *Utopian Studies*, 30 (1): 5–44.

Schreiber, M. Y. (2010), 'Kaddish: Jewish American Elegy Post-1945', in K. Weisman (ed), *The Oxford Handbook of the Elegy*, 397–412, Oxford: Oxford University Press.

Sinyangwe, S., D. McKesson and J. Elzie (2014), 'Mapping Police Violence: 2014 Unarmed Victims'. Available online: https://mappingpoliceviolence.org/unarmed2014 (accessed 6 May 2021).

Sinyangwe, S., D. McKesson and J. Elzie (2015), 'Mapping Police Violence: Troy Robinson'. Available online: https://mappingpoliceviolence.org/unarmed-2015/vlo9vfddf9bvumwoqtw3b3e4cdoqtm

Sinyangwe, S., D. McKesson and J. Elzie (2021), 'Mapping Police Violence: 2021'. Available online: https://mappingpoliceviolence.org/

Smith, D. (2014), 'Not an Elegy for Mike Brown', *Split This Rock*, 12 August. Available online: https://www.splitthisrock.org/poetry-database/poem/not-an-elegy-for-mike-brown (accessed 6 May 2021).

Smith, D. (2015), *Black Movie*, Minnesota: Button Poetry.

Smith, D. (2017), *Don't Call Us Dead*, Minnesota: Graywolf.

Smith, E. (1974), 'Phillis Wheatley: A Black Perspective', *The Journal of Negro Education*, 43 (3): 401–7.

Smith, E. (1977), *By Mourning Tongues: Studies in English Elegy*, Ipswich: The Boydell Press.

Smith, S. M. (2015), 'The Afterimages of Emmet Till', *American Art*, 29 (1): 22–7.

Sontag, S. (2005), *On Photography*, New York: Rosetta Books.

Spargo, R. C. (2005), *The Ethics of Mourning: Grief and Responsibility in Elegiac Literature*, Baltimore and London: The Johns Hopkins University Press.

Speak, G. (1990), 'El licenciado Vidriera and the Glass Men of Early Modern Europe', *The Modern Language Review*, 85 (4): 850–65.

Spencer, L. G. (2014), 'Performing Transgender Identity in *The Little Mermaid*: From Andersen to Disney', *Communication Studies*, 65 (1): 112–27.

Spenser, E. (1825), *The Poetical Works of Edmund Spenser*, V. Available online: http://www.gutenberg.org/cache/epub/10602/pg10602.html (accessed 6 May 2021).

Spilerman, S. (1970), 'The Causes of Racial Disturbances: A Comparison of Alternative Explanations', *American Sociological Review*, 35 (4): 627–49.

Spillers, H. J. (1987), 'Mama's Baby, Papa's Maybe: An American Grammar Book', *Diacritics*, 17 (2): 64–81.

Steidl, C. R. (2013), 'Remembering May 4, 1970: Integrating the Commemorative Field at Kent State', *American Sociological Review*, 78 (5): 749–72.

Sullivan, J. D. (2002), 'Killing John Cabot and Publishing Black: Gwendolyn Brooks's "Riot"', *African American Review*, 36 (4): 557–69.

Taleghani, R. S. (2020), '"Personal Effects": Translation, Intimacy and Domestication in the Poetry of Solmaz Sharif', *Middle East Journal of Culture and Communication*, 13: 49–62.

Tate, C., ed (1985), *Black Women Writers at Work*, Harpenden: Oldcastle Books.

Taylor, D. (2010), 'Three Lean Cats in a Hall of Mirrors: James Baldwin, Norman Mailer, and Eldridge Cleaver on Race and Masculinity', *Texas Studies in Literature and Language*, 52 (1): 70–101.

Tell, D. (2017), 'Remembering Emmett Till: Reflections on Geography, Race, and Memory', *Advances in the History of Rhetoric*, 20 (2): 121–38.

Thompson, K. (2005), *Moral Panics*, Abingdon: Routledge.

Tighe, S. (2014), 'Of Course We Are Crazy: Discrimination of Native American Indians through Criminal Justice', *Justice Policy Journal*, 11 (1): 1–38.

Todd, J. M. (1998), *The Critical Fortunes of Aphra Behn*, New York: Camden House, 1998.

Treloar, N. (2021), 'The Weaponization of the "Left-behind White Working Class"', *Runnymede Trust*, 14 January. Available online: https://www.runnymedetrust.org/blog/the-weaponisation-of-the-left-behind-white-working-class-harms-us-all

Tsakiropoulou-Summers, T. (2013), 'Helen of Troy: At the Crossroads between Ancient Patriarchy and Modern Feminism', *Interdisciplinary Humanities*, 30 (2): 37–56.

Twiddy, I. (2012), *Pastoral Elegy in Contemporary British and Irish Poetry*, London and New York: Continuum.

Ulanday Barrett, K. (2020), *More than Organs*, Little Rock: Sibling Rivalry Press.

US Government (1953), *Military Supply Management Program*, Subcommittee of the Committee on Government of Operations, Washington: Government Printing Office.

US Government (1961), *Dictionary of United States Army Terms*, Washington: Department of the Army Headquarters.

US Government (1969), *Logistics Management, Department of the Army Field Manual*, Washington: Department of the Army Headquarters.

US Government (1994), *Department of Defense Dictionary of Military and Associated Terms*, Washington: Joint Staff Pentagon.

van Der Auwera, J. and A. Zamorano Aguilar (2016), 'The History of Modality and Mood', in J. Nuyts and J. Van Der Auwera (eds), *The Oxford Handbook of Modality and Mood*, 9–29, Oxford: Oxford University Press.

Vickery, J. B. (2006), *The Modern Elegiac Temper*, Baton Rouge: Louisiana State University Press.

Vrana, L. (2018), 'Gwendolyn Brooks's Last Quatrain: The Ballad Form and African American Anti-Lynching Poems', *Journal of Ethnic American Literature*, 8: 5–27.

Wagner, T. (2010), 'America's Civil Rights Revolution: Three Documentaries about Emmett Till's Murder in Mississippi', *Historical Journal of Film, Radio and Television*, 30 (2): 187–201.

Wall, C. A. (1999), 'Sifting Legacies in Lucille Clifton's "Generations"', *Contemporary Literature*, 40 (4): 552–74.

Walters, J. (2000), 'Nikki and Rita Dove: Poets Redefining', *The Journal of Negro History*, 85 (3): 210–17.

Waters, E. (2017), *Lesbian, Gay, Bisexual, Transgender, Queer, and HIV-Affected Hate Violence in 2016: A 20th Anniversary Report from the National Coalition of Anti-Violence Programs*, New York: New York City Gay and Lesbian Anti-Violence Project. Available online: https://avp.org/wp-content/uploads/2017/06/NCAVP_2016HateViolence_REPORT.pdf (accessed 6 May 2021).

Watkin, W. (2004), *On Mourning: Theories of Loss in Modern Literature*, Edinburgh: Edinburgh University Press.

Watterson, W. C. (2010), 'Nation and History: The Emergence of the English Pastoral Elegy', in K. Weisman (ed), *The Oxford Handbook of the Elegy*, 135–52, Oxford: Oxford University Press.

Weeks, J. (2010), 'AIDS: The Intellectual Agenda', in C. Critcher (ed), *Critical Readings: Moral Panics and the Media*, 77–87, Maidenhead: Open University Press.

Weisman, K., ed (2010), *The Oxford Handbook of the Elegy*, Oxford: Oxford University Press.

Wheatley, P. (2001), *Phillis Wheatley: Complete Writings*, ed. V. Carretta, London: Penguin.

Wheeler, L. (2001), 'Heralding the Clear Obscure: Gwendolyn Brooks and Apostrophe', *Callaloo*, 24 (1): 227–35.

Whitley, E. (2001), '"A Long Missing Part of Itself": Bringing Lucille Clifton's "Generations" into American Literature', *MELUS*, 26(2): 47–64.

Willard, C. (1995), 'Wheatley's Turns of Praise: Heroic Entrapment and the Paradox of Revolution', *American Literature*, 67 (2): 233–56.

Wurfel, D. (1977), 'Martial Law in the Philippines: The Methods of Regime Survival', *Pacific Affairs*, 50 (1): 5–30.

ya Salaam, Kalamu (2016), 'Love and Liberation: Sonia Sanchez's Literary Uses of Personal Pain', *Neo-Griot*, 29 March. Available online: http://kalamu.com/neogriot/2016/03/29/essay-love-and-liberation-sonia-sanchezs-literary-uses-of-personal-pain-2/ (accessed 6 May 2021).

Young, J. K (2010), *Black Writers, White Publishers: Marketplace Politics in Twentieth-Century African-American Literature*, Jackson: University of Mississippi Press.

Zafar, R. (2013), 'Elegy and Remembrance in the Cookbooks of Alice B. Toklas and Edna Lewis', *MELUS*, 38 (4): 32–51.

Zeiger, M. F. (1997), *Beyond Consolation: Death, Sexuality, and the Changing Shapes of Elegy*, Ithaca, NY: Cornell University Press.

Index

Abba, Abba A. 98–9, 113 n. 10
ableism 22, 25, 170, 171–5
abstraction 24, 42, 121–2, 123, 126, 143–4, 149
Adorno, Theodor 147
Ahmed, Sara 7, 161–2, 164, 166
Aizura, Aren Z. 119, 122, 124, 147–9
anti-museum 24, 154–5
Aoki, Ryka 115, 128–39, 144, 148–9
apotheosis 51, 53, 58, 161
archive 6, 155, 160
Arnold, Matthew 3, 5, 15, 64
assemblage 5, 117, 125, 153, 157, 176
assimilation
    of grief experiences 4, 21
    of Indigenous communities 142, 144, 147
    of irregular bodies 138
    of literary work 21, 61–2, 149–50
Awkward, Michael 33, 43, 48, 62–3

ballad 67, 71–2, 112 n. 4
barricade 20, 167–8, 169–70
Bettcher, Talia Mae 116, 118, 127, 129, 149, 150
Bible 56, 85–7, 95–6
binary
    gender 115, 116–18, 119, 126, 127, 141, 143, 149
    racial 34, 37, 42, 45, 46–7, 48
Black Aesthetic 23, 34, 42–8, 49
Black Arts Movement (BAM) 42–8, 49
body
    'acceptable' queer 130, 131–2
    displaced queer 137–8, 139
    of Emmett Till 65–6, 69, 74–8
    and gender 46, 128
    and gun 125–6
    and hearing 171–2, 175
    marked 137, 141–2, 164
    of Michael Brown 103–4
    nocturnal 18–19
    objectified 46
    parts of 89, 126
    as poetic metaphor 8, 45–6, 134, 169
    politic 147
    regulation of 135
    trans* 116, 122, 128, 131, 137, 139
borders 19, 20, 22, 34, 47, 62, 96, 117, 169
Brooks, Gwendolyn
    and Black Aesthetic 34, 42–3
    critical reception 23, 35–8, 40, 44–5, 112 n. 4
    elegies for Emmett Till 66–74, 76, 77–8, 105
    elegies (general) 26 n. 3, 48–9, 52, 79
    in Ramazani 12, 31, 59 n. 1
    'the rites for cousin vit' 52–5, 56–8, 95
Brown, Michael 102–9, 111
Bryant, Carolyn 65–6
    and femininity 69, 71, 105
    and imprisonment 70
    as maternal figure 66–8
    as silent 70, 76, 77–8
Bryant, Roy 65–6, 68
    as monstrous 69–70
    trial 67–9, 73, 77–8, 110, 112. n 3
    and white patriarchy 77
    as wound 74, 77
Butler, Judith
    on gender 116, 117–19, 120, 126–7, 129, 150, 153
    on grievability 4, 6–7, 18–19, 22, 120, 122–3, 159
    on photography 75, 76
    on precarity 19, 20, 140–1
    on violence 110, 113 n. 16

capitalism
    cultural 131
    and elegy 17
    general 27 n. 7, 31, 97, 101
    and military 158–9
    necrocapitalism 119–20, 135, 145, 149
    and prisons 146

as vampire 144–5
capitalization 26 n. 1, 54, 68, 89, 91,
    112–13 n. 8, 158
carcerality 22, 145–8
Carmichael, Stokely 81, 82–3, 106
Chrystos 140–1, 148
cis-heteropatriarchy
    and abstraction 122
    and binary 127, 141
    and gaze 128, 131–2
    and hegemony 121–2, 125, 136
    and violence 124, 125–6
    see also heteropatriarchy
Clifton, Lucille
    'after kent state' 92–7, 102, 103, 106–7,
        112–13 n. 8
    critical reception 37–42, 48
    elegies (general) 12, 26 n. 3, 33, 48–9, 79
    'here rests' 55–8
colonialism
    and elegy 4–7, 23, 49, 140–8
    ideas 12, 64, 97, 111, 147
    and literature 21, 62
    systems of power 18–19, 24, 39, 64, 98,
        138, 140–2, 144, 146, 148
    and violence 20, 51, 63, 109–10, 141–2,
        144, 147, 150
complaint 9, 46
Crenshaw, Kimberlé 7, 11, 18

Davis, Angela 100, 145–6, 146–7
Day, Meg 157, 170–5
D/deafness 24, 170–5
dehumanization 22, 104, 106, 164
    and gaze 76
    and language 135, 159
    of queer and non-binary persons
        119–20, 124, 135, 149
    of trans women 122, 123, 125, 148
    and violence 89
Derrida, Jacques 24, 155–6, 176
Dickinson, Emily 1, 8–9
Dickinson, Stirling 136, 137–8
disposability
    of images 75
    of lives 20, 22, 119–20, 122, 124, 133,
        137, 139, 147–8, 149, 159
Driskill, Qwo-Li 115, 140–8, 149–50,
    151 n. 6
DuBois, W.E.B 86, 96

Edelman, Elijah Adiv 119, 123, 126, 135,
    137, 139, 145, 149
EDSA Revolution 167–8
Elegiac complaint 9, 46
Elegy
    and class bias 14–17
    'English' 3, 4–7, 17, 22, 23, 32, 44, 64,
        155
    as genealogy 2–4, 5–7
    as mode 21, 32, 33, 34, 47, 67, 100, 102,
        103, 153, 158
    as necropoetics 19–20
    and patriarchal bias 7–11
    and racial bias 11–14, 29–48
    women's 1–2, 7–10
Emerson, Ralph Waldo 138–9
erasure
    of D/deaf persons 173, 175
    of feminized labour 8
    as figurative death 115
    of Indigenous American culture 141–2,
        144, 146, 147, 148–9
    of non-binary bodies 119–20, 122,
        123–6, 129–31, 134, 135–9, 148–9
    of particularity 104
    of poverty 14, 25
    of subjectivity 52
    of women writers of colour 13, 39
Espinoza, Joshua Jennifer 115, 120–8, 132,
    143–4, 148–9
Eurocentrism 21, 61–2
    in education 144
    and elegy 32, 34, 61, 62–3, 64, 111, 150,
        153, 155
excess 10–11, 53–4, 115, 139

Fanon, Frantz 22, 77, 96–7, 109–10
Ferguson protests 102, 103, 106, 107, 108,
    110
Fordham, Mary Weston 12, 13, 58,
    59 n. 1
Fuss, Diana 1, 3, 12

gaze 74, 76, 128, 131–2, 161
gender
    and grief 10
    heteronormative ideals 6, 116–17,
        129–30
    inequalities 2, 11, 13, 14–15, 31
    and language 8, 125

policing of 118–20, 126–7, 129–30, 141–2, 146
tropes 41, 45
see also binary
Giovanni, Nikki
and Black Aesthetic 34, 43
critical reception 45, 46
elegies (general) 48, 58
'Reflections on April 4, 1968' 80–7, 91, 95, 104, 106, 108, 110
Gray, Thomas 3, 55
grief
accumulated 104
authenticity of 11
collective 1, 71, 86–7, 90, 91–2, 149
commercialization of 17
common experience of 4, 21–2, 90
as complaint 9
and elegy 21–2, 34, 48, 72
gendering of 10
inherited 165–70
and language 53, 95
militant 46–7
as performance 9
public 2
see also policing
guns 82–3, 93, 125–6, 158

Harper, Frances Ellen Watkins 12, 85, 86
healing 91, 140, 148, 173
health care 130, 140
Helen of Troy 104–5, 106
heteropatriarchy
binaries 116, 118, 141
colonial 142, 144, 146, 148
desire 126
hegemony 121, 139
ideals 46, 119, 124, 127, 136, 149
marriage structures 8, 142
Holy Week Uprising 82, 83, 85, 106, 110
hooks, bell 33, 35, 39, 40, 43–4, 62, 64, 74, 112
House Concurrent Resolution 144
Hughes, Langston 1, 3, 30–2, 47, 61, 62–3
Hussen, Aida 46–7, 84, 106, 111

identity
Black identity 43, 63
and capitalization 26 n. 1
and complexity 57, 131–2

D/deaf identity 173
in elegy scholarship 4
in elegy 21
elision of 39
enforcement and regulation 129, 136, 138–9
and gender 121, 153
Indigenous identity 144
and mourning 47, 133, 165–6
politics 25, 145
queer identity 131, 135
Two-Spirit identity 141
inheritance
grief as 165, 169
literary 3, 150, 153
Indigenous
American communities 140, 146, 148
American elegy 2, 29
American erasure, *see Erasure*
American history 141–2, 144, 149
Americans and precarity 140–2, 144, 145, 147–8
American systems of gender 141–2
American writers 11, 29, 140–8
Hawaiian *ohana* 134–5
West African drum elegies 100
irregularity 67, 90, 128–9, 130
of bodies 130, 133, 135, 136–9
of identity 117

Jefferson, Thomas 12–13, 50, 63
Job, Book of 56–7
Johnson, Lyndon B. 82, 83, 92, 95, 100
Jordan June
elegies (general) 58, 64, 80
'In Memoriam' 87–91

Kay, Dennis 1, 2, 3, 12, 27 n. 5, 30
Kennedy, David 1, 3, 7–8, 12, 30
King Jr., Martin Luther
elegies for 23, 80–92
and non-violence 79, 81, 82, 106, 107, 109–10
Kutzinski, Vera M. 5, 13, 34, 47, 61–2

Lamble, Sarah 122, 123, 127, 129–31, 132
language
and accessibility 43, 48
of Christianity 49
coded 9, 38

colonizer's 26 n. 1, 176 n. 1
in disarray 87, 92
erasive 148–9
and excess 10, 54, 115
extra-lexical 52–3
and gender 8, 125
and identity 63
Indigenous American 144, 145
rhetorical 149
sign language 173–5
US military 157–9, 160–2, 163
and violence 24, 83, 91–2, 96, 124–5, 133
as weapon 22, 146, 147–8
Lee, Spike 107, 109
Lorde, Audre
  'Afterimages' 74–8, 105, 110
  elegies (general) 12, 26 n. 3, 30, 58, 66, 79

Malcolm X
  'The Ballot or the Bullet' 81, 82–3
  elegies for 12, 33–4, 52, 55, 58, 79
  on violence 106, 107, 109–10
Marcos, Ferdinand 165, 167–8
Marlowe, Christopher 104, 106
martyrdom
  and Christopher Okigbo 98–9
  and language 161
  master narratives of 159–60, 163
masculinity
  and desire 15, 70, 76–7, 125
  and elegy 4, 6, 10, 20, 115, 153, 157
  and gender expression 116, 117
  and grieving 10
  and language 8, 95
  white masculinity 23, 64, 67–8, 69–71, 73, 76–7, 78, 105
Mbembe, Achille
  on archives 6, 160
  on capitalism 145, 159
  on colonial occupation 138, 142
  on *death-worlds,* 120, 139
  on forms of living 123
  on language 159
  on museums 6, 24, 154–5, 176
  on necropolitics *see necropolitics*
  on radical hospitality 24, 155
  on sacrificial economy 106
  on slavery 52
  on sovereignty 128, 139
  on universalism 153
  on Western culture 6, 61, 129
  on Western democracy 118–19
  on white fear 41, 77
  on writing 22
militant nuns 167, 168–9, 170
military-industrial-complex 20, 159, 162
Milton, John 2, 3, 5, 31, 64
Milam, J. W. 65–6, 67, 68–9, 73, 77–8, 110
Miranda, Deborah 140, 148
Morrison, Toni 13, 21, 23, 29–30, 30, 62–3, 64, 154
MOVE (organization) 97–9, 101–2, 104
museum
  anti-museum *see anti-museum*
  critique 6, 154–6, 176
  decolonizing of 157
  and martyrdom 159–60
myth
  and Black experience 48
  and chivalric tropes 67–8
  family mythos 166, 169
  of glass delusion 137
  and Helen of Troy 104–5, 106
  ideological myths 124
  mythification of the dead 161
  myth-making 24, 160–1, 164
  and pastoral 15–16
  and white masculinity 23, 68–9, 70

National Guard 92–3, 95
necrocapitalism 119, 145, 149
necropoetics 19–20, 27 n. 8, 157
necropolitics
  definition 18–19, 118–19
  and elegy 20, 22, 24
  and heterosexuality 119
  as ideology 25, 126
  and meaning 139
  and power 128, 129, 133–4, 135
  and precarity 20, 139, 147, 148–9
  see also queer necropolitics
nocturnal body *See body*
non-binary 64, 119, 137, 142, 146
nonviolence 80, 81–2, 83, 84, 86, 87, 91, 106, 109–10, 113 n. 16

objectification
  of Black women writers 46
  in 'here rests' 57

and language 135, 158
'Other' as object 39
in 'The Last Quatrain' 71–2
in 'the rites for cousin vit' 53–5
of trans women 123–4
Okigbo, Christopher 98–100, 101, 102, 113 n. 9, 113 n. 10
Ostriker, Alice 37–42, 42–3, 48
otherness 39, 42, 48, 145, 156, 157, 176

pastoral 1–3, 9, 14–16, 27 n. 8, 64, 89, 130
pathetic fallacy 130, 165
pathologizing
    of black urban crime 100
    of deafness 24, 173–4
    of sexuality 136–7
    of trans* bodies 129
    of 'unproductive' bodies 135, 137, 145
patriarchy *See heteropatriarchy* and *cis-heteropatriarchy*
patronage 16–17
People Power Revolution *See EDSA Revolution*
Philadelphia 97–9, 100–2, 104
photographic images
    of Carolyn Bryant 112 n. 3
    of the dead 76, 158, 161–2
    and desensitization 75
    of Emmett Till 66, 75
police
    brutality 79, 83, 97–9, 102–6, 107, 108, 121, 126, 140, 146
    in colonized world 96, 141
    in Emmett Till case 77
    in Michael Brown shooting 102–6
    and misgendering of victims 121, 122
    and MOVE bombing 97–9
    in UK, 113 n. 15
policing
    of gender 129, 141, 145
    of grief 10, 34, 47, 84
    ideological 135–6
    of Indigenous Americans 145
    of literature 34, 41, 47
    militarized 20, 23, 97, 108
    of trans* bodies 126–7, 129, 135–6
    of Western democracy 18
policy
    colonial 5, 141, 144
    discriminative 22, 94, 126–7, 144

precarity
    definition 19, 140–1, 149
    and Indigenous American body 140–1, 142, 145, 148
    material 143–4, 145, 148, 149
    and necropolitics 20, 22, 140
    and trans* body 24, 115, 127, 129–30, 136, 139, 140–1, 148
    and Two-Spirit body 140–1
    see also Butler, Judith
predation 144, 145, 147, 158
prison
    figurative 70, 78, 145–7
    and gender regulation 127, 146
    industrial-complex 20, 145, 146–7
    as necropolitical 19, 20
    and racial disparity 100, 146–7
promised land 85–6, 87, 88

queer necropolitics
    book of essays 24, 115, 119–20, 122
    definition 119–20

radical hospitality *See Mbembe, Achille*
Ramazani, Jahan
    on elegy 33–4, 58, 59 n. 1, 91, 92
    on Langston Hughes 31–2, 47, 61, 62, 63
    Poetry of Mourning 1, 2, 3, 7, 12, 30–1
Rankine, Claudia 24, 25, 111
Ray, Henrietta Cordelia 12, 13, 58, 59 n. 1
regulation
    of bodies 22, 126–7, 128–30, 138–9
    of gender 126–7, 128–30, 133, 135, 146
    of sexualities 118–9, 120, 133, 135, 138–9
    social systems of 24, 99, 117, 118–9, 126–7, 128–30, 133, 135, 138–9
Rossetti, Christina 8

Sacks, Peter M. 1, 2, 3, 7, 8, 12, 30, 58
Sanchez, Sonia
    critical reception 46
    elegies (general) 33, 48, 58, 79
    elegy for MOVE 97–102, 104
seashell resonance 171–2
Sharif, Solmaz 157–65
Shaw, W. David 1, 3, 8–9, 12, 30
slavery
    and Alfred, Lord Tennyson 5
    and George Whitefield 49–50

and John Milton 5
and language 32
and museum 154
and necropolitics 18–19
and the pastoral 14
and Phillis Wheatley 12, 49–50, 51–2
and Promised Land 85–6
Smith, Danez 58, 102–11, 121
Smith, Eric 1, 3, 7–8, 12, 30
sovereignty
   Black sovereignty 81
   and hospitality 156, 176
   and MOVE, 98
   and norms 129
   personal 134
   and power 119, 128, 135
   romance of 139
   women's sovereignty 8
Spargo, R. Clifton 1, 12, 30
spectacle
   and Emmett Till 75, 76
   and Martin Luther King, Jr. 84
   and MOVE bombing 101
Spenser, Edmund 2, 3, 5, 16, 27 n. 5, 31
Swinburne, Algernon Charles 2, 3

Tchaikovsky, Pyotr Ilyich 136–7
Tennyson, Alfred Lord 2, 3, 5
Theocritus 2, 14
Thoreau, Henry David 136, 138–9
Till, Emmett 36, 65–7, 79, 93, 110
   elegies for 23, 66–78, 105
Till-Bradley, Mamie 66–7, 71–3, 75
Transgender Day of Remembrance (TDOR) 130–1, 132, 139, 148
transcendence 38, 55, 58
transmisogyny 24, 121–2, 123, 124, 125–7, 128–9, 131–3
Twiddy, Ian 1, 3
Two-Spirit 140, 141, 144, 146, 151 n. 1

Ulanday Barrett, Kay 157, 165–70

vampire 144–5, 147
Vickery, John B. 1, 12
Vietnam War 94–5, 97
violence
   colonial 18–19, 20, 27 n. 8, 51, 63, 96, 109–10, 140, 141–2, 144, 147

and gaze 74–5, 76
genealogy as 6
and Malcolm X, 81, 107, 109–10
in pastoral 15
of pathologizing 24, 170, 174
patriarchal 94–5, 97
in poetry 42, 51, 68, 72–3, 80, 83, 86–7, 88–92, 100, 106, 120–8, 138–9, 171
and police 106–7, 113 n. 15, 126, 146
political 102, 108, 168
and precarity 19, 140–1, 146–7
and protest 92
racial 73, 80, 83, 93, 108, 130
of regulation 24, 139
threat of 24, 136, 148, 168
transmisogynistic 24, 115, 121–2, 124–7, 128–32, 148
and war 100, 108, 161, 168
white 20, 23, 64, 68–70, 76–7, 78, 81–3, 84, 86–7, 93, 97, 105–7, 140
see also Butler, Judith; language

Walker, Alice 12, 58
Walker, Margaret 33, 58, 79
Wheatley, Phillis
   critical reception 12–13, 35, 44, 59 n. 1, 63
   elegies 12, 23, 26 n. 3, 48–9, 49–52, 53, 55, 57, 58
Whitefield, George 49–51, 53, 55, 57
whiteness
   DuBois on 96
   and elegy 63, 64, 150, 154, 157
   and femininity 11, 23, 64, 69–71, 76–8, 105
   and masculinity 23, 64, 67–70, 73, 76–8, 105
   necrophilous patriarchy 64, 93, 96–7, 102–3
   in poetry 88
   supremacy 22–3, 25, 32, 35, 41, 63–4, 65, 105, 142, 156
wound 70, 77, 89, 91, 164, 173

Young, John K. 13–14, 23, 35–7, 40, 48

Zeiger, Melissa F. 1, 3, 7, 10, 12, 26 n. 2, 30
Zeus 84–5

www.ingramcontent.com/pod-product-compliance
Lightning Source LLC
Chambersburg PA
CBHW061830300426
44115CB00013B/2313